THE MALE PAGAN

JOHN SIMONE

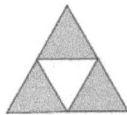

Three Pyramids Publishing

The Male Pagan

Three Pyramids Publishing
PO Box 432
Pine Plains, NY 12567-0432 USA

Manufactured in the United States of America.

First Edition, October 2011

ISBN-13: 978-1-886289-07-9

Book design, typesetting and editing by John Simone

Illustration by Carol Versace

Cover design by gnibel.com

Photograph of the author by Joe Turic, JT3 Photography, New Paltz NY

Dark Moon Invocation to the Green Man by Blayze, Applegrove, Sydney. Used with permission.

About the Author

John Simone has authored books for more than twenty five years. He has worked as an executive secretary, a computer programmer, and a technical writer and editor. He enjoys traveling and has been almost completely around the world. He has been a Pagan for more than 40 years.

Other books by John Simone include:

Pcychic Awareness: Everything You Need to Know to Develop Your Psychic Abilities. ISBN-10: 1-886289-03-4. ISBN+13: 978-1-886289-03-1 Publication Date: 1995 176 pages .

The LCIS & DCIS Breast Cancer Fact Book. ISBN-10:: 1-886289-19-0. ISBN-13: 978-1-886289-19-2. Publication Date: March, 2002. 218 pages.

Astrology for Beginners. ISBN-10: 1-886289-13-1. ISBN+13 978-1-886289-13-0. Publication Date: 1995. 40 pages. Comb Bound.

The Intuitive Tarot Workbook. Workbook, comb bound. Available from Three Pyramids Publishing: http://www.three-pyramids.com/books.

Life After Weight Loss Surgery: Achieving and Maintaining Massive Weight Loss. ISBN-13: 978-1-8862800. Publication Date: October 2010. 216 pages.

Visit Our Website

Visit our website at http://www.three-pyramids.com for links to other resources, and John's lectures and personal appearances.

Lectures and Personal Appearances

John Simone is available for lectures in your area. His talks are inspirational and motivational. John has led workshops on various topics in the USA and England.

Warning and Disclaimer

Special Sales

For information about bulk purchases or corporate premiums, please contact the Special Sales department at Three Pyramids Publishing, P.O.Box 432, Pine Plains, NY 12567-0432 USA.

Dedication

Life is a journey, not a destination. Sometimes it's like walking on a sunny beach. At other times, it's a strenuous climb up a steep and treacherous mountainside. Regardless of what the path looks like at any time, making the journey has been a pleasure because of the friends who have walked alongside.

To **Barbara Straub**: You are my protector, my mentor and a very dear friend. Most of what I learned about life, I learned from you. Nearly thirty years ago, you showed me that magic does indeed exist in everyday life. Many of my fondest memories involve you and Unicorn Books. Thank you for being my friend.

To **Sarah (Sally) Mulligan**: With a very few people, you know from the minute you meet that you will be dear friends forever. I have enjoyed every single minute that I spent with you, and I'm looking forward to many more. Life is magickal!

To **Elizabeth (Lisa) Aycock Jones**: We have traveled together, dined together, and worked magick together, with never an angry word between us. Thank you for taking time from your unbelievably busy life and spending it with me. Glastonbury is calling!

To **Nicholas Mazzacua**: My memories of my travels around the world all include you. We have had great times in the past, and I'm looking forward to many more in the future! Many of my memories of Glastonbury are linked with our visits there. See you next year on the Tor!

To **Richard Vasconi**: We've been friends for thirty years now. We are brothers who had different sets of parents. I cannot imagine a life without you in it. I hope every man finds, at some point in his life, a wonderful friend like you.

To **Lily Tomlin**: Life without laughter is no life at all. Thank you for sharing your gift of delight with us, and for being my friend.

And finally, to **all Pagans**, male and female, who are searching for a connection to universal energy. May you find many blessings on your path!

Contents

Men *and Paganism*   *1*

    What is a Pagan? 1

    What Does It Mean To Be A Male Pagan? 5

    Religion versus Spirituality 5

    What is a Spiritual Path? 6

    Defining Paganism 7

    My Personal Pagan Journey 8

    Paganism Today. 9

The *Male Pagan Survey*   *13*

    The Survey 13

    The Survey Responses 15

    Survey Says.... 15

      Sexuality 15

      In the Closet, or Out?. 15

    Male and Female Balance in Paganism 16

      About Rituals 17

      Practical Magic and Ritual Work. 18

      Using Herbs as Tools 20

      Books of Shadows or Other Written Records 20

      Practical Magick, and How It Works 22

      Effective Practical Magick 24

      Does Practical Magick Work? 26

      Percentage of Male Pagans 27

Universal *Energy:*   *29*

    How Does This Work For Magick or Ritual?. 34

The *Male Role*   *37*

    Men are Vital to Pagan Traditions. 39

    The Great Horned God 40

    Meeting the Green Man 42

Masculine *Energy in a Goddess Tradition*   *45*

    Loss of the Goddess 50

    Working With Masculine Energy 51

Gay *and Bisexual Men and Paganism*   *53*

    Historical Precedence 53

    Paganism Today 56

    Are Gay and Bisexual Men Marginalized in Paganism?. 58

    Gay and Bisexual Men and Power. 60

Ethics *101 for Pagans*   *63*

    Choosing an Ethical Path 70

Practical *Magick*   *73*

    Defining Magick 77

        Why Is Magick Spelled with a K? 78

    Making Magick More Effective 79

    When Magick Doesn't Work 81

    Timing. 82

    How to Achieve Success Using Spellcraft. 83

        Absolute Belief 83

        Total Faith 83

    Morality and Ethics 84

Your Word is Sacred 85

Everything Starts NOW 88

Working Magick for Others 89

Clean Up When You Are Finished 91

Ritual   *93*

The Joy in Ritual 95

Adapting Rituals 95

Using Goddess-Based Rituals 96

Using Rhyme and Rhythm 97

Tools to Access Energy in Rituals 98

To Access Masculine Energy 98

To Access Feminine Energy 98

Tools   *101*

Tool Basics 103

Primary Tools 104

Pentacle 104

Wand or Staff 104

Athame and Sword 104

Chalice 105

Additional Tools 106

Boline 106

Censer and Incense 106

Besom or Broom 108

Bell 109

Cauldron 109

Candles 110

Herbs and Oils 111

Book of Shadows or Journal 112

Cingulum 114

Scourge 114

Spear 114

Stang 114

Jewelry 114

Stones and Crystals 115

Ritual Robes 115

Charms and Amulets 115

Statues and Pictures. 116

Mortar and Pestle 117

Pagan Name 117

The Altar or Ritual Space 118

Tools for Working with The God 119

Tools for Working with The Goddess. 119

Divination 120

Gods *and Goddesses*   *121*

Aspects of the Divine 122

Deities and Sexuality 123

The God and Goddess Resource List 123

The Pantheon. 125

Adonis 125

Amun 126

Apollo 126

Aphrodite. 127

Apis 128

Ares 128

Artemis 129

Astarte. 130

Athena 131

Bacchus 132

Ba-Kha. 132

Baron Samedi 133

Bona Dea 134

Brigid 135

Ceres 135

Cernunnos 135

Cerridwen 136

Cronos 137

Cupid 137

Dagda 137

Damballa 138

Demeter 138

Diana 139

Dionysus 140

Ereshkigal 142

Eros 142

Erzulie 143

Faunus 143

Freya 144

Frigg 144

Gwydion or Gwyddien 144

Hades 146

Hecate 147

Hera 148

Hephaestus 148

Hercules 149

Hermaphrodite 150

Hermes 150

Herne 151

Horus 151

Hyacinth 153

Inanna 153

Ishtar 156

Isis. 156

Janus. 158

Juno 159

Jupiter 159

The Loa. 159

Lugh 160

Mars 162

Mercury 162

Minerva 163

Neptune 163

Odin 163

Osiris. 164

Pan 164

Persephone. 165

Poseidon 165

Priapus. 166

Proserpina 167

Ptah 167

Rhiannon. 168

Saturn 168

Tammuz 170

Thor 170

Venus 171

Vesta. 171

Vulcan 172

Zeus 173

List of the Gods/Goddesses in the Ancient Egyptian Pantheon 175

Conclusions   *181*

Thank You! 183

Appendix — *Magickal Correspondences*   *185*

Wood 185

    Species of Trees and Their Energetic Quality 186

Metals 191

    Metals and Their Energetic Quality 191

Color. 192

    Color Correspondences 193

Animals 195

Astrology. 195

Index   *197*

1

Men and Paganism

The original working title of this book was "Men and Wicca."

A odd thing happened as I began to more completely research the topic of the book I thought I was working on. It turns out that many of the men I talked with and who responded to my surveys and personal research questions actually identify themselves as Pagan. A bit more than half of them identified as Wiccan, leaving a large number who followed other Pagan traditions.

This discovery forced me to take another look at what I thought was the phenomenon of men and Wicca. Just as there are a number of spiritual paths that are loosely called Wicca, there are many additional paths whose influence is a bit further afield. My interest in learning how men felt about being Wiccan morphed into a genuine fascination about men and Pagan spirituality. At the end of the day, the topic was wide-ranging and very rewarding to me personally on my quest for spiritual understanding.

What is a Pagan?

In order to discuss the material presented in this book, it is necessary to first define the group of men about which I'm writing. At first glance, this seemed to be an easy task. My original definition of the group was "any and all male followers of any of a number of Wiccan traditions."

In reality, however, this narrow focus turned into a virtual nightmare! Most of the men I interviewed described themselves as Pagan; a few claimed to be Wiccan and most felt that Wiccans **are** Pagans. To complicate matters, while the term Wicca is somewhat easy to define, no two sources can completely agree about a definition for Pagans.

Is a Wiccan a Pagan? Probably, according to most definitions.

Are all Pagans Wiccan? Definitely not.

In simple terms, the term "pagan" has come to symbolize followers of any earth or nature-centered spiritual path. However, it's far more complicated than that. Even attempting to find a definition in one of the many dictionaries proved both interesting and fruitless.

For example, the American Heritage Dictionary defines pagan as:

1. One who is not a Christian, Muslim, or Jew, especially a worshiper of a polytheistic religion. 2. One who has no religion. 3. A non-Christian. 4. A hedonist. 5. A pagan.

The first and third definition are specific about what a Pagan is not. That's not too helpful. It is like trying to describe a fish by saying it's not a boat.

The first definition also ignores other monotheistic religions that are not Pagan, including the large populations of Buddhists and Hindus.

Interestingly, the second and fourth definition imply that Paganism is not a religious path by defining it as the absence of a belief in a spiritual path. That is patently untrue.

The fifth definition is useless. The definition of a term cannot be the term itself.

I found an interesting discussion about the term "pagan" at the Religious Tolerance website (http://www.religioustolerance.org).

It is generally agreed that the term "pagan" comes from the Latin word paganus. There is little agreement about what the word meant before the fifth century CE. There are three currently acceptable definitions, although none is generally accepted by a majority.

1   The word originally meant "rustic," "hick," or "country bumpkin." It is believed that Christians used the term to denigrate and ridicule those who lived in the countryside who held on to old-fashioned, familiar beliefs. Those who lived in the countryside were much slower to adopt Christianity – a new religion at the time – than people who lived in urban areas.

2 The term paganus could have signified someone who was a "civilian" instead of "military." Christians of the period often called themselves "miles Christi" or "soldiers of Christ." Non-Christians became "pagani" (non-soldiers, or civilians). The term was not used in a denigrating way.

3 The term could have represented any outsider, in a neutral sense, with subsequent implication of "hick" or "civilian" added as time passed.

After the fifth century CE, the term began to represent any non-Christian. In later times, it morphed into an evil term that implied Satanism. This definition persists even today, even though it is inaccurate.

Another rather snotty implication is that Pagans practice "primitive" religions. It should be noted that no particular spiritual path has any intrinsic value over any other path.

Most people today agree that Pagans include those who follow the Wiccan traditions and other spiritual paths. Paganism embraces a number of distinct spiritual paths, including Druid, Asatru, Green Man and ancient Greek, Roman or Egyptian religions. Some, but not all, are earth-centered and emphasize the cycles of nature and living in harmony with these cycles. Others are deity-centered.

Isaac Bonewits has noted that in the early part of the twentieth century, the term pagan was applied to agnostics, atheists and hedonists to imply "religion-less" when referring to an educated, white, male, heterosexual European, but when referring to anyone else, the term implied "ignorant savage" or "pervert."

I define Paganism as including some of the following concepts:
- ✓ Polytheistic (Pagans believe in more than a single male god)
- ✓ Nature-based, honoring nature and all life forms. Objects in nature are a manifestation of universal (God/Goddess) energy, not separated from it as Abrahamic religions believe.
- ✓ Pantheistic (any religious belief or philosophical doctrine that identifies God/Goddess with the Universe). Pagans can worship within a pantheon, a number of gods and goddesses who embody different aspects. Each of these deities embodies a different aspect of universal energy. Depending on the spiritual tradition, the deities might or might not be distinct, discrete aspects of a single universal energy.
- ✓ An acknowledgment of the divine feminine as well as the divine masculine. Abrahamic religions do not include worship of a feminine

principle.
- ✓ Animism (the belief that natural objects and phenomena possess souls). Animists believe that all things are alive and animated with spirit.
- ✓ Belief in the immortality of the spirit and in the continuous cycles of the Seasons and life itself: birth, death and rebirth. Many Pagans also believe in reincarnation.

Your definition might be very different.

Paganism includes reconstructed traditions such as Greek polytheism, Celtic, German, or Nordic reconstruction-ism as well as modern eclectic traditions such as Discordianism, Druidism and Wicca and its many offshoots.

Abrahamic religions are monotheistic faiths that emphasize and trace their common origin to Abraham, or recognize a spiritual tradition identified with Abraham. The three main Abrahamic religions are Judaism, Christianity, and Islam.

Many Pagans are indeed polytheistic. Monotheism is a relatively recent concept. There is little evidence to support a belief in monotheism in ancient times. Most civilizations about which we have some current knowledge believed in a pantheon of deities, each with specific qualities and areas of influence.

The vast majority of all humans who ever lived were pagans.

Note: The term Pagan is capitalized in the same way that Christian, Buddhist or the name of any other religion is capitalized. This practice honors Pagan traditions and elevates this spiritual path to equality with other established paths. In this book, the term pagan (lower case) is used to discuss ancient peoples who were not affiliated with organized Christian-based religions; the term Pagan is used to signify modern-day believers in one of the many reconstructed pagan spiritual traditions.

I often link the definition of a Pagan with someone who has considered various spiritual paths and decided that any of the Pagan traditions is a good fit in his particular case. In reality, each of us defines a spiritual path that might adhere to some but not necessarily all beliefs surrounding a specific religious concept or group. Humans have a tendency to accept and use what resonates within and to ignore any concept that doesn't resonate. Part of our life experience is to become an adult, with all that implies – using our intelligence and our emotions to determine what is right for each of us. The men who responded to the survey indicated in resounding numbers that they use what resonates and they ignore any aspect that does not.

So, when I prepared a survey to research topics for this book, I intended to include any man who identified himself as a Pagan, not just Wiccans. While it changed the original concept somewhat, the information that I discovered as I researched these men and their beliefs proved both enlightening and educational. Spiritual paths are all about personal growth; my spiritual path has evolved as a result of meeting these interesting and intelligent men and in working on this book.

What Does It Mean To Be A Male Pagan?

An increasing number of men are drawn to Pagan spiritual traditions. The Abrahamic, monotheistic, male-based religions that have become prevalent over the past two thousand years are becoming more and more restrictive. Both men and women feel trapped in a perpetual cycle of doing something that their religion decrees as evil and then having to petition the hierarchy for forgiveness.

Pagan traditions enable people to develop their own spiritual path. Any sense of right or wrong, good or evil, is completely personal. There is no group to approve or disapprove of a Pagan's actions.

Many Pagan traditions, if not most, include a polytheistic view: Pagans believe in both a God and a Goddess, two facets of an ultimate, universal deity.

Can men successfully work in a spiritual tradition that includes Goddess worship? And can a Pagan man access masculine God energy as well as feminine Goddess energy?

Pagan men work within a number of spiritual traditions, but all of them have many aspects in common. Learning how to access and use energy is integral to the Pagan path.

Religion versus Spirituality

There is a difference between religion and spirituality.

Spirituality is personal communication with universal energy, or God/Goddess (or whatever you call it in your tradition).

Religion is groups of people who have adopted specific principles or beliefs in their quest for this communication with the universe. A religious tradition attempts to illuminate the path for achieving this communication. Unfortunately, the tendency of religion to define the Divine as something discrete that can be discovered and understood often eliminates the possibility of accessing the actual energy of the universe. If you know what you're seeking, you won't be able to find it anywhere else other than where you look. God and Goddess have become something external; in fact, they are a part of every living thing, intimately and essentially incorporated within that life form.

Each religion believes that it is essentially correct, and therefore other religions must be incorrect by default. An ingrained belief that one is ultimately correct is a driving force in creating war and discord. A spiritual person understands that everything is essentially correct, and nothing is incorrect. If others can be as equally correct in their beliefs as you can in yours, there isn't much to fight about.

Spirituality is something you feel within you. Religion is something you agree to feel outside of you.

Spirituality is individual. You determine your own spiritual path. Religion is communal, and a group develops a concept for that spiritual path. Your personal spirituality and the spirituality found in organized (or disorganized) religion can be different, in varying degrees.

Think of religion as a container for spirituality.

What is a Spiritual Path?

What is a spiritual path? Most people visualize a long straight road stretching out ahead, green bushes on both sides and a dirt path underfoot; kind of a walk through the woods. In actuality, I think of a spiritual path in an expanded sense. Mine has a rainbow above in a bright blue cloudless sky; the path is paved with golden bricks and is easy to walk on. Beautiful vistas can be seen along each side. My point is, if you visualize something, make it as big and beautiful as you can. We're stuck with so-called "reality" in the physical world. In our imagination and in the energetic realms where spirit and magick exist, these limitations do not exist. Take advantage of that!

If you think about it, when you visualize yourself performing a ritual next to the dirt path through the dark, foreboding woods, what impact will that have on the outcome? If you visualize yourself sitting in a warm sunny field next to that golden road, looking off into the distance at the beautiful view – would this improve your results? Only you can answer that, but I've used visualizations in both ways and that golden path and beautiful view certainly helped me!

The Pagan path is whatever you determine it to be. Many Pagans take bits and pieces from various traditions. You can use whatever resonates for you, or whatever works, and discard whatever does not feel appropriate.

The only person who can determine the correct spiritual path for you is **you**.

Defining Paganism

Pagan spirituality is vastly different from the traditional, monotheistic, male God-based religions that have been popular over the past two thousand years.

One aspect popular in most monotheistic religions is that God exists somewhere outside of us. He floats above us "in heaven." When people following these traditions pray, they think of God being physically somewhere above them. The term "raise your eyes in prayer" is common.

I grew up in a Christian tradition. I remember thinking at a very young age that I didn't particularly enjoy the idea of a cranky, vengeful God hovering somewhere above me, up in the clouds, watching my every move, ready to punish me for the smallest transgression. I felt constantly threatened. And I didn't particularly feel much love beaming down at me either.

Pagans believe in a universal energy sometimes called "The One" or "All That Is." It is composed of everything that ever existed, both in the past, the present, and the future. It does not rule over the universe: it **is** the universe. Because it is difficult to visualize something that essentially incorporates everything, Pagans use the concept of a God and Goddess, both of whom are equal to each other in every way, but also distinctly different. The manifestations of God and Goddess include a pantheon of deities, each with a name and specific qualities that can be accessed to aid in manifesting change in our reality. A Pagan can use a set of specific God and Goddess archetypes, or call on any of those known or imagined, to interact with the world and effect change. Unlike monotheistic Abrahamic religions that are prevalent in the world today, Pagans are not concerned with redemption or the concepts of Heaven or Hell. Their focus is on the world we know. Rituals, along with practical magick if it is used in your tradition, can be used to effect change within an individual's reality.

Pagans universally concern themselves only with personal spiritual development; we do not believe that we can influence the spirituality of anyone else, and it is not our responsibility to do so.

Pagans view God and Goddess in a very different way. Our deities are forever within us and all around us. The essential life force that flows through us and forms the basis for being alive is part of the same energy that they are.

Quantum physics has demonstrated that we are essentially energy. See page 29 for a discussion about how science and spirituality interact.

My Personal Pagan Journey

My own participation as a Pagan began more than 40 years ago, when I was 17. During the summer, I had been invited to parties in Woodstock, NY (yes, **the** Woodstock), where I was exposed to a number of Pagan and Wiccan people of both genders. I found myself fascinated by the information they told me and before long, I had joined a rather makeshift Wiccan coven that cast circles in a local pasture, usually at midnight. I enjoyed both the ceremonies and the conviviality that followed.

Over the years, I joined other Wiccan and Pagan groups, finally deciding to practice as a solitary. In the late 1980s, I was teaching Psychic Awareness classes at a local community college for adult students. Many of the students were interested in the Wiccan tradition, so we began a study circle that eventually had about thirty participants.

A career move with my job caused me to relocate to Raleigh, NC in the early 1990s, and although I was aware of a Wiccan group in the nearby Chapel Hill area, I had been a solitary for many years at that point and didn't see any need to get involved with a group circle. Having experienced both group and solitary practice, I can honestly say that I follow a solitary Pagan path by choice. I was constantly finding circles in which there was always someone attempting to obtain power. Note that this was my experience, and does not necessarily reflect anyone else's views of group Pagan activities.

Paganism Today

In the early 21st century, some Pagan traditions emphasize feminine energy, and unfortunately, ignore or assign lesser value to masculine energy.

Feminine energy is receptive energy. In the Wiccan tradition specifically, many spiritual paths emphasize Goddess energy due largely to the greater number of women participants versus the much smaller number of male participants. This spiritual path attracts a large number of women, including many who are feminist. Many were drawn to Wicca because they no longer felt welcome and honored by Abrahamic monotheistic traditions. The ancient Pagans saw their spiritual path as balanced, with equal energy and emphasis given to both masculine and feminine energy. Separating from Abrahamic traditions meant that the feminine could be again accessed and given a place of honor. Unfortunately, many of these women equated the God archetype of the ancient pagans with the Abrahamic all-powerful, vengeful God. This God was not a pleasant, approachable figure. So, God energy was eliminated. This mirrors what happened when Abrahamic religions became popular: feminine energy was valued less, and any Goddess connections were eliminated.

Unfortunately, neither Abrahamic nor Goddess-only Pagan religions are balanced.

Masculine energy is projective energy. The world cannot exist without projective energy. Somebody has to go out and get food for dinner. Somebody has to step up and fight when people are threatened. Projective and receptive energies are neither good or bad; they simple are. Energy is energy. It has no intrinsic value. Humans have overlaid their concepts of "good" or "bad" to describe energy, but this value is not consistent: it is assigned in an individual way by each person, reflecting life experiences that are vastly different, and there is no master scale that can measure energy in a meaningful way.

In a balanced spiritual tradition, both projective and receptive energy have equal value. Neither is good or bad, and neither is preferable to the other. They simply exist. Women can take advantage of projective energy by accessing the God archetypes; men can use receptive energy by accessing the Goddess archetypes.

Women cannot continue to view the Pagan God as evil, judgmental or vengeful. The God worshiped by Pagans was powerful, but fair and loving as well. The God of Abrahamic religion and the God in Paganism are vastly different aspects of masculine energy. They are not the same God. Men in Pagan traditions have learned to see the Pagan Goddess as nurturing and loving, but also as a powerful being. The time has come for women in Pagan traditions to relax their political views and simply learn to access God-centered energy as a tool that can have enormous benefit to their lives. Pagans of both genders sometimes need to be reminded that there is no battle between male and female energy, and therefore there can be no winner or loser. These energies simply exist and are tools with which reality can be transformed and adapted.

As with many modern interpretations of Pagan spiritual paths, Wicca today contains a paradox within its structure. While it is often viewed to be a Goddess-based spiritual path, the eight Sabbats reflect the Wheel of the Year. The Wheel is a celebration of God energy and traces the symbolic life of the God from his birth at Yule through his death at Samhain. The period between Samhain and the following Yule represents a dark time: the period after death when we await rebirth.

The Wiccan Esbats reflect the movement of the moon, a Goddess energy.

Because the solstices and equinoxes are about the God and the esbat full moons are about the Goddess, the tradition is naturally and integrally balanced. Some modern Wiccan traditions have become completely Goddess-based and are attractive to feminists, who negate the masculine principles and elevate feminine energy above the masculine. While many of these traditions celebrate the Wheel of the Year, they ignore the connection to masculine energy or ascribe it (incorrectly) to Goddess energy. To me, this version of Wicca seems as unbalanced and biased as today's Abrahamic religions.

To be fair, the vast majority of Wiccans that I have met and corresponded with believe in an equal partnership between God and Goddess, and view their spiritual path as balanced.

The defining difference between Abrahamic and Pagan spiritual paths is that for Pagans, the feminine is honored and celebrated.

There is a phenomenon in the Christian world called "What Would Jesus Do?" In adapting that to your Pagan spiritual path, if you have questions, ask yourself "what would the first Pagan have done?" At that time, there were no traditions; no books in which you could research answers or how others view the topic. Looking at the issue in this way forces you to focus on your own intuition and common sense (these days, we call it "logic."). If the answer seems preposterous, then it probably won't work. If it seems correct or just sits well with you, then try that. A valuable tenet in the Pagan spiritual traditions is that all wisdom already resides within you. Rather than seeking answers from others, simply ask yourself what the answer is.

I know what you're thinking: if I know the answer, why am I reading this book? Well, would you have come up with that concept if you had not read this book? I would like this book to become a resource for Pagans, not **the** final word. My goal is to pass along what I have learned over the past 42 years and hopefully there may be something – anything – within this book will resonate within and help you along your path. I truly believe that every Pagan has an obligation to pass the information learned to others on a similar spiritual path. Nothing in this book is intended to be the source of your knowledge: it is a resource that can help you more easily walk the Pagan path. That journey is infinitely rewarding, and I wish you much success and many blessings as you follow your heart.

2

The Male Pagan Survey

The Survey

With that concept in mind, I decided to survey men about their experience with Paganism, enabling each man to define his spiritual path for himself. One of the wonderful aspects about Paganism is that there are a huge number of traditions with which one can identify. Two people can agree to start a new tradition, and it becomes reality! This is much more difficult to do if you identify with one of the mainstream, monotheistic religions.

Since I'm a member of The Witches Voice and PaganSpace networks on the Internet, I used my contacts through those two websites to locate men who might be amenable to taking my survey. I also personally interviewed a number of men who identified themselves as Pagan. The survey respondents spanned the gamut in all areas, and included gay, bisexual and heterosexual men in relatively equal numbers.

Pagans acknowledge their sexuality; the Pagan spiritual path accepts sexuality as an integral part of what we are. Many monotheistic traditions have separated sexuality from spirituality, changing it from an essential part of ourselves into an evil impulse that has to be monitored and held in contempt.

There have been many theories over the years that Pagan men are primarily gay men. I found this to be untrue; a large number of heterosexual men responded to my survey.

It has been assumed by the Pagan community in general that gay men become Pagans because it is one of few spiritual paths that does not discourage gay men simply because of their sexual orientation. But is this why gay and bisexual men become Pagans? I have long doubted that this simplistic concept reflected reality. I have personally known many gay Pagans and can honestly say that their participation was heartfelt and sincere; they were part of the tradition for the same reasons as any other participant. The survey also indicated that it is true that many gay and bisexual men are attracted to Paganism because they feel a sense of acceptance that is lacking in more restrictive, monotheistic traditions. But one cannot ignore the large number of heterosexual men who responded to my survey and must necessarily be counted. Sexual preference, it seems, did not significantly skew the results, which was a surprise.

We'll explore more about male Pagan sexuality in a later chapter. For many Pagan men, sexuality is a driving force in life, and it affects many aspects of life. To a Pagan of either gender, sexuality and Pagan beliefs go hand in hand. For most Pagans of either gender, sexuality is not something that needs to be justified or excused; it simply exists and is generally viewed as a positive.

I wanted to find out how male Pagans used their spirituality in their daily lives. Most Pagan men actively live their spiritual beliefs; this is not something that is done one night a month under a full moon and then disregarded until next month's celebration. The vast majority of men who responded to the survey indicated that every part of their day is based on their spiritual beliefs. This is often far from the norm for men in monotheistic religions, where men feel a sense of spirituality while in a church but abandon it once they walk out the door and then participate in everyday life in a manner that is very different from the life experience that is espoused in church.

The survey was designed to provide the ability to make specific comments about nearly every question. The additional information that was provided via these comments certainly informed some of the issues presented in this book, issues about which my original ideas or beliefs were often quite different.

Because many of these comments were personal in nature, I will not make them public here. However, I did include the information in various comments throughout the book. If you voiced an opinion on the survey, your voice was heard!

The Survey Responses

Here is a summary of the results of the survey that was available in early 2011. Along with written comments supplied through the survey itself, I have also incorporated other comments obtained through personal interviews with a number of Pagan men over the past few years.

Survey Says...

About three fourths of the men responding to the survey indicated (either directly or through their answers) that they were from a number of Wiccan traditions. The other 25% did not indicate their tradition, or their answers did not supply enough information for me to figure it out.

Keep in mind that, because of the large number of Wiccans, the survey is slightly biased toward the many Wiccan traditions rather than Paganism in general; however, after talking with so many men over the years and listening to their anecdotes about their traditions, rituals and practical magick work, the results are representative of Pagan men in general, as well as Wiccan men. Most Pagan traditions incorporate a similar body of beliefs.

Sexuality

One question that was asked in the survey was whether one's sexuality has had any impact on a man's Pagan beliefs or rituals. Only about 25% of the respondents mentioned their sexuality as being integral to their choice of spiritual path; the other 75% indicated that their sexuality had no bearing on their choice. If gay or bisexual men comprised 40% of the survey, this means that 15% of gay or bisexual Pagan males did not join the Pagan spiritual path because of their sexuality. Anecdotal evidence was contrary to this conclusion; the vast majority of gay or bisexual Pagan men that I had previously talked to in person had indicated that their sexuality was a driving force in their selection of the Pagan spiritual path.

In the Closet, or Out?

Ten percent of the gay or bisexual men who responded indicated that their sexuality was completely closeted. Thirty percent indicated that they were out to some friends or family, but not generally. And 50%

of the respondents indicated that they are completely out to everyone.

The comments for this section of the survey were interesting.

One man stated that Paganism influenced his sexuality, and he believed that "Pagans should not discriminate between gay, bisexual or heterosexual orientations."

Another respondent stated that he "came out fully as a gay man after becoming a Pagan. Being Pagan helped him accept himself as he was because the Lord and Lady accepted him as he was and would not want him to be anything other than that."

Two men said that "no closet could contain them!"

Another man took exception to the terms "gay" or "bisexual." He considers himself "pansexual and falls for a person, not the plumbing."

Another respondent stated that "his Pagan path started long before he had any concept of any sort of sexuality, whether his own or someone else's."

Several men indicated that they are out only to some friends or family, but that other friends, family or co-workers follow restrictive religious paths that look down on any alternate form of sexual expression. They consider themselves closeted "out of necessity," not desire or preference.

Male and Female Balance in Paganism

An overwhelming majority (85%) follow a spiritual path that honors God and Goddess equally. Only 6% follow a God-oriented path, and 9% follow a Goddess-oriented path.

One respondent noted that he "finds it easier to draw both God and Goddess energy by accepting both the Lord and Lady within himself and accepting his dual nature."

A respondent indicated that "the Green Man is his main male deity, but he uses Gaia as his consort." Another stated that he "includes both masculine and feminine energies in his work, but feels he is more Goddess oriented." A third man said that he is "more male God oriented because he is a male, but includes female deities as needed. People tend to choose gods or goddesses that best represent who they are."

Another man stated that he "did not separate God from Goddess. His spiritual path is a pantheistic religion with many goddesses and gods. He works with at least 5 Gods and at least as many Goddesses."

Another man summed up the majority when he said that his "sexual preferences don't dictate the nature of Divinity."

About Rituals

About 70% of the respondents indicated that they perform rituals or practical magick whenever it is needed. About 25% perform rituals during Sabbat or Esbat celebrations in their tradition. Five percent do not work with lunar energies and instead work only at Sabbats in their tradition. (Note: many of the respondents of the survey identified themselves as Wiccan, so results are slightly skewed, although I feel that the percentages are probably accurate for Paganism as a whole.)

The vast range of comments supplying additional information for this question was impressive. Unlike more "organized" religions, Pagan men are not stamped with seals of approval for their beliefs and practices. As evidenced by the comments, each man has taken Paganism and made it work for him.

"Every day, I live what I believe, trying to respond instead of reacting."

"Piety: it's not just for High Days anymore. We need to do work at our home shrines daily."

"Though I honor all the holidays, I work when it is needed."

"I have had subjective experiences that indicate the success of some of my workings."

"I perform daily affirmations as well as giving thanks daily to BOTH the God and Goddess."

"For me, the Sabbats are the eight holidays. I celebrate them plus the Esbats (full and new moons) plus a healing ritual called 'The Child of Light' on the first quarter moon."

"Feri's primary focus, in my practice, is to commune with deity. The two times of the year that the religion requires us to recognize is Beltane and Samhain. These are the times when the veil is thinnest, and we and 'they' can cross over the easiest. We do much work across the veil. Total possession by deity is a major part of my practice of Feri."

"I don't do lunar-based workings. I do group High Days eight times a year, and personal home practices daily."

"I sometimes go to Pagan events."

"I have my own prayer room, so I'm able to worship whenever I need to."

"I teach a children's group, so sometimes we do Rituals as a lesson as opposed to (doing them only) on the Holidays."

"All my family have chosen to be pagan/wiccan so they are learning as we go, plus I do not feel that you have to wait for certain times to practice. I enjoy it; it brings me peace."

"I work with my Earth Mother, who is a dear friend of mine and has brought me along with other friends to where I am now spiritually. I have learned so much since I have known them."

"Though I often join in with others during Sabbats and Esbats, my practice runs from daily to whenever I feel the need."

"At this time, it's not as consistent as I would like."

"I hold a special Frer/Freyjablot on every Friday the 13th."

"Ritual and magic are a way of life and not limited to any specific time."

"There are times only for certain things; everything else is just as I go along."

"(I do ritual) when the universe calls."

"Unfortunately, I only seem to realize how stressed I am and that I need to center myself when I practice. I want to practice more but have had a hard time structuring my time in all aspects of my life at this point."

Practical Magic and Ritual Work

This survey question asked about spellcraft and ritual work.

The majority responded that they create their own spells and rituals as needed. A significant percentage indicated that they use spells and rituals obtained from books, or from any source that seems appropriate. A small percentage (less than 10%) indicated that they use only spells or rituals approved by their group.

One man made an interesting point when he theorized that "if we have lived before, we would then have memories of ancient spells and rituals. I have lived before!"

"I might find spells from books and other research but I also change them and customize them to be more personal to me and to the gods/goddesses. In my view, it creates more of a relationship by making my own and customizing my own."

"I use mostly rituals from my tradition but have run an eclectic coven where we created our own rituals, and now work locally with an eclectic group for the eight Sabbats."

"I create much of my own spells. I follow many rituals handed down through Feri. In addition, I create my own rituals, and follow my intuition and create rituals and/or spells 'off the cuff.'"

"I use a Book of Shadows handed down through generations."

Another man indicated he obtains spells and rituals from any source, because "the power comes from within."

"My Book of Shadows is based on the rituals provided by D.J. Conway in her book *Celtic Magic*."

"Whatever I feel happy about and if it will not cause any harm, I will look at it and may use it."

"I have a very large library that I draw from."

"Being an eclectic, I use whatever source is available that rings true to my own beliefs. There are sources that put the High Priest or Priestess on some kind of pedestal and lose the Goddess and God in the process. These are denominations that I will not follow. There is only One deserving of worship in our belief system... not as others would have us believe."

"(What I do) depends on the nature of the working."

"I am tradition selective for I find that specific traditions resonate within me, while others are actually repellant to my sensibilities."

"(I use) what feels natural to my being and Oneness."

"No training, no choice."

"We have a set of 'standard' rituals but can incorporate others if it is appropriate."

"I look at other people's work for inspiration, then write my own."

"I do what feels like the right choice for me at that specific time."

"I haven't gained the confidence to create my own spells yet."

"I don't use whole spells that I find. If I don't write my own, I take a sentence or a small part of other spells."

"I am a group of one, made up of the female/male perspective."

Using Herbs as Tools

About 90% of the respondents use herbs (a broad category that includes herbs, incense, and essential oils) in their rituals. Ten percent said that they did not consider the use of herbs to be important.

Using Candles as Tools

95% of the respondents use candles as part of their rituals; five percent do not incorporate the use of candles.

Books of Shadows or Other Written Records

About 60% of the respondents keep records in a personal book. Ten percent included a mixture of those who use only a group's written records, and those who use records published by someone else. Two respondents indicated that their tradition forbids written records, allowing only the spoken word to be used in teaching about the tradition. About 30% don't keep any form of written record, often citing the common prohibition in traditional witchcraft or nature religions against keeping written records; it should be noted that since the time of Gerald Gardner, Wiccans have been maintaining personal records or group Books of Shadows, and today it is a common practice, as witnessed by the large number of men who do this.

One respondent stated that the term "Book of Shadows"(BOS is a shortened form) is very loosely defined. "I keep a record of all the work I do, but it's not so formal as a tightly bound book."

Another mentioned that "writing has taken many forms over the years and differences in translation can affect spells."

"We have a BOS of our tradition and then we also have a personal one with rituals that we have written.

"I am empathic. I just go on how it feels, and work from there."

"My Tradition has a BOS that is copied but we also make it personal by adding our own material to our individual copies."

"I actually write my own rituals and spells depending on what the need is. I use the resources that are available to me."

"I use a Book of Shadows that was handed down following initiation. Our tradition is deeply interconnected."

Another participant stated that he uses a book that he shares with his wife.

"I use many books for research. No book is a Bible, in my opinion."

"When going through a spell, I normally go through it three times, so that way it seals itself in my head and in the Universe."

"We no longer have to worry – as much – about being burned as a Witch. But, at the same time, I don't surrender such information to people that seem 'too Christian.'"

"I have considered making my own, but am still undecided."

"Our coven/tradition maintains a book; in addition, we have individually-kept personal books."

"I record my rituals and practice elements in my Mystic Journals."

"I use multiple sources and combine my own practices into them and modify to my own needs."

"I will be using a book of shadows. I have been moving so much of late and am afraid of being separated from it."

"I had tried the Tarot and other divining tools, but when I picked up the runes it was different. They seemed accurate. I kept a book of readings for two years until I was sure that it was working for me. Spells are written but must be memorized before use. Other than the runes, I rarely try to work magick. I was looking for a way of life, not just an advantage over others. I have never wanted power over others really, if challenged, I will face anyone, wand to wand, sword to sword, gun to gun..."

"Each tradition varies. In ours, you hand-copy each BOS after completing the degree."

"I have one, but have not updated it in forever."

"I have both a personal as well as a group BOS."

"What I know is dangerous for others to know or see."

"I have a few spells I have become comfortable with; I want to create my own book once I start to find my own spells."

Practical Magick, and How It Works

This question asked how practical magick (also called spells in many traditions) work.

About 65% said that spells take considerable attention and must be worked more than once to be effective. About 25% said that simply reciting a spell ensures its success, and doing it once is enough. Ten percent of the respondents don't use practical magick or spellcasting.

The comments in this section of the survey varied widely, and give a genuine representation of the variety of Pagan beliefs, along with how universal most of them are.

One man took exception with the way this question was worded. He felt that one option was limited by the indication that recitation without intent is enough, while a second option is limited by the assumption that you must do things over and over to get any results.

"To me, words mean nothing in the spirit world. Intent makes the difference."

"None of the choices provided are truly how I work my spells. I put a lot of time, effort and heart into my spells, but normally I do not have to do the spell more than once." (Note: I agree, a fourth option would have been appropriate, or the responses could have been worded differently; I can see where the choices could be a bit confusing, although they were crystal clear to me at the time!)

"Intent is really the key. You can perform the work only once and have it be successful so long as there is strong intent behind the work."

"It really depends on the work at hand, I believe."

"It depends on the spell and the energy one wants to raise."

"Sometimes I prepare days in advance. When I do my work, I continue to feel a certain break within my conscious. Then I know the spell is complete and sent into the universe."

"Bad question. There are many ways to cast a spell. I don't restrict myself to any one way. That said, usually once is enough."

"Initially there needs to be a lot of time and energy put into a ritual. (After) the ritual has been completed once, I remember it, and again, do other rituals based on what I have performed."

"For me, my spell work starts long before I have committed word to paper, purchase a candle, and so on. By the time I 'light the candle,' I have been working on my intent for a long time. Some spells require repeated work – depending on the working – others require only one working. This is often more dependent on the direction spirit gives me. I channel many of my spell crafts."

"The answer above is only partially correct. I feel that intent is very important when casting spells, because without it the energy of the spell will diffuse. I do not, however, feel that spells must be cast multiple times to be effective."

"(My answer is) actually a mix of the first two; it takes intent and some spells do need to be done over but for smaller tweaks, not so much."

"Spells or magick takes many layers of intent: for example, herbs, candles, and so on."

"I might be a tad more Ceremonial than that. Yes, recitation is enough if your heart is TRULY in it. I enjoy the "magick" involved in a bit more ceremony and pomp. Not to the point of the Golden Dawn's approach but I really enjoy communing with the Goddess and God for a while … even if only through meditation under a starry sky... it truly is magickal."

"Intent is key. While I have had 'once is enough' success, I find that the more energies, focus and intent I can generate, the more effective the outcome."

"I do mostly shamanic/rune and gladr work; it is not traditional spellcraft."

"Once recited the effort still needs to be performed and acted out intently in order to shift the paradigm to manifest."

"I don't believe a spell necessarily has to be done more than once, but I do believe it has to have a lot of intent."

"Sometimes once is enough; sometimes more is required."

"It all depends on what my intent is. Most often it's sex magick with a willing, knowing partner. Sometimes it's just meditation. Sometimes it's a full ritual."

"It is a fine line; there are times when once is enough and others where repetition feels right."

"Mind/Body work together through the subconscious to achieve what is intended."

Effective Practical Magick

This question allowed multiple choices; participants could select as many answers as appropriate. Therefore, the percentages will total more than 100%.

62% of respondents agreed that a spell is worked as many times as is needed.

27% agreed that a spell should be worked only one time.

33% are part of a group that performs practical magick by reciting a spell.

64% are part of a group that performs practical magick by using concentration and focus.

40% perform spellcasting by working alone and reciting a spell.

75% perform spellcasting by working alone and using concentration and focus.

Those men who added comments to these questions practice spellcasting and have a firm belief in its effectiveness.

"My belief in spellwork is a bit different; objects summon, but the intent comes through."

"(There are) many ways to work spells. Each spell is different."

"(It) depends on the spell."

"One person is better than an untrained group, but a trained group is better than one person."

"I do not subscribe to any dogmatic belief or system with regard to my religion and its practice; this includes spell crafting. Groups lend more energy, it is a math thing – more people. But an individual can do extremely powerful work as well. A group may be challenged focusing everyone's intent sharply for the working, where one person can finely focus his intent."

"It is really a factor of intent. It's better for one who really believes in it to do it than one believer and a group (of people who) don't care. Also note that at times, it's only necessary once."

"Recitation just aids intent."

"Spells are effective when you, a Solitary, or everyone, a group/coven, works and uses concentration and focus."

"All of the above. It depends on whether the ceremony is an initiation where you depend on a group reciting incantations along with concentration and focus, or a specific issue for one person to focus on."

"If I'm doing spells, I contact my many friends around the world and they send positive energy at the time of the casting."

"It is hard to get a group truly focused."

"We are taught that we are all Gods and Goddesses. We all have the spark of Deity within us. If we TRULY believe and are happy and content with our belief system then what we do magickally will manifest. Every one of us affects the entire universe with a single thought. We are truly magickal beings... and one with the universe on a GRAND scale."

"Although I work with groups, I find that the most effective workings are with one other person of the opposite sex to raise kundalini energies."

"There is definitely Power in Numbers; sometimes once is enough. It depends on what it is or if it was meant to be."

"I tend to work alone, but more voices help the gods hear your request and may show its urgency."

"We encourage doing solo spells between rites as well as group ones during them, people playing roles in groups."

"Focus of Will and Intention is everything to successful spellcraft; there is no 'wrong' way to do it."

"(It) depends on the situation."

"This is what I find works for me, but by no means do I think this is the only successful way to make spells effective."

"Change is constant so adjustments must be made."

Does Practical Magick Work?

An overwhelming 96% of the men responding to the survey believed that they had effectively caused change using spellwork and ritual. Only 4% thought that they had not been successful.

"I made it rain once, and I found a lover."

"I can produce testimonials of the work I have done."

"I have also been unsuccessful as well. I am still relatively new in spell-work, but each time it is performed is a learning experience."

"(I've been successful) too many times to list."

"I never do a spell that will not work. I am only willing to do a spell when I am ready for its outcome. Some things take time. If my spells did not work, what would be the point in doing them? I have created a wonderful life for myself through the effective use of spell work and through my practice in the Craft."

"Time will tell."

"Our group ritual is quite effective for proper purposes."

"Be careful what you spell for, it may go better than you planned."

"I have effectively created significant change using spellwork and ritual even before I was initiated into my (tradition). I resolved unimaginable issues; praise be to my spirits – ancestral, guides, and gods. Post initiation, the magic is complemented with the authority and bloodline of my ancestors and brethren. The secret to success is to believe in the ancestral spirit within the core of oneself. Therein lies the essence of our God-given power or "breath of the creator.""

"I haven't won lotto yet."

"Things around us are always relevant, so the change may not be outwardly noticeable, but you feel it. Things seem better, people seem happy, so yes, they work."

"It truly is a magickal feeling when manifestation is realized."

"Yes, with several applications for a specific spell and ritual."

"But not near as often as I would have liked. To me, spells are a prayer, a request of the gods. They will grant it if they desire. We have little force outside our own bodies. Trust them if you truly believe."

"Among other examples, I used magic to quit smoking; I did, cold turkey, five years ago. I had chain smoked for 30 years."

"I feel I have become more patient through ritual, and that in time I will be more confident in my own abilities as well."

"My weather working seems to be particularly successful."

Percentage of Male Pagans

This question asked if the respondent had worked with a group, either currently or in the past; if so, what was the percentage of males in the group?

Percentage of Males in the Group	Percentage of Responses
10	9
20	10
30	20
40	23
50	26
60	4
70	1
80	1
90	3
100 (all male)	3

"The number was determined deliberately – of the thirteen, seven were female and six were male."

"Only on a handful of occasions can I remember that there were more males than females; it was a rare thing."

"My main tradition, the Minoan Brotherhood, is all male. The NY Welsh tradition is about 50/50."

"The number varies between 35 and 65% but is usually close to 50%."

"I would say at least 50%, sometimes more, sometimes less. We never really looked at how the gender representation was expressed through the circle. I have even been brought into a Dianic ritual. Now that was a trip."

"It fluctuated a bit, and when it did, (the number of males) tended towards the lower end."

"We try not to discriminate sexually, or regarding orientation and so forth, but sometimes we have to encourage participation by minority individuals to create balance."

"Usually 40-50%."

"I have been the only male many times, but sometimes there have been as many as four. But I have been the only regular attendee."

"I was the only male."

"(It) has varied over time from 90% male to 10% male; presently about 40%."

"The Wiccan group I am with – I am not dedicated to their path, but I am invited to dedicate-only rituals due to my experience and participation and because my wife is dedicated – has only six adult males out of about 40 members, but my Heathen kindred has 50% male members who have taken an oath, and about 30% are males at our gatherings."

"Mine is a rough and tumble path that only a few women desire, but there is room and gods for all who ask."

"(Participation) has reached close to 50% in the past; (it is) around 30% now."

"I am usually the only male."

"My group workings have been primarily in male covens."

"I have met very few groups. I was invited long ago to become the first male in a coven that hadn't had a male included for many generations."

"I have also worked in an all-male group in the past."

"Just myself."

3

Universal Energy: Einstein's Theory of Relativity, Quantum Physics, and All The Other Stuff a Male Pagan Needs to Know

I could have titled this chapter "The Secret of the Universe." In fact, I almost did.

The information in this chapter provides a solid background of information that explains how and why both Pagan spirituality and magick work.

Let's face it. Many people accept the "truths" of their spiritual path with a grain of salt. Who can say what the Christian God looks like, where he's located, and what he does? It all comes down to simply accepting the "truths" of that spiritual path on faith.

Faith is important. It serves us well.

However, science has lent a hand to our quest to understand the cosmos and our place in it. Few people are exposed to it. The vast majority of public schools today teach outdated concepts about the universe, and the scientific discoveries of the past hundred years are still not discussed much in that forum.

Rituals and magickal workings will be far more effective if you get a good grasp on what is happening in actuality. This knowledge elevates your beliefs and efforts into the realm of reality; having to accept that a ritual or spell will work based only on faith that it will is not necessary if you have a fundamental knowledge of the science and philosophy behind the theory of how the universe works.

It required a number of years of study for me to be able to understand these concepts. You can get the same benefit by devoting a few minutes and reading this chapter all the way through. How easy is that?

Primitive man accepted almost everything on faith alone. As recently as three or four thousand years ago, humans assembled annually at Stonehenge to work magic that would enable another year to be born. Without that effort, they believed, night would come, darkness would settle in for eternity, and everyone would die. That's a lot of pressure. When an issue becomes one of life or death, it's quite normal for everyone to actively buy into it and do whatever they must to ensure that what they envision will happen, hopefully according to plan.

At some point, it became understood that all of that magical effort was not needed for some aspects of life. The sun, for example, would rise every day without magic being necessary. Maybe one year, everyone was busy with war or famine or some such thing, and nobody went to the annual Return of the Sun celebration, and the sun indeed returned. Other things, like successful crops, still required a bit of magical effort. The magic was needed because a dried up seed couldn't possibly change into a green and growing plant without magic, could it? So some magic persisted even into very recent times.

Some types of magic never went away. There is a woman in my town who has been making love charms since she was a very little girl, learning the craft from her mother and grandmother. She is in her late 90s now, still working to ensure the object of someone's affections will respond to them. Her clients are mostly female, young and old, attractive and not so pretty, from all walks of life. She claims great success. I hear she does quite well, selling her love spells for a few dollars. Most people would scoff at her, saying she's delusional, nobody can do what she claims she can do. Yet she has quite a few people consulting her and buying her charms. Love charms don't work? Don't ask anyone who goes to her!

Then the Church became all-powerful. While it borrowed heavily from pagans – all of the major Christian holidays were appropriated from pagan celebrations – it condemned pagans as godless and evil. Any and all magical working became taboo, punishable by imprisonment, torture, and death. I think those are great reasons to stop working magic (at least openly).

As time passed, the Church became less powerful and more segmented. There was no longer a single overpowering entity to rule over everyone.

Isaac Newton theorized that the universe was made up of what was believed at the time to be solid objects which were attracted to each other by gravity. Newton based his theory on popular thinking of the 17th century. His theory was extended in the 19th century to state that atoms were the fundamental building blocks of nature. Newton believed that atoms were solid particles; the protons, neutrons and electrons that composed an atom were a solid physical object. Newton's theory constituted Newtonian Physics – which, incidentally, are still taught in most public schools, ignoring Einstein's theory and the subsequent development of quantum physics.

In 1925, Albert Einstein took this theory to the next level. Einstein theorized that subatomic particles were pure energy. His Theory of Relativity ($E=mc^2$) states that energy is exactly the same thing as a particle of physical matter accelerated to the speed of light in a vacuum. (Okay, that takes a while to figure out.) In its simplest form, it states that energy always exhibits mass in whatever form it takes. In other words, all physical matter is energy that has slowed down so much that it forms a physical object.

That's us, folks.

Einstein believed at the time that the energy was in the form of particles: objects that had the appearance of being solid matter. Einstein was partially correct. Another physicist of the same period, Thomas Young, believed that energy existed as a wave form and was not particles at all.

Although their theories differed, they both acknowledged that all things are comprised of energy. Everything that exists is nothing more and nothing less than pure energy.

Here's a visual representation of the basis of this theory:

Universe > Galaxy > Earth > People > Organ systems > Cells > Molecules > Atoms > Subatomic Particles > Energy

In other words, we exist in an infinite field of pure energy, in the same way that a drop of water exists in the ocean. It can be part of the whole, or separated, but it is essentially the same thing no matter how it manifests.

Expanding this concept, if everything is simply energy, then the electricity that you use in your home is exactly the same as you. The gas that fuels your car is exactly the same as you. These things appear differently in the physical world because of their physical structure, the vibrational frequencies of their subatomic particles, and the varying formation of particles that comprise them.

Everything that exists – you, your dog, the chair you're sitting in, the money in your wallet, the stars, the sun, the oceans, air, your physical senses – all of them are composed of the same energy.

Another physicist, Neils Bohr, who won the Nobel prize in 1922, added to the theory. He believed that energy could be both waves (like Young) or particles (like Einstein). Einstein and Bohrs debated this theory for many years. Bohr believed that any particle could exhibit the qualities of both a wave and a particle at the same time.

Although Einstein believed that everything in the universe was composed of pure energy, he also thought that everything that happened as a result was a random event without any individual interference or participation. The only thing that could change this randomness was God.

In 1927, Bohrs and other respected scientists assembled to experiment with his theory. Their findings comprise the "Copenhagen Interpretation." This revealed that subatomic particles weren't just particles; they could be waves as well, but not both at the same time. Energy is waves, and when attention is placed on it, waves disappear and a particle is formed. The thoughts and perceptions of the scientist doing the observing determined whether it was a wave or a particle.

That is, energy that was being studied immediately took form immediately based on the thoughts and beliefs of the scientist who was observing it. If the scientist expected to see particles, he did. If he expected to see waves, he did. Same energy, different manifestations based on human perception.

So, everything in our world consists of pure energy that began as a wave and manifested into physical form based on our belief that it would be physical.

The most interesting aspect of this entire discussion is that for thousands of years, enlightened individuals and spiritual texts have taught that everything is one thing.

If everything is simply energy vibrating at different rates, then there is no separation between you and your neighbor, your dog, your house, your car, or the axe murderer in the next town because you are intricately connected to everything and anything else.

This scientific proof of what spiritual texts and teachers have been saying for several thousand years is about a century old at this point.

Take it a step further. You have the ability to see, hear, touch, smell and taste: the five senses. What about the sixth sense: extrasensory perception? If all energy is the same, then the ability to use extrasensory perception must be as available to you as any of the other five senses. And if everything is energy, then you can manipulate anything that exists. You can manifest anything you want or need. If everything that is physical is connected to everything else, than everything that is unseen is also connected to everything else.

Your thoughts are infinitely creative. You can change pure energy into a physical form or use it as pure energy depending on what you think it should do.

Now... do you see how ritual works? Do you understand how magick works?

A further discovery by a scientist named Max Planck has been named the Quantum Entanglement.

Planck hypothesized that when subatomic particles are broken in half (separated) in a laboratory setting, the two halves have the capability to communicate between themselves and that communication is received instantly from each other, with absolutely no regard to time or space. This applied regardless of how far apart physically they were.

Humans have measured the speed of light, and we know sound requires time to travel (as evidenced by an echo). The two halves of Planck's particle received the communication at exactly the same time regardless of how far away they were from each other.

This proves that communication between any two forms of energy is not subject to time or space (at least, as we understand it at present).

Newtonian Physics stated that nothing could travel faster than the speed of light. That is not true. Energy doesn't need to travel – it's already connected to all other energy.

How Does This Work For Magick or Ritual?

Just as the subatomic particles assumed the form (wave or particle) that the scientist who conducted the experiments expected, the events and circumstances that make up your reality take shape according to what you believe they will do.

Whatever you believe will happen, will indeed happen.

You create your own reality. Your life is not the result of forces outside your control, or the efforts (or lack of) of a deity. You get in life exactly what you believe you will get.

I don't know how you feel about that, but it's infinitely scary.

Another thing to remember is that your life today, right at this moment, is the result of what you were. You can change it and the change can start right at this very minute.

Your life is a painting, and you are the artist. If you don't like the scene on your canvas, paint over it.

There are people around you who appear to live a charmed life. Everything goes well for them. There are others who seem to attract every negative experience possible.

When I was young, I knew two identical twins. They lived in the same house, wore the same clothes, and basically lived the same life. They were physically separated only for however long it took to take a bath or pee. Literally. Yet one twin constantly moaned about his awful life; the other was constantly happy and enjoyed his days. Even though they were identical, everyone in my class at school could identify which was which from thirty paces, and we were able to avoid the cranky brother while enjoying the company of the more positive one. Their lives were almost exactly the same in every way imaginable. What was different? One saw life as negative, the other as positive.

What you accept as truth can be based on reality, or your perception of reality. If you don't like your reality, change it. The lesson of quantum physics is that the act of observing an object causes it to become reality and that reality is based on our choice of how we observe it. An object cannot exist independently of its observer.

How does this work in a practical way?

If, for example, you believe that money is scarce and difficult to acquire, that thought will harmonize with energy of a harmonious frequency, transmute into particles which will attract similar particles that harmonize with it, and your life will reflect a difficulty in acquiring money.

If on the other hand, you believe that money flows to you effortlessly, that energy is sent forth instead, attracting money to you.

In a spiritual sense, your rituals can become more meaningful and the results more evidential simply by changing what you believe to be true. If you work magick, you will see more success. When you connect with the God energy, you will feel it throughout your being.

I've seen the proof of this theory in my own life. In 2007, I had a serious illness that nearly killed me. I was not expected to live. I had to stop working because I was too sick to sit in my office chair and do the work. I began to feel that, without an income, I was poor. My savings disappeared. I ended up living hand to mouth for a year until I finally found a permanent home. Before becoming ill, I had always been able to enjoy an ample income; money flowed to me effortlessly. If I needed a specific amount for some reason, I always had it. Even though my circumstances are significantly reduced today, I still always have enough money to do what needs to be done.

Here's another example. I used to do psychic fairs for many years, always taking the same highway from my home to the new age bookstore about an hour away where the fairs were held. Every time I passed a small farm, I looked at the little cottage attached to the barn. It always felt so cozy and warm to me, even though it was an abandoned building that had once been an office space and most recently contained the equipment for processing milk from the dairy barn it was attached to. I always thought "I'd love to live there."

Years later, after becoming ill and having to give up my home in the south, I moved north again to be near my sister. During the sixteen years that I had lived in North Carolina, she had purchased the property that barn sat on and now owned the little cottage! She and her husband had worked to remodel the cottage into a small house. Guess where I ended up living?

Manifesting what you want is relatively easy; at least it has been for me. I've always been able to do it without much effort. You can do it too.

You just have to know that you can.

4

The Male Role

Note: While this information relates to any Pagan spiritual tradition, it was originally written about Wicca, since that is the tradition that I have followed for more than 40 years. These concepts can be applied to any Pagan spiritual tradition.

Women often outnumber men in Wiccan circles by a 2 to 1 ratio. In many circles, the number of women can be much higher; some circles have no male participants.

It is true that in general, fewer men are interested in their spiritual selves. Spirituality is often looked upon as a basically feminine role. This has been a trend that has developed over the past two thousand years, as Christianity matured. In fertility based religions, men were always important because their energy was considered integral to the process. Spiritual ritual that eliminated the male principle would not work. Both the God and Goddess were included in the tradition, both held equal places for the most part, although each was assigned a superior role on occasion, depending on the season and the reason. The Goddess was venerated during the part of the year when fertility was needed. Crops would not grow and animals would not reproduce without intervention from the Goddess. For the part of the year when the ground was fallow and animals were not actively reproducing, the God was revered; his energy was used to bring the Goddess (along with her fertility and fecundity) back into the world. Since the Goddess gave birth to the God each year, both were absolutely necessary.

When Abrahamic religions began to flourish, the need for Goddess energy was negated. Men could make anything happen, and women were subservient to the will of men. The Goddess was neglected as the world conspired to make the God a supreme being. In the Catholic church, for example, the Goddess figure was transmuted into Mary – a mortal woman who had the task of giving birth to a God figure while remaining mortal. While many Catholics revere Mary as a feminine aspect of God, the official stance of the church is that Mary is simply an adjunct, necessary to accomplish a miraculous task, but inessential enough to not be assigned a primary role.

Another issue is that in Abrahamic, male-based monotheistic religions, male priests have all the power. Outside a few very progressive denominations, many traditions do not allow women to assume the role of priest. One gender rules, while the other is kept subservient.

In most Pagan traditions, priestesses are used. By empowering the female gender, Pagans evoke a more balanced view of the world. In many traditions, male priests have roles as well, working alongside priestesses as equals to accomplish a task.

Can men find a suitable role in a Goddess-based spiritual tradition? Can they find a role in a tradition that assigns much of the spiritual work to priestesses rather than priests?

As both genders are empowered, both men and women can become fulfilled and powerful in ways that were impossible in traditions where this equality was denied.

Power, in the sense in which it is used here, is not a win-lose issue. One does not assume power in a way that makes others powerless. Each gender is able to assume powerful roles that are interdependent rather than exclusive. When two powerful genders combine, it makes an even more powerful synergy that in turn feeds more power back to the individual.

Many women have become Wiccan to avoid Abrahamic-based monotheistic religions that are male-centered, where women were required to assume a subservient role, submitting to male authority as a matter of course. The women of Neo-Pagan goddess traditions tend to relegate men to a passive role, defending this stance using the logic that men cannot possibly understand the feminine energy of the Goddess.

That's just wrong.

But it's certainly understandable. Many Pagan religions are modern adaptations of what were originally fertility religions. By its nature, fertility religion confers a high status to feminine energy. Without a female, for humans as well as for the vast majority of species, there is no reproduction.

It is important to remember that modern Wicca was brought into being by a man, Gerald Gardner. It must be noted that Gardner's practice of Wicca always involved women in a prominent role. In subsequent years, many more men contributed considerable amounts of information and theory to the practice of Wicca, including Stuart Ferrar and Isaac Bonewits among others. Christopher Penzak has promulgated what is probably the definitive information about gay Pagans and how gay men can work within the Pagan traditions.

Any tradition that emphasizes one gender over another is simply out of balance. The gender that is slighted cannot fully participate or embrace a path that essentially says "you're not worth as much as someone else."

Men are Vital to Pagan Traditions

A quick check of the Internet reveals a long list of Wiccan circles that are open only to women and have no male participants. This stance is every bit as counterproductive as the old Abrahamic model.

Are men important in Pagan traditions?

Looking at ancient Pagan pantheons, there are as many Gods as Goddesses. Ancient pagans had a balanced view of their universe. They would not have considered participating in a tradition that excluded either God or Goddess.

The Wheel of the Year provides another example of the necessity of masculine energy in Pagan traditions. More than half of the year is ruled by the God. His influence begins with his birth (or rebirth) at Yule and ends with his death at Samhain. Only eight weeks exist wherein the influence of the God is dormant.

Sabbats are God-centered. The Goddess participates and assists the God in an equal role.

Many Pagan men understand the archetypes that exist in each manifestation of the God, and because these archetypes are masculine in nature, men are more easily able to work with the energy to promulgate change and growth. At the same time, Pagan men understand the archetypes behind each manifestation of the Goddess, and are able to call on those archetypical qualities to both understand the Goddess in that manifestation and to work with the specific energies lying behind the archetype.

In all things Pagan, balance is absolutely necessary. All-female circles innately lack a definitive energy that links them to masculine archetypes; scientifically, females have two X (feminine) chromosomes but no Y (masculine) ones. Men, on the other hand, have both an X and Y chromosome. This does not in any way indicate superiority, or any lack in women. It simply restates the fact that men can access feminine energy. I look at is as a sign from the universe that is saying: "Look, this proves it. You contain a feminine side." (Note: this is my opinion. If you can prove me wrong, please write me. If not, just think about it and don't just dismiss it!)

My point is that men are essential in every spiritual tradition. They must find a way to contribute equally to their tradition, and also to receive equal benefit from it.

A gay Wiccan friend postulates that gay men have accessed their feminine energy and that they don't need to connect with God energy. I think that's wrong. Men, whether gay, bisexual or heterosexual, are still men. They contain or can access within them every masculine energy that every other man contains or can access. A gay man is not a female. He can act in a way that's more feminine than masculine (and this discussion is a road I really don't want to wander down), but his spirit is still male. Gay and bisexual men might find it easier to access Goddess energy than heterosexual men; some men are indeed innately attuned to their feminine side and instinctively understand how to access and utilize feminine energy. I think some further research should be done on that concept. But it is essential for every man, regardless of sexual orientation, to understand that the basis for everything that he is comes from a masculine energy.

Since every man can access and use his masculine energy to commune with the God archetype, it is essential to include men in the Pagan spiritual community and to ensure that their energy is used in a positive way to balance Goddess energy. Balance is essential in any magick if it is to be successful. Spells, rituals, and incantations performed with both masculine and feminine energy will always be successful.

The Great Horned God

If it can be said that there is a single archetype that can be accessed by any Pagan man, it undoubtedly would be the Great Horned God.

The Great Horned God was traditionally associated with Celts, and thereafter with Wicca through Gardner's writings, which were based in large part on Celtic mythology. This archetype has been known throughout the history of mankind. Some of the deities that were linked with the Great Horned God include:

Tammuz, the son/lover of Ishtar

Danuzi, the son/lover of Inanna

Osiris, the Egyptian Lord of the Underworld

Pan, the Greek god of woodlands and wild places

Dionysus, the Greek god of greenery and the vine

Janus, the Roman god of beginnings, transitions, endings, and time

Herne, the god of the hunt in ancient Britain

The Green Man, the god of vegetation and woodlands

Cernunnos, the Celtic god of fertility and animals and the ruler of the underworld

The Great Horned God is the symbol of the divine manifestation of male energy. He has traditionally been considered the equal partner of the Goddess, required as an essential part of annual fertility rites that ensured new crops, livestock and human babies every year. The Great Horned God rules life, death and the underworld. As every goddess archetype has represented the moon, the Great Horned God represents the sun. He rules over part of the process of birth, death and rebirth; the Goddess rules the process when life is alive and abundant, and the Great Horned God rules it when the earth is cold and desolate.

While the Great Horned God was originally associated with fertility, he also came to represent the guardian of the portal into the underworld.

The Great Horned God was such an important deity to the Celts that his image and abilities were targeted by early Christians. The beneficent image of the kindly Great Horned God was transformed into the Christian representation of the Devil, known as the "deo falsus" or "false god." As the ruler of Hell, his image was not far removed to ancient Celts from their view of him as guardian of the portal to the underworld.

Herne, the ancient British god of the hunt, played an important part in the Wild Hunt. This symbolic hunt mirrored the annual hunt for wild boar, deer and other meats by humans. There are many British people, both Pagan and otherwise, who believe that Herne, an antlered giant beast of a God, still lives in the protected forests around royal Windsor Great Park. Herne was also linked to Robin Hood in his role of protector and provider to the tribe.

As Osiris, he was the judge of the dead and the protector of the underworld. Osiris was both the brother and the husband of Isis, the goddess of fertility, and he fulfilled his role as a fertility god by fathering Isis' children.

The Green Man has been depicted as a horned man, peering out of a mask made of leaves. He is the god of the woodlands and vegetation. He represents the elemental spirits of trees, plants and foliage and promotes growth and an annual regeneration. He rules over a court consisting of fairies and nature sprites. Livestock could not survive without lush meadowlands, and the Green Man had the power to bring rain to the crops.

Whichever Great Horned God archetype feels most comfortable to you, the energy and qualities of the Great Horned God are available to all Pagan men. He simply needs to be invoked. The archetype surrounding the Great Horned God is incredibly strong because of its association over the entire history of mankind; this makes it easier to tap into it in our own time.

Meeting the Green Man

In my case, I had one very memorable afternoon with the Great Horned God. There is a small park that runs alongside a small river in Connecticut, near the New York border north of Danbury. The river is often quiet and peaceful, but in the springtime, after the snow melts, it becomes a raging river. The park is adjacent to several waterfalls; huge boulders line the banks, providing an excellent place for sitting or lying in the sun, listening to the music of the moving water, and contemplating life.

On this occasion, the park was completely empty of other humans, as it often is. I had just completed a difficult week at work, with several important deadlines and more than enough drama for a lifetime. I had spent the morning at Unicorn Books, a wonderful New Age bookstore in New Milford, CT, doing psychic readings and chatting with Barbara Straub, the owner and a great friend. Doing readings always mellows me out, so on the way home in the early afternoon, I stopped at the park to sit by the river for a few minutes and to just enjoy what was left of the day.

I had been sitting on a sunny boulder, watching the water cascade over the waterfalls and listening to the sounds of nature – leaves rustling on the tree branches, birds singing – and then I heard a rustling noise in the underbrush on the riverbank behind me. I looked around, expecting to see someone hiking past, but there was nothing there. I turned my attention back to the river and heard it again.

This happened several times. I began to think I needed medicating. The noises became louder, like someone was walking forcefully through the shrubs and underbrush. I was about to turn around again when I heard a loud snort. It wasn't human – it definitely was a kind of noise only animals make. I looked up quickly, and there was still nothing anywhere around me. Looking away again, I heard another snort and smelled a very strong musky animal smell.

Suddenly, everything went silent. The leaves stopped rustling, the birds all stopped singing. Even the dull roar of the waterfalls seemed to quiet down considerably. Now I was getting nervous. This was not a normal day. I wanted to look around at the riverbank again, but couldn't move.

There were a couple more snorts, and then a low growling noise. It didn't alarm me; it sounded more like something humming than an animal growling with aggression. I couldn't move a muscle, and realized suddenly that I did not want to move. Life was frozen, like when Samantha the Witch wiggles her nose and everything around her freezes in mid-frame.

I heard a voice talking quietly to me. It described several experiences I had been having in recent weeks. This didn't frighten me. I have channeled before, the first time many years before in the Cheops pyramid in Egypt, where my spirit guide can through loud and clear. I remember feeling just great. I had no worries in life. I felt protected and loved.

Then the growling/humming stopped, followed by more stomping noises through the brush, almost like one would hear when a deer runs away from a human. I could move, I could turn my head again, and when I did – nothing was there, except the musky smell.

I knew while this being was humming that it was the Great Horned God. I had not, at that point, been familiar with that archetype and was completely unaware of it. Having encountered it in person, I was fascinated by it and began to research it.

More than a year later, in a Wiccan circle, one of the other men mentioned that he had just had an encounter with the Great Horned God the previous weekend while on a camping trip. His description of his experience matched mine exactly, although the two happened mile apart (in two different states) and more than a year apart in time. In his case, the buddy he was camping with also heard the same noises, had the same experiences, and investigated the area surrounding their campsite thoroughly. We had never mentioned our experiences to each other.

The Great Horned God is easily accessible. Sometimes he comes when he is needed, or simply because he wants to. Ours were not isolated experiences; other men over the years have described nearly identical experiences to me. The one thing we all had in common was that we were open to experiences like these, and we did not discount them by saying, "that couldn't happen, the Great Horned God isn't real." Reality is what you know it is, not what others experience.

Seek the Great Horned God in the daytime, in wild places where you are undisturbed. In many cases, we who have experienced him did not hear words and sentences; we simply understood instinctively that some information of great importance was being imparted to us. Don't try to apply logic to it; it's not a logical experience. Enjoy it when it happens to you!

5

Masculine Energy in a Goddess Tradition

The term "masculine" relates to two similar but slightly different concepts: sexuality and gender.

In a sexual sense, men are masculine and women are feminine. (And yes, a few people are born who are both male and female, but let's ignore that issue for the purpose of this book, because I have neither a solid answer or even a theory on this topic.) You are either male or female. It's simple.

When masculinity refers to gender, it's a different and far more complicated story. If you are born male, your energy is masculine. You have within your essential being many masculine traits, such as strength, courage, or power. Your sexual preferences do not matter; you retain masculine traits regardless of who you sleep with. If you're born female, your energy is feminine, and your essential being has feminine traits, such as nurturing, compassion, or humility. Mankind has assigned a masculine or feminine energy to virtually every trait that we can exhibit. It is important to recognize that men can possess any trait traditionally considered to be feminine, and vice versa.

But – and this is important – within each of us lies the complimentary energy. Every male has both an X (feminine) and a Y (masculine) chromosome. The energy of every male includes a feminine component that can be demonstrated scientifically.

So, logically, within each male, one can find the Goddess.

It is important to remember that masculine or feminine traits are *archetypes*. Archetypes are defined as the original pattern or model from which all things of the same kind are copied or on which they are based; a model or first form; a prototype. Spirituality and religion rely almost completely on archetypes. God and Goddess are both archetypes. Archetypical meanings come from deep within the human psyche and often are developed throughout the history of mankind.

Why, for example, is bravery considered masculine? Maybe it was a man who first ventured forth from the cave and smacked a huge animal on the head. If a woman had done it, maybe bravery would be considered a feminine trait. The point is, some event, somewhere in time, associated almost every archetype with either masculinity or femininity. That link, however, is not absolute. Joan of Arc exhibited bravery, as did the first female astronaut. The act of being brave does not make them masculine.

It is this concept that is vitally important in understanding how men can exist and thrive in a spiritual path that, as a Goddess-centric path, has long been considered essentially based in feminine energy.

It also indicates that Pagan men need to develop and access masculine archetypes if they pursue this spiritual path. Men need to learn to access and use God (masculine-based) energy to work effectively.

A Pagan spiritual path includes both God and Goddess. Men are reluctant to join a religion that focuses only on Goddess energy, and rightfully so. Pagan spirituality is not a religion only for those with wombs. Both masculine and feminine energy are essential if one seeks a balanced perspective. Many traditional Pagan spiritual paths have always reflected a balanced view of God/Goddess energies; in recent years, beginning in the 1970s, the emphasis has shifted as fewer men joined these groups.

It is also unfortunate that most of the books published in recent years on Pagan spirituality, and especially those on Wicca, tend to emphasize Goddess worship and relegate the God to secondary status. Gerald Gardner did this in his writings, so perhaps the bias is so long-standing that it has become pervasive. Women who have found Abrahamic male-centric religion too oppressive have hijacked several Pagan traditions as they revolted against the status quo. It is up to Pagan men to remind other Pagans with whom they interact that a balanced view of life is needed. Women can be comfortable accessing God energy, just as men have learned how to work with Goddess energy.

Many men coming into Pagan paths in recent years have been much younger than those in the past, who often turned to Pagan spirituality because Abrahamic monotheism no longer worked for them. This happened as they matured. Pagan spirituality now attracts much younger men, many of whom begin in their late teens or early twenties. Developing some masculine traits, such as the warrior spirit, requires a man to live in the world for many years. Some Pagan paths, like Asatru, seem to attract mature men who innately have a warrior spirit.

Over the past two thousand years, masculine energy has been defined primarily as a warrior type: man goes out into the world and conquers it, and brings home the spoils. Today, Pagan men are assimilating the warrior aspect with the artistic, creative aspect of masculinity, and bringing the concept of what masculinity is back into balance.

Modern man craves masculine energy. Over the past several decades, fathers became distant figures, always away "at work," while mothers essentially raised their sons. Absentee fathers cannot effectively demonstrate masculine energy to their sons. And mothers cannot teach their sons how to be masculine. Many men have no idea what masculine energy is, or how they can access it. This revelation can occur through their spiritual path – as long as God energy is as revered as Goddess energy.

Another issue that is off-putting to both men and women is the trend toward superficiality. There are a large number of Pagans who sport bumper stickers, wear pentacles and loudly proclaim their Paganity to the world at large, but who can't perform a ritual or even explain what Pagan spirituality is and is not. Few men are attracted to a spiritual path that can be purchased at the local New Age store, or one that seems to hinge on lighting candles and reciting poetry and then going home. Every Pagan needs to learn how to connect to spirit on a deep personal level. That does not happen simply because your Acura sports a cute bumper sticker or because you never leave the house without your pentacle.

When a man allows himself to become an overfed couch potato, it becomes far more difficult to access masculine energies. A recently as a hundred years ago, our ancestors spent most of their time out in nature, observing seasons, feeling the cold in winter and the warmth of the sun in summer, watching the cycle of birth and death, tending animals, and connecting in a basic way to the energies of the Earth. That connection is missing if you live in suburbia, have a lawn service to maintain your property, and never go outside except to get into the car. Several Pagan men mentioned in our survey that they take time each day to get outdoors and really connect with nature and the Earth.

Maybe you live in a highrise apartment in the city and work in an office. Your environment is urban; you are surrounded by streets full of vehicles and a lot of concrete. Your apartment doesn't even have an balcony or outdoors terrace. Is it possible to connect with Earth energies?

It is, and it takes a bit of effort. Every neighborhood has a park; go there and sit for a few minutes as often as you can and observe nature and whatever is going on around you. Visit a botanical garden. Take a bus to the seashore, if that's possible. It might take some planning and a bit of effort, but every human can find a way to communicate with nature without giving up an urban lifestyle and moving out to the woods. That connection to nature is essential if you want to understand the Pagan spiritual path.

And, whenever possible, avoid Dianic or other Goddess-based groups! If a more balanced group does not exist in your area, form one! If you are solitary, your spiritual path can reflect exactly what you want it to reflect.

There are Pagans who realize that the scales have tipped dramatically toward Goddess energy. This is a natural response by female Pagans who come to the Pagan spiritual path because they no longer can feel comfortable in any of the Abrahamic male-oriented religions. Taking back the feminine spirit is fine, and necessary. However, it can be done in a more balanced way than simply ignoring God energy while venerating the Goddess. Women must be willing to view their Pagan traditions as balanced between God and Goddess energies.

Men are as spiritual as women. They instinctively understand concepts like love, spirit, nature and balance. It is not the principles behind Pagan spirituality that alienate men: it is the practice. If all concentration and power is allocated to the Goddess, there is no masculine based energy that attracts men. Men view a spiritual path that is out of balance as out of bounds. Nobody wants to go there.

I don't think that women are willfully ignoring masculine energy in order to alienate men from participating in their tradition. I think it is an unfortunate by-product of the excitement of having a Goddess-based tradition to call their own. In their haste to accept the new order, God energy has been forgotten, left along the wayside and treated as an adjunct to the important feminine energy.

Unfortunately, women who alienate themselves from masculine energy can begin to find it difficult to access masculine traits that are necessary for them to survive and thrive. Women who are in the work force often have to access masculine traits simply to survive in the business world. If they can't compete with men at work, they will be relegated to inferior positions and lower salaries. It can be difficult to access masculine traits if a woman believes totally in a spiritual path that excludes masculine energies.

In Wicca, the move toward Eclectic Wicca and books by feminist writers like Starhawk, Zsusana Budapest and Silver Ravenwolf (among many others) have encouraged the abandonment of balanced spirituality and fostered the Goddess-centric world that so many men find today when they search for a spiritual path. Starhawk's seminal book *The Spiral Dance* is Goddess-centric and ignores male energies for the most part. Although it professed to be a book about Wicca, it was in actuality a book about Goddess worship. Even Stuart Farrar's *Witches Bible* stated that a Wiccan coven can only be run by a woman. This imbalance and female bias has attracted many women who have a hatred for men. Their tradition has become peace-loving, feminist and anti-male. Their spiritual path is totally unbalanced. What man, other than one filled with self-hate, would consider joining such a tradition? Many men have abandoned Wicca in favor of Asatru, Druidism, or one of the Reconstructionist traditions based on Celtic, Norse or Greco/Roman spirituality, where masculine energy is considered an essential part of the tradition. These traditions have a warrior aspect that is highly attractive to men.

Another aspect is how men are expected to behave in a Pagan tradition. Masculine males might find it difficult to be enthusiastic about wearing floral headbands and dancing in a circle. Some men even object to having to wear robes. The ritual practices of some traditions might need to be overhauled to enable men to express their masculine energy in a way that is appropriate to them. So much of Pagan spirituality is feminine-oriented out of necessity; communicating with spirit is essentially accomplished by our feminine receptive energy, not a projective masculine energy. Much of the energy used in any Pagan undertaking is feminine in nature. We ask the God and Goddess for information or help (a feminine, receptive form of energy), we don't order them to help us (a projective, masculine energy).

One man who took the survey made an interesting observation about why he was considering leaving the Pagan group that he had been with for more than ten years. He noticed that the majority of women in his group were extremely overweight, chain-smoked, or had serious addictions to alcohol or drugs. The last two High Priestesses in his Wiccan tradition had been on serious power trips; neither knew much about Wicca but both reigned over the group like queens. Everything of any nature had to be cleared through them. He was trying to reconcile how a spiritual path attracts people who are addicted to alcohol, drugs, food or power, and how they can profess to live a balanced life when their own lives are so completely unbalanced. I don't think his complaint is uncommon; I remember participating in a group more than thirty years ago that sounds strangely similar to the one about which he comments. I left that group for many of the same reasons, and ultimately worked as a solitary to avoid these poisonous group dynamics that never felt very spiritual.

Loss of the Goddess

In pre-Christian times, anthropological research has found evidence that the people of the times acknowledged a balance between masculine and feminine energies. Indeed, many ancient spiritual paths included both God and Goddess worship by groups that included both men and women.

For the two thousand year period in which masculine-based monotheistic religions were in the forefront, emphasis shifted from a balance of masculine and feminine energies toward a concept that masculine energies were the primary life force. Although feminine energy was essential, it was considered a compliment to masculine energy. These monotheistic religions are called Abrahamic because they were all based on Abraham, a father figure in the Old Testament. Christian, Judaic and Islamic traditions are all based on this archetype.

Religion shifted to a patriarchal model. In the Christian world, men controlled everything and women were subservient in nearly every way.

As time passed, this view became more toxic. Women were equated with evil. Eve was blamed for Adam's fall from God's grace. If a man wanted to follow a spiritual path, he could assume any office in the Church, even rising to the topmost posts. If a woman wanted to follow a similar path, she could become a nun and spend the rest of her life serving the men of the Church.

In some traditions, women were so spiritually reviled that they were relegated to sitting in spaces removed from the main area of worship. Orthodox Jewish women sit separately from men. Islamic women must be totally covered and are physically separated from the men in mosques. Fundamentalist Christian churches constantly preach the inferiority of women and harangue them to accept whatever the man of the house decrees.

For Pagans, this model simply does not work. Pagans acknowledge both masculine and feminine energy; they are considered equal and complementary. One does not exist without the other. It is impossible to define something as masculine without the concept of femininity. This is especially true of archetypes. For example, it is impossible to define beauty unless the concept of ugliness is considered. Beauty is relative, as are many other archetypes, such as power, love, empathy, and so on.

Pagans understand the need for balance. Balance is a defining principle in the scientific world. For example, a 200-pound man cannot play on a seesaw with a 30-pound child. Neither can two 30-pound children play seesaw if they both sit on the same side. Balance is the essential component.

Working With Masculine Energy

How then does a male Pagan work effectively in spiritual traditions that, in current times, often emphasize the feminine?

The Wiccan tradition is a good example. Wicca has evolved in some circles from a balanced God/Goddess philosophy into a Goddess-based, Goddess-centric form that emphasizes feminine energy and relegates masculine energy to a God who is "less than," a form of consort. In these traditions, the God is considered as an adjunct to the Goddess, necessary for several discrete purposes but not essential to many. Magick is worked within the circle that evokes the favor of the Goddess. Altars are decorated with Goddess images; rituals that honor the Goddess and rarely mention the God are used.

It is true that not every Wiccan circle (or every Wiccan, individually) has become Goddess-centric. There are many Wiccans who understand the concept of balance and who actively use God energy in their rituals.

On the other hand, some feminist Wiccans focus completely on Goddess energy and do not include God in their rituals. This has evolved as a form of resistance to the monotheistic God-based religions of the last two thousand years. Feminists say that they are taking back their feminine energy by participating in a spiritual tradition that honors only the Goddess. This concept, however, is relatively new. There is no evidence that ancient people worshipped only a Goddess and excluded a God. While feminists claim that they are taking back their tradition, they are in fact rewriting it. Ancient civilizations understood that they would not survive without both masculine and feminine energies.

The need for polarity remains essential to any tradition. Ritual relies on archetypes, and archetypes are innately masculine or feminine. For example, the Wiccan "great rite" (the conjoining of male and female to create new life) is celebrated symbolically through ritual every time an athame is plunged into a chalice. The athame represents the masculine, the chalice represents the feminine. Very little can be accomplished using magick that ignores polarity. Placing two chalices side by side provides little energy. Rubbing two athames together might sharpen the blades, but in a magickal sense, not much happens.

Polarity can be viewed like electrical energy. A battery has a positive and a negative terminal. If you connect one battery's positive terminal with another battery's negative terminal, electricity will flow between them. Connecting either the two positive or two negative terminals together produces nothing. Electricity is simply the flow of energy. Magick is exactly the same thing. Without energy moving from one thing into another, magick does not happen. Both require polarity in order to work.

6

Gay and Bisexual Men and Paganism

It has become an urban legend that many gay and bisexual men and women are attracted to Paganism. I have seen several estimates that more than 50% of Pagan men are gay or bisexual.

In my survey, the majority of men (about 60%) who responded identified themselves as heterosexual, with about 40% identifying as gay or bisexual. My survey was taken by men from all over the USA as well as worldwide; there were responses from all of the continents, although the numbers heavily favored North America and Europe. Obviously the responses were limited by the necessity of being able to access the Internet, where the survey was hosted and which was the origin of the survey announcement, and this definitely skewed the results to some degree.

Historical Precedence

Greco-Roman mythology features male same-sex love in many of the myths that fostered Paganism. These myths have been described as being crucially influential on Western LGBT literature, with the original myths being constantly re-published and re-written, and the relationships and characters serving as icon for gay and bisexual men today.

In comparison, lesbianism is rarely found in classical myths. However, several traditions, including Dianic Wicca, have become attractive to lesbians because they consider only the feminine aspect of Divinity. In some Dianic groups, men are banned outright. In most groups, men are welcome, although most men are not likely to join a spiritual tradition that, in essence, demotes them to a secondary place. It can be argued that over the past two thousand years of Abrahamic religions, women have had that same experience. Indeed, the concept of a spiritual tradition that honors feminine energy must seem highly attractive to women today. The virtual lack of balance in Dianic Wicca is one of its main criticisms.

In mythology, the patron god of hermaphrodites and transvestites was Dionysus, a god gestated in the thigh of his father Zeus, after his mother died from being overwhelmed by Zeus's true form.

Other gods are sometimes considered patrons of homosexual love between males, such as the love goddess Aphrodite and gods in her retinue, such as the Erotes, Eros, Himeros and Pothos.

Eros is also part of a trinity of gods that played roles in homoerotic relationships, along with Heracles and Hermes, who bestowed qualities of beauty (and loyalty), strength, and eloquence, respectively, onto male lovers. Apollo and Heracles both had a number of male lovers, both with other gods and with mortal men. In the poetry of Sappho, Aphrodite is identified as the patron of lesbians.

Aphroditus was an androgynous Aphrodite from Cyprus, and in later mythology became known as Hermaphroditus, the son of Hermes and Aphrodite.

Wikipedia lists many same-sex pairings in ancient history. They include:
- ✓ Achilles and Patroclus
- ✓ Achilles and Troilus
- ✓ Ameinias and Narcissus
- ✓ Apollo and Branchus
- ✓ Apollo and Hyacinth
- ✓ Apollo and Hymenaios
- ✓ Apollo and Iapis
- ✓ Chrysippus and Laius
- ✓ Daphnis and Pan
- ✓ Dionysus and Ampelus
- ✓ Dionysus and Prosymnus
- ✓ Euryalus and Nisus
- ✓ Heracles and Abderus
- ✓ Heracles and Hylas
- ✓ Heracles and Iolaus

- ✓ Ianthe and Iphis
- ✓ Poseidon and Nerites
- ✓ Poseidon and Pelops
- ✓ Polyeidos and Glaucus
- ✓ Orpheus and the Thracians
- ✓ Orpheus and Kalais
- ✓ Apollo/Silvanus and Cyparissus
- ✓ Zeus (Artemis) and Callisto
- ✓ Zeus and Ganymede

More information is available at http://www.wikipedia.org.

If Pagan religions in ancient times were rife with stories of same-sex love, it must be assumed that there was no moral judgment about gay or bisexual men in existence at that time.

The more or less complete lack of evidence of same sex love between women begs the assumption that this form of homosexual love was not considered as lightly. Alternately, since most of the historical accounts of ancient times were written by men, it could simply be that men had no concept of what women did. The existence of various feminine mysteries, in which the participants were strictly female, with no male allowed to observe them, could indicate that this aspect was kept securely hidden from all men.

It is likely that we will never know what is true about these relationships; we have only a few written records to illuminate a deeply personal area of life.

Several gay men have pointed out that homosexuality has been tied to paganism for eons. The term "flaming faggot," used in a derogatory way to describe gay men, was coined during the witch trials in the 16th century, when small branches (called faggots) were used to light the pyres and stoke the flames beneath a man who had been condemned for witchcraft and was being burnt at the stake.

Fortunately, gay and bisexual Pagan men today have a number of myths from all of the ancient civilizations that can enable working with a God or Goddess archetype (and both are important) that has some connection to their own sexuality. For more information, see the chapter "Gods and Goddesses" on page 121.

Paganism Today

In our own times, gay and bisexual men feel welcomed and honored in many Pagan spiritual traditions.

Paganism honors a feminine principle and elevates it to an equal status with masculinity,.

One of the overriding points of the ancient myths surrounding the gods and goddesses was that in almost every case, if you were not true to your self, you'd end up suffering through some overwhelming experience that had to be dealt with. Although the deities led what seem like extremely complicated lives, much of what they experienced resonates throughout mankind. If a god went a bit berserk because of jealousy, then a man could feel the same passion and understand that it was a normal part of his life experience. In most myths, jealousy – an emotion seemingly felt by every god or goddess of antiquity – caused a lot of bad behavior that ultimately needed to be resolved, either by the deity or by the intercession of others. Jealousy wreaked havoc in the heavens, just as it causes issues for us today. The myths describe the often long and tedious process of having to put right anything that was disrupted by a jealous response.

These myths also indicated that those emotions we perceive as "negative" are really just emotions, with no intrinsic value of "good" or "bad." If the gods felt the same emotions, they could scarcely be considered to be wrong. After all, they were gods, and were all-powerful. The fact that a deity had suffered through the same issue and ultimately resolved it points the way for humans to attempt the same thing. Just do it, go through it, and if you make an effort, everything will be right in the end.

This ultimate acceptance of any action, whether it is perceived as a positive or a negative one, has freed gay and bisexual men (along with heterosexual men, and women as well) from the intense pressure of Abrahamic guilt and disapproval inherent in the monotheistic traditions today. Indeed, the same prohibitions have been an integral part of Abrahamic traditions dating back to the days of Christ.

In Pagan traditions, all men and women are honored for the individual, however flawed or gifted, that they are. All are equal in the eyes of the Gods and Goddesses, and this concept is strongly held by Pagans. If everything in our physical world is an integral part of the universal energy, and not at all separate from it, then how can any single expression of that divine connection be incorrect or inappropriate?

There are those who argue that gay and bisexual men are highly attuned to their feminine side, and this is a major reason why they are drawn to a spiritual path that considers feminine energy to be part of the ultimate expression of a deity. I believe that any man, gay, bisexual or heterosexual, can access his feminine energies. This energy is an essential part of every human being, male or female, and is available to anyone. There is no reason that I can determine that indicates a heterosexual man cannot be as attuned to feminine energy equally as much as a gay or bisexual man. I am sure that many heterosexual men feel a societal pressure to be "real men." Many of them have demoted their own feminine energy by refusing to acknowledge it. In Pagan spiritual traditions, it becomes nearly impossible to ignore this issue, and I believe that all men, regardless of their sexual preference, can access and work with Goddess energy.

By understanding the myths of individual Gods and Goddesses, it is possible to attune to specific qualities presented by each deity, and to use those qualities in ritual work or spellcasting. Making an emotional connection to the qualities of a deity enables us to attune to their energy and to manifest change if that is what you seek.

It is important to remember that our God and Goddess archetypes represent specific qualifies manifested by what might be called an incarnation or manifestation of universal energy. All of the archetypes are merely aspects of one all-inclusive energy. Those individual aspects were provided to humanity so that we can more easily identify with Divinity. Many Pagans get caught up in their reverence to the individual manifestation (for example, invoking Apollo or Diana) rather than making the essential connection to the universal energy that embraces and includes all archetypal instances of the deities. For magick, whether it is spiritual magick or practical magick, to work, this connection to universal energy is essential. For many Pagans, it is easier to focus on a specific archetype; doing so makes their work easier. However, I have always had better results (particularly with practical magick) when I invoke an archetype and then acknowledge and include universal energy. To do this, I invoke the archetype, and then allow an all-consuming white light to flood my aura, building the energy and then with a single thought, igniting a spark that flashes the white light out into every corner of the universe.

Are Gay and Bisexual Men Marginalized in Paganism?

Much has been written about the power that can be raised through male/female sexuality. Gerald Gardner based many of his beliefs about Wicca on this concept. The same can be said about the work of Aleister Crowley, although research into Crowley's life revealed a man who was misogynistic and a voyeur. Alexandrian Wicca, founded by Alex Sanders, an associate of Gardner, holds many of the same beliefs. Alexandrian Wicca emphasizes the polarity between male and female energies. The English witch, Sybil Leek, also fervently believed that both male and female were necessary in order to work magick.

There is no argument that the polarity between male and female can raise abundant energy. Many of the books describing ritual assume the participation of both a high priest and high priestess, working in a coven with both men and women.

However, the sexual energy that can be raised by male-male or female-female is every bit as effective. In ancient Egypt, the male priests of Isis were exclusively gay men, and the worship of Isis was incredibly powerful.

In her book, *Drawing Down the Moon*, Margot Adler notes the powerful energy contributed to magickal workings by gay men and lesbians.

In many cultures, a particularly strong energy was attributed to gay men or lesbians. In native American spiritual traditions, for example, gay men are considered closer to the Great Spirit than heterosexual men. These men are called berdache ("two spirits"), and their place in that society is honored rather than reviled. Pagan traditions have long been considered to work "between the worlds."

This concept is an important one. In ancient times, the village witch or wise man would live at the edge of town, between civilization and the wilderness. The mystical Isle of Avalon exists in the mists, not quite of the earth, but not completely beyond it either. In fact, all humans live in the biosphere, a thin layer of atmosphere that is separate from both the earth and space. Just as humans rely on their ability to live in a "neither earth nor sky" place, Pagans realize that we work somewhere between the divine universal energy and the highly restrictive physical world.

Gay and bisexual men are aware that, in many ways, they already exist in a reality that is different enough to make them feel removed from other men in society, but yet not completely separate. In following a Pagan spiritual tradition, these men have an advantage. In performing ritual or working practical magick, their mindset is already attuned to a quality of energy outside the physical world. Gay and bisexual men must take advantage of this privileged aspect of their reality.

Some of the old prejudices from mainstream society were still rampant when I became a Pagan. Men did not work with men, or even touch them in some circles. Most circles at that time (the late 1970s and early 1980s) enforced the rule of polarity by insisting the participants arrange themselves within the circle in boy/girl pairs. In my first coven, the High Priest could not work without the High Priestess at his side (and vice versa).

Thankfully, this rigid system has largely been abandoned in recent years. Pagan men in the circles I have attended do not feel constrained in any way about working with, or touching, other men. The concept of circle pairings has mostly been abandoned; participants now work anywhere in the circle that feels comfortable to them. In one circle, there were no women who felt comfortable acting as a high priestess (the degree system does not exist in that group; any woman can act as high priestess at will). The circle was led by a high priest, and the ritual was just as effective.

We, as Pagans, have never felt as constrained as many of those who participate in mainstream, Abrahamic religions. Our entire system operates differently. We have little hierarchical structure, and we do not hire people to act as interpreter between humans and the gods in the way that mainstream religions do. Authority, for Pagans, is not taken from church headquarters or a book. It comes from within, and every member of the Pagan community has exactly the same right and privilege as any other. This attitude removes barriers that can be burdensome to others. The Pagan community is inclusive rather than exclusive.

Pagan traditions are able to maintain their traditions while still honoring and acknowledging the diversity of paths that others might follow.

It is unfortunate that many gay men remain in the closet. Even more unfortunate is the concept that a gay Pagan is in a closet in the back of the other closet. Breaking out is difficult, although as with any effort one makes in life, accomplishing a task once makes it far easier the next time.

Gay and Bisexual Men and Power

Many gay and bisexual men have issues with power. They are told from an early age that the essence of what they are is "wrong." The manifestation of this lack of power is a too-compliant personality. I see this frequently in the gay men I know, although there are many exceptions. Some of these men refuse to take a stand in an argument, throwing hands into the air and walking away instead of stating what they feel. They become quiet when men with stronger personalities, physical traits or voices are in the room.

The Pagan path enables any man to understand that he is as valuable as any other man. He is part of universal energy. Others might be louder, or swagger when they walk, but often those traits are compensating for an internal sense of lack. In his Pagan spiritual practices, a man can understand that he is every bit as effective in the world as any other man.

And what about that so-called "feminine energy" with which gay or bisexual men are so familiar?

It's an interesting phenomenon. Heterosexual men associate everyday tasks with being either masculine or feminine. Mowing the lawn: that's masculine. Cooking and washing the laundry: a feminine thing.

My own mother was quite brilliant, in her own way. She raised four children, two boys and two girls. The boys learned how to cook (both my brother and I are far better cooks than either of my sisters), clean, sew, and do laundry. I know how to knit and crochet. My sisters learned how to mow the lawn, fix something when it breaks, and both of them went out to work at an early age. They know construction and are good with hammers and drills. All of us went to work as soon as we left school, and we all fully expected to spend a lifetime being useful, productive people.

If a heterosexual man swaggers when he walks, and talks loudly, but can't do his laundry and eats only take-out, is he a fully-developed human being? I think not, based on how I was raised. Most gay and bisexual men can do all of these things. Being in touch with their feminine side is an advantage, not something for which they should apologize. Only a few days ago, I noticed a man walking through a construction site that I passed on my drive into town. He had the swagger, puffed on a big cigar, and was yelling something across the parking area. But he had a huge hole in his pants, just below the crotch. I thought to myself, I would have sewn that up before going out of the house. Not out of any sense of modesty, but because if something had gotten lodged in the opening, it could have caused problems for him, in more than one way.

Some men also develop "planned incompetence." Usually after taking a partner, a man "forgets" how to do things that he used to do perfectly well on his own, because his partner has taken responsibility for them. The partner also "unlearns" some tasks as well. After more than forty years as a Pagan, having met literally hundreds of Pagan men, I have not seen much of this phenomenon in the Pagan world. Pagan men, who readily acknowledge both their masculine and feminine energies, tend to be far more accepting toward doing any household task that needs doing, rather than assigning tasks based either on some outdated notion of whether a task is masculine- or feminine-oriented, or through the aspect of planned incompetence. The Pagan men I know change diapers without being asked. They gladly make dinner and take the kids to soccer practice. I don't see many nagging wives at the side of Pagan men. And as Martha Stewart says, I think that's a very good thing.

7

Ethics 101 for Pagans

People of both genders are often attracted to the Pagan spiritual path because of the relative lack of dogma, doctrine and rules.

In monotheistic religions, participants are instructed very specifically about what they can and cannot do, what choices they can or cannot make, and how they must live their lives in order to be an active, acceptable participant in that tradition. There are long lists of rules: these things are allowed, these things are not acceptable.

One common thread in the so-called "organized religions" is the determination that a participant should not have to do any thinking about his spiritual path. Follow the rules and regulations, and everything is fine. Break a rule, and you have to figure out how to make things right again. In some religions, you consult a church official, who proscribes what must be done to resolve the issue. In others, the entire group is consulted and comes to an agreement about the next step and how it should be accomplished. If you are successful, everything is back to normal. Woe to the individual who, for whatever reason, fails to come back into line with the group's paradigm!

Pagans are what I like to call a "disorganized religion." Pagans are disorganized in the sense that there are few or no lists of rules and often no group that expects compliance with a list of regulations. A Pagan determines for himself what the acceptable boundaries are and how to maintain them. Some Pagan groups (often called circles, groves, or covens) favor a group approach to resolving an individual's issues, although this is far from the norm. Ultimately, each Pagan assumes responsibility for acting ethically and honorably. The way that a Pagan interacts with the world around him is not based on rules originated and enforced by other people. It is based on individual ethics, morality and the concept that we all have to get along together to live in this physical world.

So if Pagans don't have proscribed dogma, doctrine or rules to guide them, how can this spiritual path work in the real world?

Pagans do indeed have some guidelines for how a Pagan life should be conducted. The essential difference is that for Pagans, the person who writes these guidelines and then enforces them is you. Pagans accept the notion that in the end, each man is responsible for his own actions. As a corollary, no person is responsible for the actions of others. This "live and let live" theory is one of the base tenets of the Pagan spiritual path. Pagans believe that every man and woman has the right to determine their own path in life, and that path must be honored.

This overreaching acceptance of every person's right to determine a life path is the reason why Pagans do not proselytize or actively seek converts to the Pagan spiritual path. A path that is absolutely right for one person is not necessarily right for any other person.

If there is one rule that is common to most Pagan paths, it is the concept of what is called in the Wiccan traditions the Wiccan Rede: if your actions harm no one, do as you will. Although Wiccans adopted it formally, most Pagans subscribe to it in some form.

But as with any aspect of life, at some point issues arise.

Harm nothing. That's easy to figure out and to put into action, right? Or is it?

What if you want a steak for dinner? Somebody has the kill a steer and that probably hurts the steer. Bulls are not euthanized like your pet Yorkshire Terrier; a vet does not give them an injection that allows them to gently go to sleep and never awaken. They are killed in a very active way. You're eating the steak, so who is responsible for the steer's death? Would the steer still be alive if you, personally, didn't buy a steak? Probably not. The guy behind you in the grocery check-out line probably has a steak in his shopping cart, and it had to come from somewhere.

If everyone on the planet stops eating beef, there would be little reason to slaughter a steer. (Oh, wait; we'd also have to stop buying anything made of leather too. Life sure gets complicated, doesn't it?) But realistically, is this going to happen?

Humans are part of nature, and in nature there exists something called a "food chain." Almost every living species is part of this interdependency. Plants grow to feed animals; animals grow to provide food for other animals. Our existence on the Earth is a cycle of life and death, birth and rebirth. Everything that is born will, without exception, die. The food chain is an integral part of the cycle of life. The only advantage humans have is that we are rarely food for other species. That is not always true: ask the children who fall into a river each year and become dinner for an alligator in South America. I doubt they would agree that they are at the top of the food chain. But in general, we have an advantage, because we are not actively hunted by any other species.

Pagans have to decide, each man for himself, about how he wants to fit into the cycles of the existence that we have created here on this planet. Is it unethical to eat a steak? It is, if you apply a literal meaning to the rule. It is not, if you subscribe to the concept that man is part of a food chain; he must honor his own part in it and also honor the plants and animals that provide him with his food. But how does the "if it harms none, do what you will" concept fit in?

I believe that the Universe (which is just another term for God/Goddess/All That Is, or whatever deity you believe in) has given me awareness and conscience. That part of my consciousness understands right and wrong: a moral and ethical standard by which I attempt to guide my life. These standards connect me to the Universal energy in my everyday life. I use my ethics and morals to determine if an action I contemplate taking is driven by anger, greed, envy, pride or any other motivation that I think is less than honorable. If the action I'm contemplating taking is connected with any of these negative impulses, I try to understand what is behind that feeling. I carefully reconsider. And then, I might do what I was planning, or I might not do it. Frequently, I choose not to go ahead with that action. I understand that if I do take an action, there is karma to consider. I believe that every action returns to me three-fold. By stopping to contemplate and then making a conscious decision to proceed or to not proceed, I can guide myself through my daily life.

When I do something that I know will bring a karmic response, I realize that whatever the response is, I've earned it through my own actions. But I'm human. I make mistakes, and sometimes I do something that might affect someone else in a way that I have not considered. I also realize that there are times when doing something that will result in the universe slapping me in the head is worthwhile, even if there is a price to pay. At least I considered the action, and when the energy returns to me, I don't complain about it or try to negate it. I know that I will get back exactly what I earn by my actions. I always invoke the God and Goddess in these situations, and part of my ritual or spellcraft will include asking them to act in a way that is just and fair for all.

I think most Pagans believe in much the same way.

With all of this in mind, my actions are usually well-intentioned. I do not need a priest or other human telling me what I should do; it's always obvious to me. For example, I wouldn't think of kicking a dog. And although there are times when I think I'd really enjoy slapping someone who's behaving very badly, I don't do it. As a conscious being, I realize that I need to deliberate about any action I contemplate taking.

But what about something simple, like picking a flower? Isn't that causing harm to the plant?

As Pagans, we are obligated to honor all other living things. The plant grows, flowers, and dies. If I pick a flower because I find it to be a thing of beauty, and put it in a vase and enjoy it for several days, have I harmed the plant? The vast majority of plants can create additional flowers. I view the flower as the plant's gift to me. It will produce another flower, one that I'll leave alone to blossom, wither, and form seeds. As a Pagan, I am willing to allow the plant to give me its gift – a flower. It can't give me money or a new car. All it can provide me is its flower. I can enjoy the beauty of the flower, smell its essence, and let it remind me of the principles of life. What a great gift!

Everything living being in the universe has the right to offer a gift to anything else in the universe.

Unfortunately, the current interpretation of the Rede has become "do what you want, but don't hurt anything." How can any man who understands what masculine energy is subscribe to a "law" that says you can't hurt a fly? It is unreasonable to expect a man – or indeed anyone – to live this way. It just won't work. I think that this too-literal interpretation of this guideline tends to alienate men from following a Pagan path.

The ethics that you have adopted for dealing with the real world are the same ones that work in your Pagan spiritual path. One can find many books on Pagan philosophy, ritual, and spellcasting (also called folk magic).

Many contain lists of rules that are patently ridiculous. You can only do a love spell when the moon is full and Venus is well aspected, in the summer because you need a specific herb that is in blossom only in July and August and you must use pink candles, not white or blue or orange ones. You can only invoke a specific God to perform a particular task. It's nonsense.

If you want to work practical magic and it fits in ethically and morally with your personal world view, it will work regardless of the color of the candles you use, the phase of the moon, or the specific herb that you use. The God and Goddess do not care about the external trappings of your rituals. The only energy that is accessible to them is your emotions, whatever it is that you feel with passion and act upon with determination and focus. Why would an all-knowing, all-powerful being care about whether your candle was red or yellow? It's ludicrous and it defies logic. To believe that we are so restricted in our ritual that we need to slavishly follow these restrictions denigrates the power of the universe. It also denigrates your personal power. If the trappings you use are vital to ensure success, then all anyone would have to do is use the same materials and their rituals would always work. Anyone who truly believes that would likely also believe that Rapunzel is still in her tower and the dwarf in the cottage next door is still weaving gold out of straw.

Within the practice of folk magic, there are guidelines that might enable you to achieve greater success IF you subscribe to them (that is, believe in them wholeheartedly, without reservation or doubt) and IF they make logical sense. If you subscribe to them because they seem logical, then follow them. But be aware that you are actively choosing to do this: it's not required at any time. You can perform a ritual silently while riding a bus during rush hour, and it can be every bit as effective as the two hour full moon incantation. This kind of thinking is rather the same as believing that you can pray only inside a church. Humans love restrictions, it is true, and all of the world still dearly loves a cage. (Yes, that's a line from the movie *Harold and Maude*.) But the powers that govern the universe are so much stronger than anything else we can know or even imagine. If you limit them in your mind, you also limit what you can achieve using those powers. You are not limited, restricted or caged!

You can, however, add to your rituals any concept that aids your concentration and focus, or any that you deeply feel will help bring about the results you seek. For example, you want to do a spell to attract a loving partner. For humans, red is a sexual color; all of the areas on the human body that are sexually sensitive are red (lips, nipples, and genitals). On a subconscious level, you know that if you use red or pink as part of your magickal working, it will resonate to a greater degree and help ensure positive results. So use the red candles, and see if it helps.

But what if your love life in the past has been sadly lacking? Green is a healing color; maybe you need to find a lover who can help you heal from your past encounters so that you can discover love in a new way. So in that case, using green can work, and it might be a better choice for this particular spell. How about white? The color white contains all of the other colors, so you'd be getting the benefits of both green and red.

Using this example, you can see that there are a number of choices that can prove helpful in your spiritual work. On the other hand, you can also see that it becomes easy to introduce indecision and chaos if making a choice becomes difficult. (In the case of the example, I'd probably choose whichever color I thought of first. Remember, your intuition is always working to help you get where you need to be!)

Note: When working with color, remember that color is determined by a particular vibration of a ray of light. The color white contains all of the other colors (except black, of course). Black is the total absence of color; there are no rays of any kind of light in the color black. So white works for most magick; black is used only when you want to banish something from your life.

Here is where ethics enters into it. Actually, the question of ethics is an essential part of every aspect of life, including your spiritual path. Is using folk magick and ritual an ethical way to bring a person into your life?

I believe it's ethical to perform a ritual or work magickally to bring a person into your life: any person that would fit. It is unethical to determine a specific person who you think would satisfy your need. In other words, you can ask for a lover, but not for Mary Smith from down the block. We only know what we think we know at any time. Our knowledge at any point in life is derived from what we have experienced. The universe (call it God/Goddess, your higher self, your guardian angel, or by any other name) knows what would be best for you, given your current incarnation and what you determined you wanted to learn and experience in this lifetime, and this can free you from having to rely only on what you have experienced firsthand.

This relates to driving a car down the road at night. Yes, we're all living in the dark, for all purposes! Your headlights can enable you to see a hundred feet or so down the road. You can't know what is on the road a mile away; your headlights don't illuminate your path that far ahead. And you don't need to know what is that far away. You can only act on the present: the past is a done deal, and the future changes constantly based on what you do in the present. All you have to do is stay on the road that you can see in your headlights – all hundred feet of it – and by the time you're at the end of that section of the road, your headlights will illuminate the next hundred feet. In this way, you can drive cross country, one hundred feet at a time, and do it safely and successfully.

Life is exactly like that. You only have to deal with what's in front of you at the moment. If we had the ability to illuminate the entire road from east to west coast, there would be no surprises. There also would not be any room for negotiation. What if the road was blocked and you wanted to veer north and go through Wyoming instead of Colorado as you made your cross-country trip? If you could only take a single, pre-defined route, you would have no ability to make different choices: the end result would already be illuminated on the road ahead, as would the path you had to take to get there. Your life would be predestined; you'd be consigned to follow the road your headlights illuminated and would, by necessity, eliminate any other possibilities along the way. Life most assuredly does not work that way! All living things have the ability to make choices; humans are able to make many choices that other species cannot. A human can choose to live anywhere; a plant has to live where its seed sprouts. Because we are human, we are obligated to take full advantage of the fact that we CAN move from place to place. Yes, there are people who never venture over 70 or 80 years out of the small town where they were born. Has such a person been wrong not to have used his ability to move about? Possibly. And possibly not, if his life plan was to stay in one place and experience everything that small town could offer.

An ethical love spell would be one that seeks to concentrate on improving yourself with the goal of making you more attractive to others – not in a physical sense, but because you begin to manifest positive personality traits that are in themselves attractive to others. You could also design a ritual in which you simply ask that more love be attracted into your life. Let the universe determine what person might be a good match for you (and you for that person). You might not have met in the physical world yet; the universe can manipulate events using time and space to put both of you in the same room at the same time. Or there could be someone out there who is already attracted to you, but is too shy or insecure to let you know. Your spell could help that person find the courage to speak up and make the attraction known. Although being specific is usually best, this is why sometimes being too specific can actually prevent the outcome you seek.

And please don't waste your time by specifying that you want only persons of a certain height, weight, hair color, eye color, or any other physical trait. It should be obvious that if you are open to various physical types – and remember, each soul has the right and the responsibility to determine his or her physical manifestation in a lifetime – you stand a far greater chance of finding someone than if you allow an arbitrary list of rather ridiculous restrictions impede your search.

Our personal preferences are determined through our past experiences. If you think only a brunette will do, it might be because there were blonds or redheads in your past that you didn't particularly like. But that does not mean that a blond whom you have not yet met will not be a perfect fit; it only means that your past didn't include such an encounter. Growth and change are integral parts of life. Enabling new experiences outside the ones you already have had will always prove beneficial!

Choosing an Ethical Path

Ethics are completely personal, and it is this aspect that Pagans often struggle with. It is far easier to let a group of people determine our life's path. I often wonder if that is why so many people who participate in organized religion remain within that faith. Doing so provides them with a life path that, although proscribed by others, is acceptable enough to them. They don't have to think about many things, and they don't have to take responsibility for their decisions. They are not driving that car from coast to coast; they are sitting in the back seat.

There is another aspect to the "harm none" rule. What if your ritual causes harm to someone that you never hear about? Not doing magick that you know will cause harm is one thing. If the end result is manipulative, it's harmful. If it causes harm to someone or something outside your knowledge, it is harmful. One example is casting a spell to attract money. What if you get a huge sum, but it was the result of the death of a loved one? Is that the kind of magick you wanted to work? You always have to think through the intention of any ritual or spellcasting effort and ensure that it will harm no one. The best safeguard is to state, very specifically, as you work the ritual or spell, that the results do not harm anyone or anything. That simple statement can prevent unforseen chaos from occurring as a result of your intention. If you want money, do a spell for good luck and start buying lottery tickets.

There are few other absolute rules in a Pagan spiritual path. Each tradition has a tendency to impose its rules on the participants; this is a natural part of human nature. Everyone wants to fit into a group, and the easiest way to do that is to outline what is expected. An individual can either buy into the group consensus, or walk away. It makes life very simple.

If you find yourself participating in a group that has decided to begin imposing rules, it is a good time to sit down in a quiet place and review the rules in your mind. Can you accept them without reservation? Do you believe that the rules are necessary? If so, no problem. But if you can't, maybe the rules should be reconsidered, or maybe you should find a new group with less restrictive rules. The point is, a Pagan is not obligated to simply buy into the rules and principles espoused by others, regardless of who they are. You absolutely must follow your own ethical path, or your spiritual path will become lifeless and unsatisfactory, and your magickal workings will fail.

Solitary Pagans have an easier time of it. From the first moment, they realize that they must determine their own path. Having to formulate a working construct for your spiritual path can be difficult, but it is immensely rewarding. When you connect with the God and Goddess, you know what you've done to achieve that is correct. It does not need to be vetted by a group of others; the evidence that it is right for you and that it works is sensed in the connection you made to spirit.

Whether you work with a group or alone, you must develop your ethical beliefs on your own. Your ethics should fit within the spiritual path that you have chosen. You should not derive a set of ethics by subscribing to a particular spiritual path. And if others on the same spiritual path insist on imposing ethics on everyone, that set of ethics must exactly match your own, or at least work within the ethics you have determined for yourself, and of necessity, those ethics must resonate completely with you. Anything that does not work will be stressful, and any undertaking associated with it will not be successful.

These ethics form a basis for your magickal work. Anything you do magickally must work in accordance with your code of ethics. If it does not, it will fail. Fortunately, you cannot work around your own ethics when performing magick. Your subconscious mind is adept at filtering your intent with your ethical understanding of the world in which you live, and it will not allow you to generate enough energy to make that magickal effort work in the real world if it is personally unethical.

Pagans are very fortunate in that almost all Pagan spiritual paths have few rules and regulations. A developed sense of ethical behavior is highly compatible with any or all of the Pagan traditions.

Pagans often have good intentions, but it is essential to remember that our view of our world is always based on our experiences in this incarnation that led up to this moment. Nobody is all-knowing; nobody has a better overview of what our reality is than does anyone else. And, being human, we can never really know if what we want to accomplish at any given time fits well with our life plan.

To ensure that the outcomes I visualize have a positive effect and are part of my overall life plan, I always, without fail, include the words "for the good of all" in any magickal or ritual work. I really don't want to gain anything that is not in my own best interest, or the best interest of those around me.

Working ethically is always its own reward.

8

Practical Magick

Most Pagans acknowledge two components of their spiritual tradition: spiritual magick and practical magick. While essentially the same thing (magick is magick), some Pagans use only spiritual magick as part of their ritual devotions to the God and Goddess. Others use spiritual magick in communicating with the God and Goddess, and also use practical magick (also called spellcasting) to influence events in daily life. Practical magick, also known as folk magick, uses the energy of our mind, through will and intention, to manifest a change in a situation or event.

While there is no requirement in many Pagan traditions for working practical magick, doing so seems to be nearly universal. The responses to my survey indicated that Pagan men accept spellcasting as an integral part of how they exist and interact in the physical world.

All forms of spiritual ritual are actually a form of magick. We invoke a deity and ask for guidance, and at times, intercession.

I remember being taken to the local Catholic church when I was 8. My grandfather had died, and my mother believed that children should get acquainted with death at the earliest opportunity, since death is an integral part of life. I had never been inside a Catholic church before. The funeral mass at that time was still conducted in Latin. Although I could not understand a single word, I loved the ritual and the drama of the service. The robes were spectacular, not like the drab black robe our minister wore, and there were candles burning everywhere, and incense smoking, and water being shaken out of a little stick with a ball on the end. It was fascinating.

Because I didn't understand the connection between ritual and magick, I was quite annoyed when communion was offered. I had often heard about Christ's ability to feed the multitudes. Yet when the communion was given, there was no sign of any real food – just a smallish tasteless cracker and a swig of grape juice. I asked my mother if that was all we were going to get, or if they would be back with more, and she pinched my arm and shushed me. It seemed to me that day that the Catholics were quite miserly with the food, and I thought to myself that I wouldn't want to have to go to another Catholic service.

The Latin mass has always seemed more mystical to me than the other funeral masses I attended later in life, after the church began doing them in English. I believe it is because the Latin mass, which I did not understand, forced me to sense the meaning emotionally rather than logically.

Our own church was relatively somber (we were Methodists). The pews usually contained a lot of old ladies who spent quite a bit of time before and after the services gossiping about everyone else. The sermons usually exhorted us to get back on the right track, whatever that was. Frankly, I have never felt that anything I did was inappropriate, so I never could grasp what I could have done otherwise in any situation. The congregation had many men on the books, but not often in the pews. At Easter, everyone attended the service, dressed in fine new clothes and at that time, usually a new hat. The Christmas service was the one I liked the best because there was no admonition about how we were behaving, simply an acknowledgment of the baby Jesus' birth; that tale was hardly fire and brimstone material to begin with.

I must admit that I spent a lot of time attending church or Sunday School as a child. I was in the building so often that I knew what lay behind every door. The last time I went was for my mother's funeral in 2005. Everything was exactly the same as it had been nearly 50 years earlier. Sure, there were some colorful banners and flags on display, but the effect was that of an old women who had tarted herself up for one last dance. What overwhelmed me was the sense of being contained in a building while trying to commune with the God and Goddess. My Pagan practices occur wherever I am, often outside if the weather is decent, but never in a building that is used only for spiritual work. I was not able to access an emotional connection to spirituality, however it was defined, that day.

The connection of emotion to magick is inescapable. If you think your magick, it will never work. If you feel the projected outcome, it has a very good chance of creating the change you seek.

Magick can be defined as transformation, creation, and manifestation.

Magick is exactly the same thing as creative visualization. Whatever you can visualize in your mind, and then sense through your emotions, you can create in reality.

Consciously and unconsciously, you create your reality at every moment. Your reality is always in alignment with your imagination.

Unfortunately, much of what we visualize consciously is negative.

A friend and I discussed this last evening at dinner. Her husband Michael was terrified of getting lung cancer. I would have thought he was relatively safe: he never smoked, his lungs were healthy, he was active and vital. But he developed throat cancer, and it spread – to his lungs. He died of complications from lung cancer. He spent many of his waking hours thinking "I never want to get lung cancer." It was a powerful thought. And it attracted what he was thinking about: lung cancer.

In a very real sense, you use magick all of the time – whenever you want something enough to devote a significant amount of time to getting it, you're working with magick.

Magick happens in the energetic realms before it manifests in the physical world. You have probably heard of your astral and spiritual bodies; these are energetic parts of ourselves that manifest in realms that are composed of higher vibrational rates. The dream world, for example, is part of the astral. In the physical world, our world is relatively concrete. If you walk into a wall, you'll notice how solid it is. In the astral world, however, that wall is fluid. In a dream, you can walk through it, or it can disappear if you don't need for it to be there. This is why our dreams are so fluid, changing easily and inexplicably as we dream. The "rules" of the physical world do not apply to other energetic realms, and they can be manipulated in whatever way we want.

If you understand quantum physics (see "Universal Energy: Einstein's Theory of Relativity, Quantum Physics, and All The Other Stuff a Male Pagan Needs to Know" on page 29), you will understand that science has proven over the past century that these principles are accurate. All matter is energy; if we can manipulate anything in the astral world, we can manipulate it here in the physical world just as easily. The difference is that in the astral world, time and space do not play an integral part. In the physical world, they both seem to cause limitations. For example, if you want to whisper something to your cousin Fred, and Fred is two thousand miles away, space provides a limitation. If you use a telephone, the limitation of space disappears. In the astral world, the limitation never existed in the first place.

I have manifested many changes over my lifetime.

I've always been abundant; money flows to me as I need it. I never have to say I cannot afford what I need, although I might not be able to always afford what I want. I've always been lucky. I've survived five or six times from physical injuries that could have killed me (giving rise to my idea that as a Leo, I have nine lives…).

I used to pass a small cottage on the road to Unicorn Books in New Milford, CT, where I did psychic readings and other workshops. Every time I passed it, I always thought "I'd love to live in that little house." Guess where I live today? And I didn't buy it. While I lived in Raleigh, NC, my sister purchased the farmland on which the cottage stands. I had never mentioned the building to her. She and her husband started remodeling it, and when I became ill and needed to move closer to family, the little cottage was the place where I moved. I live in it rent-free, too. How's that for a manifestation?

When I started looking for my first house, I did it with only about a thousand dollars in the bank. How much money I had – and it was nowhere what was needed for a down payment at the time – was never important. I just wanted to buy a house and live there. I looked at a couple dozen houses and found one that I really liked. Within a couple of days, my manager at work called me into her office to tell me I had won an award for some software that I had developed to make my own job easier. The award was significant; I was able to put nearly $30,000 from it into the down payment for the house that I had already decided I wanted to live in. That whole process took less than two weeks!

I also have a cautionary tale to share. Over the years, I constantly wished that I could retire early, in my 50s. I retired at 56 – on a disability pension after a serious illness that prevented me from going back to work. I see now that I should have been a bit more specific and included the thought that I would retire healthy and well enough to do everything I envisioned doing at that age. I can't say I'm disappointed, since I got what I asked for, but I should have taken the time to think it through really well.

When my friend Rich bought a baby grand piano more than 20 years ago, I remember thinking when I first saw it that I wished I owned a piano just like that one.

Twenty years passed. The piano moved from upstate New York to North Carolina, then back again with Rich's ex-wife. A month ago, she told me she wanted to get rid of it because it took up too much space in her living room, space she now needed for other things. Guess where the piano is today? It's in my living room, and I enjoy playing it every day!

So now when anyone asks me if magick really works, I have to say yes, it really works! I have too much evidence that it does to declare that it might not be viable. Do I use it every day? No. I use it when I want something that seems to be outside my ability to achieve. If there are obstacles in the physical world (like the lack of a down payment to buy that first house), magick enables me to work around those limitations.

Defining Magick

Magick is the process of transformation, creation and manifestation. Magick acts in the energetic realms – using what we now consider quantum energy.

For a more complete discussion of quantum physics, see page 29.

The energetic realms determines what happens in our physical reality. For anything to happen in the physical world, it must first happen in the energetic realm.

So, to manifest something here on Earth, you must first create the possibility for that in the energetic realm.

Your spiritual beliefs are integral to creating effective, evidential magick. As a spiritual being, you access the energetic realm constantly.

The principles of magick exist in everything we do, even if we are not conscious of it. Therefore, magick is not something that must be learned; it is inherent within your subconscious and has been available since the day you were born. Making effective magick in a conscious way is a skill that anyone can learn. There is, however, a limitation on us humans. We cannot shift the physical world when we need it to shift. If that were possible, walls would vanish, people would change into other people, and you could fly or breathe underwater. Neither time nor space would matter; both could be altered at will. Sounds like the dream world? That's the difference between the physical world, which is full of limitation and challenges, and the dream world, which is the energetic world in which any change we desire simply happens because we think it. If you understand that the energetic world is exactly the same as the world of your dreams, you will be able to assimilate why and how you can work magick. You do it all the time in your dreams.

You can access this energetic world through your connection with the God/Goddess.

Whether they acknowledge it or not, all Pagans create magick.

Magick is the process of aligning ourselves with universal energy to influence our destiny.

Magick does not include working with blood or with elemental energies. Those activities are in the realm of sorcery: manipulating the universe to create specific change.

The difference between magick and sorcery is that in performing magick, we enable whatever destiny is appropriate for us. This changes constantly. Magick does not require a specific outcome in order to obtain our heart's desires. Sorcery uses natural energies, including elemental beings, to manifest a specific destiny. It involves force and manipulation.

The problem with using sorcery is that elemental beings are involved. Elementals are single-minded energies, each with specific purpose and limited capabilities. The Fire elemental, for example, cannot create rain needed for your crops and thirsty cattle. Logically, anything that is limited from the start can only obtain limited results. Manipulation works, but because of the nature of the universe, any time you manipulate, you can expect to be manipulated at least three times. Some Pagans believe energy is returned seven times; others, ten times. At any rate, is whatever you might use sorcery for worth being subjected to negativity three or more times? Probably not.

Spiritual magick allows universal energy to manifest a desired result in whatever way is appropriate for you at the time and in the place where you are when it happens.

Why Is Magick Spelled with a K?

Pagans spell magick with a "k" to differentiate it from stage magic, which is sleight of hand. Stage magic is illusion: something appears to change form, but in reality, one object has been substituted for another. In practical magick, success results in manifesting an actual change in the real world. What was one thing becomes something else, in some way.

Making Magick More Effective

Here are some points to keep in mind that will help you to be more successful in manifesting the results you desire.

Determine the real issue underlying the problem you perceive. If you are not totally clear about what you want to achieve, the universe will not figure it out for you. Your intentions have to be specific and crystal clear.

Focus clearly on your intention. To create magick, you must be extremely focused. This is the reason why magick is often worked at night; we perceive fewer visual clues in the darkness. The area where you work should be relatively clean, free from disturbance of any kind, and private. In an emergency, you can work a simple ritual on a crowded bus, but for the kind of change that alters a life path, you need to go deeply within, and solitude and privacy help ensure that this is possible.

Be very specific in what you want to manifest. For example, you want to attract a new lover into your life. You need to be very specific about what qualities you want that person to have, and if there are qualities that you do not want to see, include them as well.

Do not concentrate on what you don't want. Leave physical qualities out of the issue. If you decide you want only a lover with blond hair, you place an unreasonable limitation on both yourself and the universe. If you can't love someone with brunette hair, then why would someone love you? Working to attract love in the most general sense is probably a wiser move.

After you perform the ritual associated with the results you seek, let go. Allow the universe to work to bring those results to you. Do not hold onto the energy by constantly worrying about the issue, imagining ways that it can be resolved, or trying to rethink it. By freeing the energy surrounding your issue, you enable the universe to resolve it as quickly and easily as possible.

Eliminate doubt. A single doubtful thought can alter the end results. However, it has often been said that one positive thought can override ten negative ones. If you doubt, stop it as soon as you realize what you are doing, and begin thinking about the fact that your intention is already manifested in the energetic realms and the end result you seek is being worked out by the universe.

Ensure that you invoke the "if it harms none" law. Remember that karma exists. Many Pagans believe that any energy they send out returns three times. If you do something that is negative, or manipulative, expect to be subjected to negativity or manipulation three times.

When you create magick in the energetic realms, it happens immediately. Before you see the results in the physical world, time and space must be manipulated to allow that event to occur. For example, you visualize owning a house. Maybe that house is not yet built, or someone else owns it. The universe needs time to arrange for the house to be built, or for the current owner to have a reason, such as a job relocation, to move from that house into a new one. The point is, as soon as you complete your magickal working, the results are assured.

Magick can fail to produce the results you envisioned. In some cases, what you think you want is actually counterproductive to your life's goals, and obtaining the results you seek would alter your life path. Your higher self has the task of making sure you stay on a life path in which you will learn and experience certain things. If what you want to accomplish is counter to that end goal, it simply won't happen. Manipulative magick can also be short-circuited, again by the intervention of your higher self (or spirit guides, or whatever you call this energy). These beings are like highly protective guard dogs; nothing is going to climb over the fence into your life.

Not all Pagan men practice spellcraft or magick. While I originally believed it was an essential part of Pagan belief, my survey revealed that there are many men who do not use spells to change their world.

I use the term magick (with a K) to differentiate it from the kind of magic performed by stage performers – such as pulling rabbits out of hats and manipulating playing cards. Most Pagans add the K at the end of the word to indicate that it refers to a type of spiritual endeavor that has great significance to them.

Spellcraft is, essentially, folk magic. It is the manipulation of natural forces to affect a specific outcome. Folk magic has been practiced since mankind first began walking the earth.

When Magick Doesn't Work

There is a scene in the movie *Little Big Man* in which Chief Dan lies down and asks the Great Spirit to take his life because he believes that it is his time to die. Nothing happens; as he lies there, it begins to rain, and he stands up and says to Dustin Hoffman's character that "sometimes the magic works, and sometimes it doesn't."

This can happen for a number of reasons, and you will probably encounter this phenomenon somewhere along your spiritual path.

Sometimes we ask for something, and the answer is "no." We might request something before we can appreciate having it. What we experience in life prepares us for our future experiences. Perhaps your experiences up until this point have not adequately prepared you to receive whatever you requested.

If you acknowledge that a spirit guide, a guardian angel, or even your higher self acts in a protective way, it could be that gaining what you requested will not be a positive or helpful experience for you. Your guide has the task of ensuring that your life goes according to your life plan; often this life plan was determined before you incarnated. If a life plan included some "definitely must have" experiences, your guide will manipulate energy in whatever way is necessary to ensure that you are guided to those experiences. It might be that what you requested will take you so far off your life plan's path that the guide has no alternative but to ensure that you maintain the original plan.

Can this be changed? You can argue that we all have free will. I believe that these life plans are an agreement made on a soul level and "signed off" by our spirit guides or higher self. We can exercise free will in determining how we deal with the items on the life plan, but I believe that the life plan itself is a contract that we already agreed to abide by, before this incarnation.

Another aspect is when we try to use magick or ritual to bypass good old-fashioned hard work. We live in a physical world. There are expectations for each of us about how we use the lifetime we have incarnated into. Nobody gets to waste a lifetime, or to coast through one. Magick and ritual cannot be used to avoid doing the work necessary in the physical world to achieve certain ends.

For example, you want to work a ritual to make you a famous writer. You will enjoy fame and fortune, and people will eagerly await your next novel. That's fine. But if you never sit down and actually write anything, there is absolutely **no** chance that any of this will happen. You must work in the physical world to manifest what you desire.

How does this work if you want to manifest great wealth, as we discuss in another chapter? If you expect to sit around, slothlike, doing nothing, giving nothing, being nothing, how can money manifest for you? To win the lottery, you have to buy tickets. If you visualize putting your wealth into the bank and using it to control other people, you won't get it. Money is a tool; it only works when it's circulating and being used to accomplish something. Money in the bank is a figure on a bank statement. If your cousin is losing his house and you have six million dollars sitting in the bank, how is that a positive thing for either of you? Your cousin loses his house, and you're content to sit around the house, being an idiot. I sincerely doubt that any amount of magick exists that can make that happen. You cannot use a spiritual path to manifest negativity. Your guardians or higher self will see to that.

On occasion, you can work magick or ritual for the wrong reasons, and see an outcome. It might be what you visualized. It might not be. It definitely will be a learning experience for you. I doubt that it will be a pleasurable one.

Timing

I'm not sure at all that magick or ritual works only when we observe specific stages of the moon, or use only a certain color candle, or have to travel extensive distances to pick the correct herb.

Yes, there are correspondences that aid in how effective the outcome might be.

But I don't think any of them are written in stone.

The timing that is of importance is how the outcome of the ritual or magick fits into your life. You have to be in a specific place in life to get certain outcomes. Your guardians or higher self will not allow you to achieve things at the wrong times. Magick cannot be wasteful: the outcome must always have impact, somewhere, somehow.

Magick or ritual that prevents spiritual development will also fail. Your energetic self (higher self or astral self) will short-circuit any attempt that will alter your life plan and spiritual evolution. That is why we incarnate. Everything else — money, jobs, lovers, children — is just "stuff." We will always learn the life lessons that we planned to work on in this incarnation. If magick or ritual interferes with that, it will fail.

How to Achieve Success Using Spellcraft

Note: The best resource I've found for explaining how "magick" works is in a book called *The Secret* by Rhonda Byrne. Also be sure to read the chapter on quantum physics starting on page 29 in this book. That combination of information is a complete course in how to manifest anything in your life that you want to manifest.

Absolute Belief

One essential ingredient is an absolute belief that your magickal working will produce the appropriate results. Any amount of doubt dooms the outcome. If you do not believe that whatever you want is achievable, there is no way for your mind to access enough energy to create that reality.

Total Faith

Another essential is that you must, from the first moment you begin, act as though the result has already been achieved. For example, you want to attract a lover into your life. You don't care if this person is fat or thin, young or old, handsome or hedge fence ugly. You eliminate all of the superficial conditions that have no impact on your happiness in finding someone special. This opens up a huge number of possibilities. If you think you only want to attract someone of a specific age, body type or personality, you severely limit the people that the universe can bring into your world.

So your mind is open to any possibility, as long as that person is compatible with you, and you can both grow together and find love together.

But think about this: are you acting like that person is already in your life?

Do you take only one shower a week, because you don't have someone in your life right now? Are the clothes that you wear clean and pressed? Have you had a haircut recently? Is your house clean or is it full of clutter?

How can you attract love if you don't love yourself? If you smell bad, look unkempt, or live in a rathole, what kind of person do you think that will attract? Is it someone you want to include in your life?

You absolutely must act as if what you seek is already part of your life.

Here's the secret: you attract the same thing that you project.

Think about a spell to attract money. Do you feel poor? You'll attract no money, because the energy you're sending out is "no money." You have to feel abundant – and live as if you had unlimited funds – to attract money. If you feel or act stingy, that's a very restrictive energy, and you'll get back very little from the universe.

Morality and Ethics

If whatever you want to achieve does not resonate with your ethical and moral view of life, you cannot cause it to happen. You can work a lifetime at the task, but it will never be successful. Your ethics and morals form boundaries within your mind. Like the invisible fences used to keep dogs within a yard, you cannot bring yourself to step outside that boundary.

You already realize that each human forms his own set of moral and ethical codes.

These codes of behavior are developed by your higher self. They intimately and essentially reflect your spiritual values. Your higher self is able to say, "In this lifetime, you agree to follow these rules." It's that simple. There are no policemen to hand out ethical violation tickets. You cannot, at any point, cross the lines that you have determined are essential for you as a living being in this incarnation, so there is no need for a police force to enforce the rules. You are your own policeman.

This can explain why most love spells that are directed at specific individuals usually fail miserably. If your manipulative spell didn't fail, you will probably realize at some point that what you got was nowhere near what you wanted. Your "reward" becomes your punishment for violating basic universal principles; in this case, it's the "harm none" one. Manipulation always causes harm because it affects someone's ability to make choices.

Understand, however, that the term manipulation in itself is not negative. For magick to work at all, something has to be manipulated into changing itself into something else.

One aspect I always found useful in working with magick was to eliminate wherever possible the concept of good and bad. There is nothing in our universe that is intrinsically good or bad. These are value judgments we overlay onto something, based on our limited perception of it in the moment. Is a tsunami that kills five hundred people bad? Not essentially. It probably resulted from an earthquake, caused by excess stress in the teutonic plates of the earth. It is a cleansing and corrective action. The same is true for a volcanic eruption. While it might kill living things or spoil the planet's surface in the surrounding area, it results from the condition of too much pressure below the surface of the earth. It is both a good thing and a bad thing, depending on your point of view.

But if you want to work magick, you must rise above the concepts of good or bad. As soon as your mind associates the concepts of good or bad to a magickal working, it is doomed to failure. Your ethical and moral boundaries will not allow you to create something you view as bad.

Good or bad are simply value judgments that reflect our very limited knowledge based on our very limited life experiences up to that point. Rise above making that judgment, and your magick will be more successful.

We will discuss ethics further in another chapter.

Your Word is Sacred

Your word is your bond. You've heard that before, I'm sure. What does it mean?

It means that whatever you say – everything you say – must be true. If you have a tendency to tell a friend you'll go out with him the following Saturday and then break that date, your word no longer represents your true intentions. If you commit to something, you must commit to it absolutely. If you think you might not want to go out next Saturday, then tell your friend exactly what you mean. He will feel far better if you tell him you're not sure right at the moment, but you'll let him know by Saturday if you can go out with him, than if you agree to go and then cancel.

You cannot work magick effectively if you do not honor everything you say, without exception. Your subconscious mind realizes that a lot of the time, you're talking crap. It knows you don't mean what you say. How can it summon enough energy to make a meaningful change in the real world if you might change your mind at the drop of a hat? Guess what? It won't bother doing anything at all. You are defeated before you begin, hoist on your own petard, so to speak.

I realize this sounds sanctimonious, but I never cancel when I agree to do something. Even if something else comes up that might be more fun, I stick with the plan I've already agreed to. My friends know, without any doubt, that I will follow through on anything and everything I say.

A few weeks ago, I mentioned to a couple of my friends that I had to get this book written on a very tight time schedule. Nobody said "oh, you can't do that, there's not enough time." They knew that if I said I'd get it done, it would be done. This served me well when I worked as a technical writer. I could make some relatively outlandish promises, but the people who paid my salary never doubted that what I said I'd deliver, they'd get, and they'd get it on time.

Simply eliminating self-doubt in your own mind is satisfying person-ally, but it also ensures that when you attempt to change the world around you, your chances will be greatly improved because your subconscious knows that you mean business. Since you're not waffling about whatever it is you want to work on, your subconscious can get to work immediately to effect that change.

Aligning your thoughts and your spoken word with whatever you want to accomplish has often been referred to as the spiritual principle of "as above, so below." Intent and reality become one thing, and results are automatic.

The key here is that your subconscious mind, **not** your conscious mind, is in complete control. It is entirely possible for you to say one thing con-sciously yet believe something entirely different subconsciously. In that case, there's a real problem.

The reality you experience is the result of what your subconscious has set up, not what your conscious mind wants to happen. Your subconscious can only activate whatever you truly believe. One iota of doubt removes any possibility of success in the future. You can visualize being wealthy in the future, but if you subconsciously feel that you don't deserve to be rich, it just isn't going to happen.

But who says wealth comes only to those who deserve it? A ridiculous rule, if ever there was one. There are a number of very wealthy people in the world who are totally selfish and self-centered, giving no joy or comfort to anyone, treating other people badly, living dissolute lives just because they can. Do they deserve the money they have? I don't think so! And there are people who are practically saints who never have an extra dime. Mother Theresa was a good example. She was one of the most selfless humans to walk the earth. Was she rich? No. Did she deserve to be? Absolutely, without any doubt. It just doesn't work that way. So if your subconscious believes that wealth is something that you have to deserve to have, you have to change that concept.

How do you work with the subconscious?

You cannot talk to the subconscious; you cannot use words to access it. The subconscious exists only in an absolute place where words are pointless.

To access your subconscious, the only tool you have available is your emotions. You access emotion by visualizing and then feeling what you visualize. You have to hold a very clear picture of what you want. And you have to feel as if you already have it, and act that way in the physical world.

Say you want unlimited wealth. Visualizing that is relatively easy. We can access a number of visual representations of what wealth looks like: a Rolls Royce instead of a Volkswagen bug; ornate oriental carpets instead of rag rugs; a wallet bulging with currency of large denomination (don't call your paper money "bills" because your subconscious immediately visualizes the kind of bill you have to pay, and you don't want more of those!). But you also have to feel wealthy. Now this does not mean that you will run out and buy everything in sight if you only have five hundred dollars in the bank! Remember, we live in the physical world, and we have to honor the fact that the physical world is one of limitation. But in your creative mind, you can act like you have unlimited cash. Go to the Mercedes or Rolls Royce dealer and look at cars, and pick one out that you like. Save a few dollars and buy a ticket to the opera or go to a museum. These are traditionally places where the wealthy are found; go to those places and mingle. Wear your most elegant clothes whenever possible. Eat off your best china, and use the good silverware and fine crystal. Who are you saving it for anyway? Get rid of the junk art on your walls and buy one or two pieces of genuine, original art. They don't have to be expensive pieces, they just have to be the real thing. Make your own, if you must. Wealthy people do not have posters on their walls!

As you live what you dream, your subconscious registers your new life. At some point, it has to deliver some cash so you can continue to live this way.

Above all else, do not put physical world conditions on what you want to manifest. Time and space are meaningless. They do not apply in any way to magick. Magick works in spite of time and space. And don't worry about quantity. If you can manifest a dollar, you can manifest ten million dollars, or indeed any amount. The universe does not have limitations, other than those you believe you have. It is just as easy to visualize something huge as it is to visualize something miniscule. And when (not if!) you get what you visualized, don't apologize to anyone, including yourself, for having what you wanted. You don't have to earn anything. Nobody else is going without because you have something. There is more than enough for everyone. If you manifest a huge amount of money and then find yourself saying, "oh, I didn't earn it, I was just lucky and won it," guess what happens? It disappears: you blow through it and end up with nothing, or someone steals it from you, or you make a bad investment and lose it. Any way you look at it, you'll lose what you gained, because you didn't feel you deserved it. Is there any value in that?

It is important to remember that old concept of "if it harms none." Magick that is worked without sufficient contemplation can be harmful. You might get the immense wealth you visualized, but what if the one person you love above all others, your (wealthy) grandfather, had to die to leave it to you? Is being fantastically wealthy worth it if you lost someone dear to you?

Everything Starts NOW

Your history does not determine your future. What you visualize determines your future.

Your life up to this point reflects what you used to believe, up until now. You can change that, starting within this minute. You've been sick for thirty years? That's history; whatever is in the past is done with and gone. You can't rewrite what you've already experienced. Trying to do so is futile and a huge waste of time. Nor would you want to rewrite your history. You had those experiences because you needed to experience them at that time. You could not have arrived at the point where you are today without every minute of the life you've already experienced. Each step defines the possibilities of the next step that follows it. And nobody ever said life was going to be a hayride. Remember: balance. Without the experiences that you rather would not have had, you could not have enjoyed some of the ones you did enjoy. A person who has a perfect life could never be aware of how perfect his life was, because he would have nothing to compare with it.

Instead, your subconscious has to believe, from this moment forward, that you are well and healthy. Visualize a healthy body. What would you be doing if you had excellent health? Playing racquetball, taking a hike, swimming a few laps? Visualize that. Do it in your mind. Keep doing it.

Scientifically, it has been proven that the body reflects what the mind believes. In an experiment several years ago, scientists took some DNA from test subjects, and then instructed them to perform specific tasks only within their minds, like imagining they were running a race. The tissue samples of their DNA reacted as if the body was actually doing that task. There was absolutely NO difference between the reactions of the DNA that was still in the body of a test subject and the DNA that had been removed and was physically a distance away from the subject.

In another test, scientists used imaging devices to view the brains of test subjects. The brains of people doing specific tasks showed exactly the same activity as the brains of people who were only thinking of doing that task but remaining absolutely still.

Quantum physics has demonstrated that time and space are not involved in transmissions of energy. Unlike our perception of light and sound, which require very small amounts of time between transmission and reception, a transmission of energy is received at exactly the same time as it is transmitted. This is amazingly powerful. If you think about something, it already exists at that very instant.

Working Magick for Others

It seems to be a relatively universal Pagan belief that we are all responsible only for our own reality. With that in mind, we have to make an ethical decision about whether we will use what we know and believe to help others.

If you decide to do ritual or magickal work for others, there are a couple of caveats to keep in mind.

Any work that seeks to control someone else is best avoided. That includes spells done "for someone's own good." There are spiritual busybodies who feel some obligation to improve the lives of everyone around them. Every person is responsible for ONLY his own life. If someone asks for help, I try to do what I can, but I don't make decisions that are that person's responsibility to make, and I don't attempt to direct someone else's life.

In some cases, you can reasonably take the responsibility for your actions on behalf of others. You can legitimately work magick or use ritual for animals (because unlike humans, they can't do it themselves) or for minor children for whom you are responsible. That does not include any other children – only those you are directly responsible for. The kid from down the street is hanging out with the wrong crowd, and you would like to do a ritual to make sure he takes the best path for his own good? Let his parents deal with him: he is their responsibility, not yours. If you want to fix the world, use a ritual that is oriented to bring good change to everyone; remember, it is not your responsibility to fix anyone else's life.

If someone specifically asks me to work a spell or ritual, I usually do it. But, in any case, I do only what they asked for, nothing more and nothing less. I don't attempt to influence anything based on my own views, and I always specifically state that anything I do must be part of their life plan and for their own good. If what I attempt has a negative implication for them, it simply won't work.

I never advise someone about what I think they want or need. If they don't know what they want, or have no clue about what they really need, then I tell them to go home and think about it until they get a clear answer, and to come back to me for help at that point. The danger here is that the outcome that someone states they want might not be what is best for them, or aligned to bring them happiness or satisfaction. What people want is rarely what they need in a real sense. I cannot know what they are truly trying to accomplish, and I insist that they understand that before they seek help from me.

You must be responsible. I used to love thunder storms, and watching lightning is a real pleasure. I used to bring relatively violent weather when I was very young (teenage years); I had a genuine ability to create a real banger of a thunderstorm out of a few clouds. The day the lightning struck the barn next door, however, I began to realize that I was diddling around with some very powerful forces, and for the most part, it was only for my amusement. Luckily the neighbor's barn did not catch afire (although it did put out quite a bit of smoke for a few minutes), but the resulting rain coming off the hillside behind our house flooded the lower part of our driveway and nearly caused my mother to have an accident with the car when it slid off the hard surface and got stuck in the mud that formerly had been part of the lawn. I quickly realized that my actions had caused a series of other things to happen, none of which had occurred to me before that moment.

Often, what we visualize has a number of implications that affect something outside of what we imagine.

One of my early Wiccan teachers used to discuss the projected outcomes for which we wanted to work magick; she would tell us to go and think about what would happen if we did what we wanted to do. When we thought we had it all figured out, she would point out something we had never considered and tell us to go think about it some more. No matter how much thought we put into it, she could always come up with something else we hadn't considered. To this day, whenever I decide to use magick to accomplish something, I start thinking about what it is I want to accomplish, and then go back many times to consider it further. It is only when I can't come up with anything else that might apply that I feel safe in doing that work.

Clean Up When You Are Finished

After your magickal working is complete, remember to remove anything that you brought into your circle or ritual space. Remove any visual representations, like signs or symbols, and sweep up any residue if you left physical evidence behind, such as a circle of salt where your ritual circle was cast. When you are finished, there should be no indication that you were there, or that anything was done. Magick works best when your intentions are focused inward; leaving external evidence dilutes the efficacy of your working.

In the same way, do not share with other people (anyone who was not directly involved in the ritual or magickal working) any details of what you have done. Doing so dilutes the energy, and if someone who does not believe the magick will work overhears your discussion, that negativity can work against your projected outcome. Ever hear the old saying, silence is golden? Keep your energy close to you.

9

Ritual

Mankind loves ritual. We use ritual in a spiritual sense to access and commune with the Divine energy of the God and Goddess, to ask for their support in an undertaking, and to connect universal masculine and feminine energy with our own personal energy. Using ritual rather than everyday language enables us to go deeper into our subconscious and unconscious minds, where their energies are more refined than that used in the physical world of everyday reality.

It is important to remember that we do not have an absolute, concrete concept of ancient Pagan traditions. The knowledge was possess today about ancient peoples is a combination of the translations of a few historic documents, some archeological research, and myth and legends. These data, combined with the "best guesses" of scholars who are trying to create a genuine picture of ancient civilizations form the background of modern Paganism. Anyone in a modern tradition who claims to retain the knowledge of an ancient tradition is, at the very least, inaccurate. Because there is no true history of Pagan spirituality, all modern day Pagan beliefs have been developed relatively recently. This is why there are so many traditions; anyone can piece together some ancient information – assuming that everything we know today is an accurate representation of ancient practices.

Many Pagans realize that their spiritual path is one of lifelong learning. Human spirituality develops over time as one becomes exposed to new concepts. Pagans must not be in a rush to solidify their spiritual beliefs or practices; new information is constantly being revealed that cannot be assimilated if the mind is closed to it.

Ritual is often performed by rote. Doing things the same way time after time is a human trait. For example, when I eat a muffin, I take the crusty top off and eat that first. Then I nibble the sides, then the bottom, until only the soft center remains. Then I enjoy that. I have no idea why I eat a muffin this way, but it's an automatic behavior. Most of us go through life in much the same way. If something worked once, it will probably always work. So we mindlessly repeat the task the same way we experienced it the first time.

If I approached my spiritual workings in that way, however, not much would happen. A task done from memory can never have as much energy as one done while you are actively thinking and altering your behavior.

Fortunately, many books on Pagan ritual honor this concept. To raise energy, for example, almost every source mentions the need to chant or move about, increasing both volume and speed, until the proper energy level is reached. No book can tell you what that energy level is; you have to feel it for yourself. And when you experience it, you'll know that your energy is at the right level. Anything less will feel inadequate, and it's impossible to generate too much energy.

Pagans who are new to this type of spiritual path often rely on rituals that are described in books or by other Pagans who have experienced them in the past. Learning always has a starting point. Pagans must remember that rituals passed along from others worked for those people, and that same ritual might not work as well for you. There is no restriction on whether you can adapt a ritual to suit your own purposes. I've read a huge number of books, all of which profess to have the knowledge you need... and remember, this is one of them! I write about Paganism from my own experience, not from anyone else's viewpoint. What works for me might not work at all for you. Then again, it might, or you might be able to adapt something that has worked for me and make it work for you. The point is, you are always free to do that, with any ritual. These principles also work for spellcasting. Both require you to visualize an end result or an ideal with which you want to connect. Both require you to raise your energy so that you can access a higher vibration of energy than we use on Earth in our physical incarnations. Rituals are done to focus on connection; spells are done to focus on creating change in the here and now, but to attain either end, the process is the same.

I think the difference between ritual and spellcasting is that in ritual work, you raise your energy to create a connection, whereas in spelllcasting, you make a connection and then raise your energy level. It's rather like driving down the same road, but going in opposite directions depending on where you want to end up.

The Joy in Ritual

All ritual must be approached with joy. Even a ritual to celebrate a death (and yes, it is a celebration) is joyful. There is nothing we can experience in the physical world that is removed from our joy. I do know a few Pagans who spend a lot of time whining about their life, but if they approach a task with that attitude, I sincerely doubt that they will be able to effect any amount of real change.

People who seek joy in their lives are always fortunate. Good things happen to them because they know they will. Change that is viewed as a joyful experience is far easier to deal with than change that is viewed as negative. The parts of your life that change don't do it to annoy you. There is no consciousness behind change. It happens as circumstances in your life dictate. You can resist change, but you can't avoid it altogether. Accepting the changes along your life path with grace and dignity make them far easier to tolerate. And if you can do that joyfully, change becomes completely unimportant.

Change is something that humans like to avoid, but it happens anyway. I've always said that I abhor chaos but embrace change. Chaos is change that you resist. It's viewed as a negative; what logical human would want his life constantly disrupted with negativity? Change in a positive sense fosters growth. That's why we're on the planet: to learn and grow.

Adapting Rituals

No ritual is written in stone. You are always free to rewrite anything and everything in a way that will make it more evidential for you, so that it resonates within your being. In that way, it becomes effective and you will see results in the physical world. If even some small aspect of a ritual doesn't sit well with you, it will prevent you from achieving success. The part of the ritual that seems out of place is probably something that does not fit well with your code of ethics or your morality.

For example, some aspect of a ritual feels manipulative. Your ethics do not allow you to do manipulative work of any kind, without exception, because you believe that manipulation is always negative. Your subconscious mind will prevent you from raising sufficient energy to achieve the goal of that ritual. You can perform the ritual many times, but it will never feel right to you and it will always fail.

So change it! Remove whatever you feel is blocking your success. Your intuitive mind can point this out easily. You might have to change a few words, or eliminate a section, or even stop doing the ritual entirely. Do what feels right to you. Your ethics are a tool that can help you achieve success, but you cannot work around them successfully.

Using Goddess-Based Rituals

Rituals that are feminine oriented can often be rewritten to include masculine energy. For example, if a ritual includes the statement "I am a woman of the Goddess," you can freely substitute the masculine, changing it to "I am a man of the Goddess." The statement is essentially the same, but the language ensures that masculine energy is honored as much as feminine energy.

Some rituals need to be edited for men. A ritual that states "My womb is dedicated to the Goddess" obviously cannot be used by men. I might reword it this way: "My ability to create life is dedicated to the Goddess."

A ritual that is completely female-based must often be abandoned by men. These kinds of rituals usually address a woman's menstrual cycle, her ability to bear children or some other biological function. If it cannot be reworked in a sensible way, don't use the ritual. The intent of that ritual, however, can often be accomplished by simply using another kind of ritual.

Whenever a ritual is worded in a way that does not work for you, change it. Adapt it in a way that is meaningful to you. The God and Goddess could not care less about the words we use when we call on them. If the words are wrong for your specific situation, you will not be able to raise enough emotion (or energy) to make contact or to effect change. They're just words. The way that you feel about the words you use is the energy that makes the connection and accomplishes the goal. Using words that are not correct for the situation means that the emotion behind them will never be sufficient enough to attract the universal energy needed to affect the change you seek.

Regardless of the words you use, your ritual or spellcasting will work only if you can summon enough energy to send out a ripple into the ether. This can be done only through emotion, not through thoughts. Remember, words are thoughts. You must connect to the emotion behind the words to be successful.

Using Rhyme and Rhythm

There are two additional tools that are useful when used for rituals or spellcasting: rhyme and rhythm.

Rhyme and rhythm work together. Sentences that rhyme are easier to remember; once memorized, you can allow your subconscious to repeat them over and over, while you concentrate on raising the necessary emotion in order to create and send forth energy. Sentences that are rhythmic in the same way that songs or poetry are rhythmic also penetrate the subconscious more effectively. Using a series of sentences that do not rhyme or are not rhythmic tends to create a feeling of chaos. Your subconscious has to increase the effort required to remember the words, and that results in less energy available to send forth.

If you can't write in rhyme or have a problem with rhythm, you can always fall back on rituals or spellcasting that someone else wrote. While it might not be as efficient as something you created yourself, it can still accomplish the task. I feel that both rhyme and rhythm are so important that any ritual will have better results if they are incorporated.

Keep your sentences short to maintain a rhythm. Longer sentences can be rhythmic as well, but if you aren't familiar with writing in that style, it can be difficult. Your subconscious will notice any sentence where the rhythm is off, just as it will notice a poor rhyme.

Some words are difficult to rhyme. Try to find something that really rhymes with "orange." If you have a word that's difficult to rhyme, change the sentence structure so that the difficult word does not occur at the end of the sentence. You might have to fiddle a bit with other sentences as a result, but the longer you work on your ritual, the more effective it will be. This preparatory time counts as well. Every time you speak the words, your subconscious notices and records them.

If you really have difficulty with this, you can take a poetry class. Look for a class that emphasizes rhyme and rhythm over more modern poetic forms, such as freestyle poetry. Alternately, you can ask someone else to help you, but rituals that you create yourself are almost always more effective.

Tools to Access Energy in Rituals

Pagan traditions encourage the use of ritual to raise energy to accomplish a goal or seek a change. Within a ritual, we can use whatever tools complement the goal.

To Access Masculine Energy

Use any of the following to link to masculine God-based energy:
✓ Animal horns or antlers
✓ Bones
✓ Feathers that have a quill and hard, defined edges
✓ Leather
✓ Gold, iron, steel bronze or brass (any metal that can be forged). Copper has both masculine and feminine qualities since it can be forged but is also a soft metal.
✓ Certain tree branches (see the list of masculine/feminine correspondences below)
✓ Tall, reedy grasses with sturdy stems, dry hay or straw
✓ Leaves that have turned brown or gray but are still intact
✓ Rough stones
✓ Noisemakers (drums, rattles, bells and so forth)
✓ Sour or bitter foods
✓ Statues or representations of one of the ancient Gods
✓ Scents that are woody or spicy
✓ Both runic writing and the Theban script are masculine in nature, due primarily to their straight lines and sharp angles. Write an incantation or prayer in runes or Theban and place it where you can see it.

To Access Feminine Energy

Use any of the following to link to feminine Goddess-based energy:
✓ Seashells
✓ Downy feathers
✓ Green plants or green leaves
✓ Sprouting plants, or plants with flower buds or flowers
✓ Silver (any metal that is relatively soft and that must be worked gently). Copper has both masculine and feminine qualities since it can be

forged but is also a soft metal.

- ✓ Certain tree branches (see the list of masculine/feminine correspondences below)
- ✓ Soft green grass or any plant with soft or hollow stems
- ✓ Smooth stones (like river stones)
- ✓ Melodious bells, singing bowls, or anything that makes a pleasant musical sound
- ✓ Statues or representations of one of the ancient Goddesses
- ✓ Sweet foods
- ✓ Floral scents
- ✓ Script writing or any typestyle that is flowing and contains curves

INVOCATION TO THE GREEN MAN (DARK MOON)

O Lord Of The Forest
King of Night's embrace
Green and Golden is thy ever-changing face

Whisper thy hidden Mystery
In the fall of the leaves
That shroud thy branches
Strong and bold
Green and gold

Sweet is thy sap,
Thy blood rising in the dawn
Bearer of secrets from deep within thy verdant realm.

Wild and untamed
Thy song is carried by eagle, robin and wren

Thy Truth, the acorn that calls to rampant boar
Thy spirit crowned in Sovereignty!

We call to thee O Green Man
Send thy leaves to leap and spin

From root and branch
Thy sacred dance
Let thy magic doth begin!

Blayze, Applegrove, Sydney

10

Tools

The responses to my survey indicated that a significant majority of men use various tools in their rituals. A few men noted that tools are not necessary for creating a connection with God/Goddess energy, or even for spellcasting. Your will and your intentions, along with significant emotion, connect with universal energy; tools are an adjunct to this connection.

As with any topic, how you personally feel about using tools determines whether you use them. If you feel that using tools deepens and strengthens your connection to universal energy, then by all means use them.

If you use tools, remember that they have no power of their own. They are used to focus, direct and refine the power within you. They serve as props to help you maintain focus. Humans are visual beings; observing the act of plunging an athame into a chalice helps you make a more genuine connection to the spiritual intention behind the physical act.

This chapter outlines some of the tools that Pagans use. This is not a comprehensive list. Various traditions include a type of tool that is unique to that tradition. My familiarity with tools is through my personal experience as a Wiccan, so the list is biased toward that tradition. However, not all Pagans use all of these tools, and some use no tools at all.

You are always free to choose or ignore a tool, based on your personal preference. I knew a Wiccan years ago who was terrified of knives. She was convinced that she had died at knifepoint in a previous life. Using an athame was out of the question for her; she would focus on the negativity she felt about knives in general and it affected her ability to connect to universal energy. She eliminated the athame from her rituals, and her tradition was not one that used swords. She adapted the ritual tasks usually accomplished by using an athame to other tools, most frequently the wand. She used a wand of oak, which has a very strong masculine energy.

Many traditions believe that if you need to use a tool, it will be attracted to you at the right time. There is no need to rush out and purchase ritual tools from a list. Allow the universe to deliver an appropriate tool to you at an appropriate time.

Tools in some traditions are consecrated before their first use. This involves bringing them into the circle after purifying them with salt or smoke, dedicating their use to the God/Goddess, and then using the tool only for ritual or magickal purposes. Consecrated tools are not used outside the ritual space. In some traditions, tools are consecrated by the group and presented to their owner after this is complete. This is done to imbue the tool with the energy of the group. Other traditions do not consecrate their tools, feeling that God/Goddess is all-powerful and does not need any earthly consecration efforts to enable that tool to work with their energy. As with anything Pagan, do what feels right to you.

Some tools are traditionally made of wood: the wand and the pentacle. If you use either of these tools, consider the type of wood from which they were crafted. The type of ritual you want to perform can be more effective if you use a type of wood that has a link to that type of energy. (For a list of God/Goddess correspondences and associations with various uses, see the Appendix.)

Again, with any tool, its effectiveness is a result of your intent and will. You can use a wand of any type of wood to do any task. To choose a wand, hold several species of wood in your receptive hand (not in your projective hand at this point). See which woods feel suitable. It is likely that more than one will feel effective. After you select one or two that seem workable, hold them each in your projective hand and see if you get the same feeling.

The chalice is another tool that can be made of wood. If you use a wooden chalice, choose one that is made from one of the wood species that are feminine-oriented. The chalice represents feminine energy, and using a tree species that has masculine energy can interfere with the intention of your ritual.

There might be some tree species that you do not feel comfortable working with. Many years ago, I had a beautiful willow wand that a friend gave me. I never had much success when working with that wand, but I'm not sure why that is. It might be that I grew up with weeping willows growing in our back yard, and that type of tree is constantly losing branches that had to be collected and hauled away, which I hated because I was usually given that chore. I also considered the wood to be flimsy; it is difficult for the mind to think powerful thoughts when you are directing your energy outward with a type of wood you consider unsubstantial.

Other species might resonate better with you. On a trip to Salem, I picked up a maple tree branch from the cemetery where some of the Salem witches were buried. A strong wind had come up while we were wandering in the cemetery, and the branch broke from the ancient tree above me and fell at my feet, as if the tree was giving me its gift. That wand has always been extremely effective for me. While many wands are sanded down and polished, I left that wand exactly as the tree gave it to me, with broken ends and chipped bark. But if I purchased a wand, I would like it to be sanded and polished so that I could see the beautiful grain and colors of the wood.

Tool Basics

In Pagan traditions, a range of magical tools is used in ritual practice. Each of these tools has different uses and associations, and are used primarily to direct magical energies. In many traditions, they are used at an altar, inside a magic circle.

Four tools are used by many traditions as their primary tools. A number of additional tools are available and are used or ignored, depending on the history of the tradition or the preferences of the practitioner.

Generally, tools are consecrated before the first time they are used in ritual. Consecrated tools are usually not used in everday life, although there are many Pagans who believe that their tools are intended to be used in daily life so that the universal energies that the tool can access becomes available to the person in daily life.

Primary Tools

The primary tools are the Pentacle, Wand, Athame (or Sword) and

Chalice.

Some traditions require that new tools be purchased for ritual use. Others believe that any item with which the participant feels comfortable will be equally as effective.

Pentacle

The pentacle represents the element of earth.

A pentacle is a flat, round disk that resembles a plate. It usually has a pentagram engraved on it. Pentacles can be made of wood, metal, or stone. Offerings to the Earth can be placed on the pentacle, or it can be used to hold bread or other food which is eaten as part of a ritual.

Wand or Staff

The wand represents the element of air. Gardnerians associate it with the element of fire.

Wands or staffs are used to direct energy. A wand can be made of any material, such as wood, metal or stone. Wands sometimes include crystals mounted on the ends; crystals are believed to be efficient in directing energy.

A staff is often made to correspond to the exact height of the person who uses it. In some traditions, a stang (a double-headed staff – see below) is substituted for a staff.

Athame and Sword

The athame represents the element of fire in most traditions; Gardnerians associate it with the element of air, because when you use an athame or sword, you are actually slicing through the air.

In some traditons, an athame or sword is never used to cut. It is used to direct energy or control spirits or elemental energies. In other traditions, it is used for cutting, and is used instead of the boline.

Determine whether you want to use an athame with a sharp or dulled blade. If your athame is used strictly in a symbolic way in ritual, a dulled blade is safer and easier to handle. If you want to use your athame to actually cut something (replacing the boline), choose a sharp blade. The length of the athame is subjective; choose one that resonates for you. Some athames, like the Scottish dirk, have very short blades; others have blades reminiscent of a small sword. The length of the blade becomes important if you want to carry your athame to a ritual space.

An athame or sword is never used to draw blood. If it touches blood, it must be destroyed.

In some traditions, a sword is an entirely separate tool. It is used to command and is most often used in magick. In a spiritual sense, most Pagans do not believe that they can command; instead, they prefer to request.

The sword is frequently used in the Norse, Celtic and Asatru traditions, since they are associated with the warrior spirit.

If you use a sword, make sure you can handle it. Swords are usually heavy, have sharp edges and must be treated respectfully. If you work with a group in a ritual circle, additional space might be needed so that the sword can be used without endangering others.

Note: In some Pagan traditions, the athame or sword is replaced by the sickle, a crescent-shaped knife used for harvesting grasses or grain. This was usually done in ancient times by women, so the sickle is associated with Goddess energy. It is not used in conjunction with a chalice, as the athame often is, but instead is used separately.

Chalice

The chalice represents the element of water. In some traditions, it is called the Goblet or the Cup.

Some traditions do not consider the chalice a tool, but instead believe it links directly with Goddess energy and represents the Goddess in rituals or magickal workings. It often is used to represent the womb of the Goddess. It can be used to hold water, wine, fruit juice, milk or other liquids.

In some traditions, the chalice and its contents are intended for the Goddess; the chalice is not used by humans since it is intended to contain the essence of the Divine. In other traditions, humans are viewed as an integral part of the God/Goddess energy, and therefore anything that is intended for the deity can also be intended for the human. In these traditions, there is no restriction about drinking from the chalice. Pagans are always free to follow the teachings of a tradition, or to adapt it to whatever feels appropriate.

If the chalice is made of pewter, which contains lead, you should not drink from it. Wine can leach lead from pewter very quickly. If you must have a ritual drink, put the liquid in a crystal cup and drink from that instead. Avoid "lead crystal" because it is associated with Saturn energy. Silver and pewter are commonly used, along with ceramic chalices. Any chalice from which you drink should be coated in some way, or of a metal, like sterling silver, which is safe to use for drinking.

In some traditions, the liquid contents of the chalice are poured onto the Earth as an offering to the God/Goddess.

Additional Tools

Various Pagan traditions use other tools within rituals or to create change. Some common tools are listed here; this is not an exhaustive list, and a tool that might be common within your tradition might not appear. Pagan traditions are constantly changing, and using what was common yesterday might not apply today.

Boline

The boline is a small knife. It often has a crescent-shaped handle that evokes the crescent moon. Whereas the athame is used only for ritual purposes, the boline is used in practical ways, such as harvesting and cutting herbs, inscribing candles, or cutting ritual cords.

Like the athame and sword, if the boline is exposed to blood, it must be discarded and cannot be used again. Pagans revere all life forms and do not do any ritual or spellcasting that involves blood.

Censer and Incense

The censer is used to hold incense. It relates to both fire and air. You can burn raw incense, herbs or resins in the censer atop a lighted charcoal briquette or disk.

Censers are also called thuribles in some traditions.

Choose an incense that contains natural essential oils or herbs. Some incenses are made of fillers that have been lightly scented with artificial scents. Most of the better incenses are in powder form and must be burned on top of a lighted charcoal disk.

Light the charcoal by holding the disk over a match. Both matches and charcoal disks contain sulfur, which helps it to start burning. Sulfur is used for banishing; if that is not the intent of the ritual, you might want to strike the match and light the charcoal disk outside of your ritual area. When the charcoal no longer sparks, the sulfur is gone and it can be brought into the ritual area.

To ensure safety, put a layer of salt or sand in the bottom of the censer. This will prevent it from getting hot enough to burn whatever is under it, like your altar or the floor. I usually choose a censer that has feet or is raised on some sort of stand to avoid the possibility of setting my house afire. If you plan to move the censer during the ritual, it should have handles or a chain so that you can pick it up without getting burnt.

Any household item can be used as a censer, as long as it will be safe to use after the charcoal is lighted. Charcoal burns slowly but can get very hot. The use of salt or sand beneath the charcoal is always recommended.

Unless a ritual specifically calls for damping the incense to stop the smoking and release energy, the incense should be allowed to burn down until it is completely consumed.

The censer can be used for smudging, or you can burn smudge sticks, which are bunches of herbs that are tied together. In smudging, the air within the ritual space (or physical room) is cleared of negative vibrations, including emotional and psychic "trash." These negative energies can accumulate over time and tend to get trapped within the physical confines of the room or space.

Smudging is used to banish stress, eliminate negativity and promote the flow of positive energy. Most frequently, white sage is used (which results in part from native American traditions), or you can use highly scented herbs like rosemary or lavender. The herbs must be dry or they will not burn correctly, or might not even burn at all, if they are very damp. For this reason, fresh herbs are not used, and of necessity, smudging requires a bit of planning in advance.

Incense or smudge sticks should not be used if you have asthma or any form of chronic obstructive pulmonary disease, if you are pregnant, or around infants and very young children. The area being smudged must have some ventilation, which is needed both for physical safety and to allow the negative energies a pathway out of the room or ritual space. If you use a match to light the smudge bundle, strike the match outside the ritual space; remember that modern matches use sulfur and saltpeter to ignite and burn. These two compounds are used to banish and suppress

– two types of energy that you do not want associated with many rituals. After the smudge bundle is burning, it is safe to bring it into the room or ritual space.

Besom or Broom

Frequently used in Wicca, the broom is used to ritually cleanse the area where a circle will be cast before a ritual is performed. It is also used in some traditions for handfasting (marriage) ceremonies. Frequently, the besom is laid on the floor within the ritual space, and the two people who are being handfasted jump over it together in a joyful way. In some traditions, handfasting is a lifelong commitment; in others, a handfasting lasts for a year and a day, after which time the couple can part without rancor, each free to go in separate directions, or the handfasting ceremony is repeated to join them for another year and a day.

Why a year and a day? That period equates to 366 days. If you add the three digits, the result is 15; add 1 and 5 and the number reduces to 6. In numerology, the number 6 is ruled by Venus (the goddess of love). It evokes harmony, balance, sincerity, love and truth. The number 6 also represents compassion and the ability to forgive – both important qualities in a relationship!

Some Pagans insist that a ritual besom should be made of broom, a flowering species of plant commonly found in Europe. In ancient Sussex, there was a superstition about using flowering broom to sweep the house in the month of May; it was believed that doing so would cause harm to the head of the household.

In America, brooms were made from broom corn, which was assembled in a flat package. The sweeping straws of a besom are traditionally assembled into a round bunch and tied to a handle. While either configuration will work equally well, most Pagans prefer the look of the ancient besom, believing that it enables them to more easily visualize the magickal act of ritual cleaning than does a modern flat commercial broom.

Most brooms are made of straw, but you can easily make your own broom. Find a sturdy branch that is between 4' and 6' long, and preferably straight. At one end, attach dried grasses, straw, or other scented plants such as lavender and rosemary, and tie them together with a natural twine.

In the circle, sweep from center towards the outside edges. Many Pagans do this in a clockwise motion to invoke good energies.

Many Pagans place a broom with the sweeping end up near a door in their home to promote good energy and to keep negativity out. My grandmother, who was born in a very rural area in the mountains in upstate New York, used to say that if you put a broom behind your open door, unwanted guests would stay away. I'm not sure if that ever really worked, but it was an interesting observation!

Bell

The bell is associated with the Goddess. A bell can be rung during rituals to increase the participant's vibration and to purify the ritual space. A bell is rung once, twice or three times, but never continuously because the jangling noise of a constantly ringing bell is disruptive.

Bells were originally hung on doorways to improve the vibration of the house within. One can often see bells hung on doorways of shops in modern times; their protective aspect is transformed and they are now associated with security (that is, to prevent customers from walking out with the merchandise without paying for it). Bells also halt storms and evoke good energies.

Choose a bell with a pleasant smooth or mellow tone. Every bell has a different sound; try several until you find one that resonates with you.

Cauldron

A cauldron can be of any size. Groups often use large cauldrons, whereas solitary practitioners often use a much smaller version that can fit easily on a table or altar. Cauldrons, like the chalice, represent the womb of the Goddess, and Goddess energy. They represent the element of water.

Traditionally, a cauldron is a round iron vessel with three legs, but you can use any vessel that fulfills the requirements of your tradition.

A cauldron represents bounty and blessings. It was commonly found in every home in ancient times, since it was used to prepare meals. It is also linked with reincarnation and the cycle of birth, death and rebirth.

Cauldrons can be used to make brews (such as oils), burning incense (to replace or supplement a censer), to hold large pillar candles, or filled with water and used for scrying or divination.

If your ritual calls for lighting a candle and allowing it to burn completely down, put some salt or sand in the bottom of the cauldron and nestle the candle in it. The candle is secure and can burn itself out, and any wax drippings will fall onto the salt or sand and can easily be removed. The layer of salt or sand also protects the bottom of the cauldron from overheating and possibly causing a fire. Using pillar candles, which have a wider base, also ensures their stability.

The Celtic Goddess Cerridwen is associated with a cauldron, in which she prepared a magical brew that required a year and a day to create.

Candles

Candles are associated with both fire and air elements. They can be used to provide light for the ritual space, or in specific spells. While any type of wax works equally well, I prefer candles made of pure beeswax. Waxes that are petroleum-based emit noxious gases; pure beeswax burns completely cleanly. Be aware that what is often described as "beeswax candles" are not 100% pure beeswax; they can contain a large percentage of other types of wax (including petroleum-based ones) while still carrying the "made of beeswax" marking.

Early candles were made of vegetable waxes and animal fats such as tallow. These candles were time consuming to make; they smoked as they burned and they often smelled badly since animal fats can become rancid. Candles made of vegetable waxes, such as soy, are less toxic than those made of petroleum derivatives. Paraffin, a petroleum derivative, burned with less smoke than vegetable or animal fat based candles and with less odor.

Candles made of soft waxes are usually formed in containers to prevent the wax from melting and dripping. Pillar candles are wide and thick and quite stable. Tea (or votive) candles are very short and are either free-standing or formed in small metal containers. As they burn, the wax melts and the wick is able to burn the liquid completely. Tapers are tall, slender candles that are made to fit into a standard sized candleholder. Depending on the wax used, they can form drips or be dripless.

The colors of the candles you use can be important. Many traditions connect various colors with specific powers or attributes. Participants in these traditions believe that their magickal working will have a greater chance of success if they use candles of the correct color.

Regardless of the color, the visible light that all candles produce is the same. If you feel that the light has been imbued with specific qualities based on the colors of the candles you use, this belief can have a significant impact on whether your ritual will be successful. For information about color correspondences, see "Appendix — Magickal Correspondences" on page 185.

It is a good idea to always place a candle in a candleholder before lighting it. This protects your ritual space from unwanted fires, and also confines any dripping wax. You can use a candleholder that you already own, or find a decorative one available commercially. Pagan or Wiccan supply stores usually carry decorative holders that reflect the intention of your ritual.

Herbs and Oils

Herbs are used as ingredients for incense and in ritual and spellcasting. When using herbs for incense, use dried herbs and burn them on charcoal blocks. Essential oils are used for anointing candles, tools, the altar and the body in rituals and spell working.

Herbs and oils are associated with the element of earth. Since all plants have specific energies, you can use plants in association with the ritual to be performed. Specific herbs often have associations with specific types of tasks. Using a herb that is aligned with your intention can't hurt and might help. Trust your intuition to guide you to the correct herb for a specific task. Just because a herb has not been associated with the task or ritual you are undertaking in the past does not mean that it is not appropriate for you on this occasion. Pagans should never be afraid to try something new. Humans are conscious, sentient beings and we can access great wisdom if we are open to it. Let that ability guide you when making choices. If your task or ritual is not effective, you can always do it again, using different materials.

Book of Shadows or Journal

Some Pagan traditions encourage the use of a journal in which rituals are described and spells are recorded, along with any rules or requirements the participant wants to observe, inspiration, and general philosophical thoughts about the tradition itself. This journal, often called a Book of Shadows in Wiccan traditions, is a personal record of the ritual and magickal work the person has done over his lifetime. Because it is a personal record of your spiritual journey, you can include any information that you want to include.

Note: In some Pagan traditions, this journal is called a Grimoire or a Book of Mirrors.

You can purchase a blank Book of Shadows from many vendors. If you use a commercial Book, use it as if it were a blank journal. If a page has a heading that you feel is unnecessary, ignore it. Some of these commercial Books can be beautiful, with appropriate typestyles and artwork that is designed to put you into an appropriate frame of mind when using them. However, any journal will work. As you include more information, whatever form of journal you selected becomes more personal to you.

A few traditions discourage keeping any form of written record. All information in the tradition must be transmitted from person to person orally.

Some groups maintain a basic Book of Shadows, a copy of which is given to anyone joining the group. It contains some of the basic information pertaining to that tradition. Each person is expected to add personal information to his private copy, truly making each one a personal record.

Several working Books of Shadows have been published over the years, along with many that are partially complete or are completely incorrect. Take information from other Books of Shadows with a grain of salt; remember that you can (and should) choose what information resonates with you personally and disregard the rest.

While a Book of Shadows was often required to be handwritten, Pagans today use computer files audio tapes, or any other method of recording the information they want to preserve. If you use computer files, remember to back them up onto separate, removable media every time you make a change. Remember to print out the files every so often so that you also have a paper record. A hard drive crash can erase all of your records about your spiritual path!

While you can use permanently bound blank journals, they are difficult to update. Instead, you can use a three-ring binder in which pages can be added, removed, or replaced as needed.

While some traditions specify the type of paper or ink that should be used, it must be kept in mind that neither paper nor type of ink has any special powers. There is no need to go on a search for bats blood ink, or parchment paper made from Egyptian reeds on a Wednesday afternoon.

My Book of Shadows uses handmade papers, not because of the energy behind their manufacture, but because I happen to like the look and feel of handmade paper. I travel often to Glastonbury, England and there is an old paper mill in the nearby small town of Wookey Hole. The mill is shut down, but it is part of a tourist attraction and handmade papers are still made there in small batches as part of the tourist experience. I love the area and enjoy going to Wookey Hole, so I use handmade papers from that mill.

Some traditions call for the use of a "Pen of Art" for transcribing information into the Book of Shadows. While it's a lovely thought, it's also counterproductive. Why devote a lot of time to finding exactly the right magickal pen when you can use any pen with the same end result?

I use a commercial pen, usually containing liquid black ink because it is easy to use and readily available when I need a new one. When I first began my studies, I used a fountain pen with peacock blue ink (a personal peccadillo, I suppose, not because it was required). Fiddling with bottles of ink and having to refill the pen constantly, not to mention the frequent smudges of excess ink, made me look at that practice and refine it. While I still like the way my writing looks if I use fountain pens, I no longer have the time for all of the overhead they require. A liquid ball pen that I can buy in the local office supply store works every bit as well and doesn't need all that extra attention. After all, it is more important to record the information than it is to spend a lot of time preparing to write it. I think people who insist of having very specific tools spend too much time looking for them or preparing them when they might instead be using something equally as good. It seems more productive to devoting all that time to actually doing something rather than preparing to do it!

Cingulum

The cingulum (also called a singulum) is a girdle or belt that is tied around the waist. In some traditions, a cingulum is presented to initiates and subsequently worn in rituals. Traditionally, a cingulum is nine feet in length (representing the number 3 times three) and can be used to measure and cast the ritual circle.

In some traditions, the color of the cingulum indicates the level of achievement that the person has attained in that tradition.

In some traditions, the cingulum is not worn and is kept only for ritual tasks. It can be used to bind. Some Pagans tie a knot in their cingulum for every year and a day that they've participated in that tradition.

Scourge

Primarily associated with Gardnerian Wicca, the scourge is used to flagellate members of the group. It is often used in initiation rites.

Most other Pagan traditions associate the scourge with pain, and because pain represents a negative form of energy, it is not brought into ritual use.

Spear

Used by Seax Wiccan and some Nordic traditions, the spear represents the power of God. It is used to summon spirits and direct energy.

Stang

The stang is a staff that usually has two heads on its top that are created by using a forked tree branch or animal antlers. It is not frequently seen in most traditions, although some plain staffs (without the double head) are used in some traditions in place of, or in association with, the wand.

Jewelry

Various traditions use ceremonial jewelry; many Pagans own pieces of jewelry that they associate with rituals or magickal workings. A piece of jewelry that is reserved for ritual use can be worn to help the bearer attune to the energy of the ritual. Most often, silver is used, or gold. Some magickal jewelry is made of base metals, such as pewter, bronze or brass.

Stones and Crystals

Colorful stones can be used in ritual and spellcasting. You can use any stone or crystal in ritual work. Hold the stone in your receptive hand and gauge how its energy feels to you.

Crystals – especially clear quartz crystals – are excellent conductors of electricity or energy of any type. You can leave them in their natural state; crystals that are cut or polished are no more effective than one that is in its original condition.

Crystals that naturally form points, like quartz, are effective for directing energy. They are often embedded in the end of a wand or staff to help direct the energy you raise.

Stones and crystals are associated with the element of earth.

Ritual Robes

While a few Pagan traditions require participants to work skyclad (nude), other traditions advocate the use of ceremonial robes for rituals. Using a robe that is reserved only for spiritual endeavors helps the participant get into an appropriate frame of mind. Other traditions have no requirement for special forms of dress; participants can wear whatever they choose.

It is not necessary to use an actual robe. You can wear sweatpants and a sweatshirt, as many of my Pagan friends do. These garments are kept for use only inside their ritual space and never worn in everyday life. If you use a traditional robe, it can be of any color and fabric, and you can choose any style you feel is appropriate, unless your tradition has specific requirements for ceremonial robes.

If you wear flowing ceremonial robes, be careful around the cauldron, candles, or ritual fires. In the Wizard of Oz, the wicked witch could disappear in a puff of smoke, but she was able to reappear again. I'm not so sure that the rest of us can manage the same trick!

Charms and Amulets

Pagans use physical representations of the end result of a ritual or spellcasting to help them with visualizing the outcome. Charms or amulets are graphic representations of your ritual or magickal intentions. Simply seeing a charm reconnects you to that ritual or spell; these constant reconnections help reinforce your intention and ease the way for the end result you visualized.

There are many commercial sources for charms and amulets; a large number relate to Kabbalistic magic. If you aren't happy with this relationship to the Kabbalah, use a charm that is based on a naturalistic form (like animals) or create your own using the interpretation that resonates best within you.

It has been noted by many scholars of ritual and spellcasting that a charm or amulet that you create and make yourself will allow you to direct significantly more energy toward the end result you visualize.

Charms can be created from wood, clay, or any other substance. While you are molding the charm, visualize the end result that you seek. You must imbue the charm with this energy in order for it to resonate in the universe and draw complementary energies to you that will ensure the success of your ritual or magickal working.

Note: there has been a lot of misinformation about the use of the five pointed star in charms and amulets. Should a single point be at the top, or two points? Some say that a pentagram with two points at the top relates to Satan, the Christian concept of ultimate evil, and therefore should never be used. Just a reminder: Pagans are not Christians. As a group, however loosely organized, we generally do not buy into the Christian concept of Satan, the Devil, Lucifer, Beelzebub, or whatever it is called. Pagans do not believe in either heaven or hell. There is no reason why you should not use a pentagram with two points at the top, if you feel using it will be effective for you; the two "horns" at the top can be related to the Great Horned God. Never allow other people to make decisions for you that are yours alone to make! If you prefer a pentagram with a single point at the top, use that, and don't apologize for your choice.

Statues and Pictures

Many Pagans place a statue or a picture of the particular God or Goddess that they are invoking within their ritual space. In the vast pantheon of Gods/Goddesses, there is most likely an aspect that resonates with the ritual task you want to perform. A number of stores carry these statues; searching the Internet for the particular representation of that God or Goddess will usually turn up a statue or a picture that you can use.

Some Pagans, like myself, do not put representations of God/Goddess within their ritual space. While I acknowledge that various archetypes of Gods and Goddesses exist, I do not want to limit my perception of that deity to a single aspect. I prefer to visualize a connection to the universal energy of a God or Goddess and allow that energy to permeate my ritual.

Mortar and Pestle

The mortar and pestle are used to grind herbs and resins. These tools are not usually kept routinely within the ritual space, but instead are brought out only when needed. They should be made of a natural material, like stone or wood. They relate to the aspect of earth.

Pagan Name

While not everyone will consider the name you took when you became a Pagan as a tool, it really should be viewed that way.

Pagan names are used within the circle to identify you to the God/ Goddess. They also link your magickal works or rituals to you.

When a Pagan is initiated into a group, or begins working as a solitary, it is customary to take a name that has some significance. The name you were given at birth was chosen for you by your parents. This Pagan name is completely your choice, and it should reflect the person that you are. This name can be revealed to you in a dream, or through meditation. You can use numerology to determine what kinds of energy you want to embody, and then choosing a name in which the letters are based on numerology. You can also name yourself in accordance with a quality you want to bring into your life (like Patience or Honor).

Some Pagan names are a combination of two words or syllables.

It is not advisable to use the name of one of the God or Goddess archetypes. Doing so can cause you to bring into your own life some of the experiences faced by that deity. This is a powerful form of attraction. It is better to pick a name that is meaningful to you for other reasons, rather than to have to endure personal issues brought about by connecting to the life story of that deity. Life is difficult enough as it is!

The Altar or Ritual Space

Some traditions, such as Wicca, use altars for ritual and spellcasting. Other traditions that use a ritual space do not include a separate altar, possibly because they find them reminiscent of Abrahamic altars.

If you use an altar, it can be a piece of furniture, like a small table, a coffee table or a dresser, or it can be constructed specifically as an altar. Altars can be purchased commercially and are constructed specifically for that use. Some include drawers or cabinets where ritual implements and supplies can be stored. If you don't have the funds, or if you don't like the idea of purchasing a commercially made altar, use a piece of furniture. While commercially prepared altars scream **Pagan** to anyone who sees them, your ritual and magickal workings are more discreet if you use a common household item instead. Few people would make a connection to Pagan ritual upon seeing a dresser in your living room, but a commercial altar, with its distinctive markings or colors tends to advertise its function.

Some Pagans believe that their altar should be kept in a room specifically set aside for ritual purposes. Others do not have the extra space and must of necessity create a ritual space in a room commonly used for other purposes.

The altar is used to hold ritual items and as a place of focus. While some traditions indicate a special place for the altar (for example, in the East or South, or in the center of a circle), you can put an altar anywhere that feels appropriate. Those who insist that an altar must always face East, for example, have bought into that belief. For them, rituals will always work better if the altar is where they believe it belongs. Personally, I have never felt that the God or Goddess particularly cares about the physical placement of anything. They exist in a realm of pure energy; physical placement is a construct of the physical world, where we have to deal with the limiting concepts of time and space. For the same reason, I doubt that the God/Goddess care in the least whether your ritual is being done at midnight during a full moon, or Wednesday afternoon at 3:11 PM on a bus traveling to Cleveland. I have always felt that any tradition that is restrictive in any way is going to put limitations on my ritual or magickal works, and I simply do not acknowledge any restrictions on my spiritual efforts.

You do need to be practical when deciding where to place your altar. It should be in a place where you can see it and the items it holds, where you do not trip over it, and where you can easily reach anything on it.

An interesting fact about Christian churches is that the Christian altar was usually placed in the East. If a church was established on a site that was formerly associated with Paganism, often a second altar was placed in the North. The presence of two altars (not usually equal in size, shape or visual importance) is a sure sign that the area is known for its Pagan associations. These altars were common and persisted until about the 11th century. After that time, doors (and the associated Pagan altar) in the North were walled over. An ancient church with no North exit most likely had Pagan associations.

Placement of ritual items on the altar varies according to the spiritual tradition you observe, but in Wicca, the right side of the altar is devoted to the God and the left side to the Goddess. Ritual items are placed on either side, depending on their correlation to God or Goddess energy:

Tools for Working with The God

✓ Candle (most Wiccans use white or gold)
✓ A small statue of one of the Gods (in some traditions; in others, no

visual representation is used)
- ✓ Censer
- ✓ Wand
- ✓ Athame (and boline, if used)
- ✓ Salt (used to purify)

Tools for Working with The Goddess

- ✓ Candle (most Wiccans use white or silver)
- ✓ A small statue of one of the Goddesses (in some traditions, in others, no visual representation is used)
- ✓ Chalice
- ✓ Pentacle
- ✓ Bell
- ✓ Cauldron *
- ✓ Water
- ✓ * If the cauldron is too large to fit comfortably on the altar, it can be placed nearby, usually on the left side.
- ✓ The besom is usually placed near the left side, resting on the floor.
- ✓ Additionally, any evocative items, such as berries, twigs, seashells and so forth, can be placed on the altar to help you connect with the energy that you are trying to access and channel. These items are different, depending on the specific task at hand. In some traditions, they are placed somewhere inside the ritual space, but not on the altar proper.

Divination

There are a number of methods used to determine future possibilities. Some of the more common methods include:
- ✓ Tarot
- ✓ Scrying (including scrying mirrors and crystal balls)
- ✓ Runes
- ✓ Meditation
- ✓ Dream interpretation
- ✓ Ouija or other board-based methods

Each of these methods relies on how effectively you can access your psychic abilities. Note that these methods are not only used for divining the future; they can also be used to answer questions or seek direction. And please don't call any of them "fortune-telling!"

There are many books devoted to these topics. You can use a search engine on the Internet to locate some resources, or visit your local library. Asking other Pagans about the resources they use and recommend is also helpful.

11

Gods and Goddesses

As civilizations rose and fell throughout time in ancient history, each civilization that used writing left a record of the Gods and Goddesses they worshiped. One can see a certain similarity between the deities of various civilizations. The civilizations that left no written record presumably had their own deities, but unfortunately, much of this information has been lost or assimilated into the beliefs of civilizations that followed.

There are those who believe that God and Goddess are primary archetypes; that any form of deity other than a pair of all-powerful deities are simply facets of the whole. In the same way that loving and nurturing are similar yet totally separate archetypes, I believe that each manifestation of a God or Goddess is a specific, distinct and separate archetype. In ancient times, each deity assumed responsibility for various aspects of life. The deity who was invoked to ensure the growth of crops was not at all the same as the deity who was responsible for childbirth.

With that distinction in mind, this chapter contains a list of deities from many civilizations. As a Pagan, you are free to use the deity that resonates with you, for a specific task or undertaking. You can access any of these archetypes and are free to use another archetype if you believe it will enable you to be successful.

The list is alphabetical (instead of being a hierarchy). Some deities can be considered to equate to a deity from another civilization, although each civilization added its own interpretation of the quality of that deity. The deities in this list are ancient Greek, Roman, Sumerian, and Babylonian, along with the major Egyptian deities; a section at the end of the chapter identifies all of the currently known gods and goddesses in the Egyptian pantheon.

Aspects of the Divine

Wiccans, along with some other Pagan traditions, identify the Goddess as a triple goddess with three different aspects, often simplistically stated as the Maiden, the Mother, and the Crone. Other traditions equate three forms of the Goddess as the Goddess Above, the Goddess Within, and the Goddess Below. The Goddess Above is seen in the moon, stars and night sky. The Goddess Within is the earth and the harvest. The Goddess Below rules the underworld, death and destruction. Still other traditions see the three forms as Goddess of the Past, Goddess of the Present, and Goddess of the Future.

Goddesses of the Maiden or the Goddess Above include Aphrodite, Aradia, Artemis, Astarte, Athena, Inanna and Kore.

Goddesses of the Mother or the Goddess Within include Cerridwen, Demeter, Diana, Isis, Gaia, Luna and Selene.

Goddesses of the Crone or the Goddess Below include Arianrhod, Ereshkigal, Kali, Morgan and Persephone.

In a similar way, some traditions identify the God with two aspects: Light and Shadow. The God of Light is a solar god, ruling growth and the fertile half of the year. The God of Shadow is the horned god, the king of the underworld, lord of the hunt, bringer of death, the trickster. He lives in the shadows, ruling the half of the year when the earth lies dormant.

Gods of the Light include Apollo, Dionysus, the Green Man, Horus, Lugh, Mabon and Ra.

Gods of the Shadow include Adonis, Cernunnos, Chronos, Hades, Pan, Osiris and Tammuz.

The three forms of the Goddess and the two forms of the God are different aspects of the same energy, representing a slight but significant change in the quality of the energy of that deity. These aspects of divinity exist simultaneously. Within the Maiden, the Mother and Crone also exist. Within the God of Light, the God of Shadows exists.

Deities and Sexuality

In ancient times, gods and goddesses took lovers of either gender. Sexuality in the ancient world was a simpler concept than it is today, with our modern concept of sin and morality. In those times, you saw, you liked what you saw, you did what you both wanted to do, and then you moved on. The restricted morality that is seen today was not part of life in ancient times. Gay and bisexual Pagan men can find many deities with which they can feel comfortable. Unlike the Abrahamic religions, alternate sexuality is not considered immoral or sinful; it simply exists as part of life.

Many of the men who took the survey expressed their delight in the knowledge that as Pagans, they were free from the intimidating image of a judgmental deity who looked down on them with scorn simply because they were expressing the essence of what they are.

Say you wanted to ask the deity for a favor. You could pray to the cranky Abrahamic God or to a Pagan god who is associated with pleasurable acts and who had a lover of the same gender? Which one could you envision granting your request?

The God and Goddess Resource List

It would be nice to supply a nice list of each deity and to indicate what problems or issues with which each one was associated. That was my original thought when I began this chapter. As I researched the deities, I began to realize that by hearing their mythologies and developing an image of each one, that they deserved far more than a place in a reference table.

I have participated in several Pagan traditions (almost all Wiccan of various flavors). In all of them, we were held responsible for our own ritual and spell work – and since I have long practiced as a Solitary, this has become the norm for me. I don't use packaged spells taken word for word from someone's book. I have little confidence that someone else's spell will work effectively for me. I realize that any ritual or practical magick that I attempt has to reflect my will and my intent. I have to believe in the outcome in order for it to work. There are Wiccans who work towards attaining the preposterous, but they aren't generally effective in getting what they envision because it's so far removed from their reality.

Instead, we learned to research and meditate about the results we seek. If I wanted financial success, consulted a list of deities and correspondences, and chose an "appropriate" god or goddess from the list, plopped a little figurine of that deity on the alter and worked the associated ritual, it might work. Maybe... but probably not. In order to petition a deity to help you with your request, you have to understand that deity in order to make an effective connection with the archetype.

One of my responsibilities as an Elder in my tradition is to help educate others. Including a list of God/Goddess correspondences and therefore eliminating any work you would need to do is not my idea of education. I enjoy learning about any topic. As a Pagan, it is essential that you develop this connection. By researching and meditating about what you truly want to manifest, you make an internal connection between that goal and the Divine. That connection, expressed through intense will and with focused intention, is what makes rituals or practical magick work.

Consult the information provided here about the deities and determine which of them can be helpful in your quest to achieve a goal. This is your work, your responsibility. Sure, it would be great to have a list to consult for the moment when you really need something. (Solution: create your own list and add it to your journal, or look up keywords in the Index) In my traditions, we don't rely on quick fixes to resolve life issues.

The problem with such "instant magick" is that it rarely works. Without concentration and focus, your subconscious does not have the time or training to make the connection between the results you envision and the energy you need to access to achieve that vision.

Read through the information presented here. Various deities might resonate with you. You might discover an attraction or affinity for a deity with whom you have not previously worked. That is what being a Pagan is all about: opening up your world. Resist the urge to let someone else make this kind of connection for you. To be powerful in the world, you must accept it and own it.

Within the deity's myth, you will find enough information to determine which deity might be helpful in your quest to manifest change.

The Pantheon

There are literally hundreds of God and Goddess archetypes to which you can relate. In Greek mythology alone, there are twelve Olympians (Aphrodite, Apollo, Ares, Artemis, Athena, Demeter, Dionysus, Hephaestus, Hera, Hermes, Poseidon and Zeus), along with other major deities (including Asclepius, Charon, Eos, Eros, Gaia, Hades, Hebe, Hecate, Helios, Hestia, Ouranos, Pan, Persephone, and Selene). And that's just the contribution of the Greeks! For any activity in which humans might participate, there was most likely a deity devoted to it in ancient times.

The same group of deities can be found during Roman times; although given different names, their qualities are similar. There are also corresponding deities in Sumerian, Babylonian, Egyptian and Phoenician cultures. While the names change within various cultures, the archetypes remain constant. Every civilization has deities for common human issues (such as love, abundance and death).

The deities that we are aware of today are depicted in art and writings from ancient history. All of these civilizations used writing; consider how many more deities existede whose history and significance was not recorded because the civilization that worshiped them did not leave records or art for us to view today.

For this reason, when you meditate to discover which deity resonates with you, allow your subconscious to provide a name, whether it is contained in traditional lists of deities or not. All god-forms and goddess-forms are accessible to us, including those about which we have no current information. You can work as effectively with a deity whose record has not persisted into our times as you can with the pantheons that we know and understand.

Adonis

In the central myth in its Greek telling, after being wounded by Cupid's arrow, Aphrodite fell in love with the beautiful youth. Aphrodite sheltered him and entrusted him to Persephone. The latter was also taken by Adonis' beauty and refused to give him back to Aphrodite. The dispute between the two goddesses was settled by Zeus (or by Calliope on Zeus' behalf): Adonis was to spend one-third of every year with each goddess and the last third wherever he chose. He chose to spend two-thirds of the year with Aphrodite.

Adonis was killed by a wild boar, said to have been sent variously by Artemis, jealous of Adonis' hunting skills; by Ares, who was jealous of Aphrodite's love for Adonis; or by Apollo, to punish Aphrodite for blinding his son, Erymanthus. Adonis died in Aphrodite's arms, who came to him when she heard his groans.

Amun

In ancient Egyptian mythology, Amun was a god who, in the form of Amun-Ra, became the focus of the most complex system of theology in Ancient Egypt. Amun represented the essential and hidden, while in Ra he represented revealed divinity. As the primary creator deity, he was the champion of the poor and central to personal piety. Amun was self-created, without mother and father, and during the New Kingdom period he became the greatest expression of transcendental deity in Egyptian theology. He was not considered to be immanent within creation nor was creation seen as an extension of himself. Amun-Ra did not physically engender the universe. His position as King of Gods developed to the point of virtual monotheism where other gods became manifestations of him. With Osiris, Amun-Ra is the most widely recorded of the Egyptian gods.

Apollo

When Hera discovered that Leto was pregnant and that Zeus was the father, she banned Leto from giving birth on earth. In her wanderings, Leto found the newly created floating island of Delos, which was neither mainland nor a real island, so she gave birth there where she was accepted by the people, offering them her promise that her son would be always favorable toward the city. This island later became sacred to Apollo.

Hera kidnapped Ilithyia, the goddess of childbirth, to prevent Leto from going into labor. The other gods tricked Hera into letting her go by offering her a necklace, nine yards long, made of amber. Artemis was born first and then assisted with the birth of Apollo, or possibly one day before Apollo, on the island of Ortygia. She helped Leto cross the sea to Delos the next day to give birth to Apollo. Apollo was born on the seventh day of the month Thargelion – according to Delian tradition – or of the month Bysios – according to Delphian tradition. The seventh and twentieth, the days of the new and full moon, were afterward held sacred to him.

Four days after his birth, Apollo killed the dragon Python, which lived in Delphi beside the Castalian Spring. This was the spring which emitted vapors that caused the oracle at Delphi to give her prophesies. Hera sent the dragon to hunt Leto to her death. In order to protect his mother, Apollo begged Hephaestus for a bow and arrows, and used them to corner Python in the sacred cave at Delphi. Apollo killed Python but had to be punished for it, since Python was a child of Gaia.

Hera then sent the giant Tityos to kill Leto. This time Apollo was aided by his sister Artemis in protecting their mother. During the battle Zeus finally granted his aid and hurled Tityos down to Tartarus.

When Zeus struck down Apollo's son Asclepius with a lightning bolt for resurrecting Hippolytus from the dead (transgressing Themis by stealing Hades's subjects), Apollo in revenge killed the Cyclopes, who had fashioned the bolt for Zeus. Apollo would have been banished to Tartarus forever, but was instead sentenced to one year of hard labor as punishment after his mother, Leto, interceded.

Apollo had a number of female lovers, along with two male lovers: Hyacinth and Cyparissus.

Aphrodite

Aphrodite is the Greek goddess of love, beauty, and sexuality. Her Roman equivalent is the goddess Venus. Historically, her cult in Greece was imported from, or influenced by, the cult of Astarte in Phoenicia.

According to legend, she was born when Cronus cut off Uranus' genitals and threw them into the sea, and from the sea foam (aphros) arose Aphrodite. She was born as an adult, never having had a childhood.

Because of her beauty other gods feared that jealousy would interrupt the peace among them and lead to war, and so Zeus married her to Hephaestus, who was not viewed as a threat. Aphrodite had many lovers, both gods like Ares, and men like Anchises.

In another version of this story, Hephaestus' mother Hera had cast him off Olympus, deeming him ugly and deformed. His revenge was to trap her in a magic throne, and then to demand Aphrodite's hand in return for Hera's release. Hephaestus was overjoyed at being married to the goddess of beauty and forged her beautiful jewelry, including the cestus, a girdle that made her even more irresistible to men. Her unhappiness with her marriage caused Aphrodite to seek out companionship from others, most frequently Ares, but also Adonis.

Aphrodite also became instrumental in the Eros and Psyche legend, and later was both lover and surrogate mother to Adonis. Many lesser beings were said to be children of Aphrodite.

Aphrodite is also known as Cytherea and Cypris after the two cult-sites, Cythera and Cyprus, which both claimed her birth. Myrtles, doves, sparrows, horses, and swans are sacred to her. The Greeks further identified the Ancient Egyptian goddess Hathor with Aphrodite.

Apis

A bull-deity worshipped in ancient Memphis, Apis was a fertility god connected to grain and the herds. In a funerary context, the Apis was a protector of the deceased, and linked to the pharaoh. This animal was chosen because it symbolized the king's courageous heart, great strength, virility, and fighting spirit. The Apis bull was considered to be a manifestation of the pharaoh, as bulls were symbols of strength and fertility, qualities which are closely linked with kingship ("strong bull of his mother Hathor" was a common title for gods and pharaohs).

Ares

Ares is the Greek god of war. He is one of the Twelve Olympians, and the son of Zeus and Hera. As the Olympian god of warfare and courage; he was the lover of Aphrodite.

Deimos ("terror") and Phobos ("fear") are his companions in war and his children, borne by Aphrodite. The sister and companion of the violent Ares is Eris, the goddess of discord or Enyo, the goddess of war, bloodshed, and violence. He is also attended by the minor war-god Enyalius, his son by Enyo, whose name ("warlike") also serves as a title for Ares himself. Ares, was referred to as "The Father of Victory," was accompanied by Nike, the deathless spirit of victory.

The presence of Ares is also accompanied by Kydoimos, the demon of the din of battle, as well as the Makhai ("battles"), the Hysminai ("manslaughters"), Polemos (a minor spirit of war) and Polemos's daughter, Alaha, the goddess or personification of the Greek war-cry, whose name Ares uses as his own war-cry.

Ares represents aggression, courage, boldness, divine law, freedom, masculinity, and righteous indignation.

Artemis

Artemis was the daughter of Zeus and Leto, and she was the twin sister of Apollo.

Hera forbade Leto to give birth on either terra firma (the mainland) or on an island. Hera was angry with Zeus, her husband, because he had impregnated Leto. But the floating island of Delos (or Ortygia in the Homeric Hymn to Artemis) disobeyed Hera, and Leto gave birth there. The myths also differ as to whether Artemis was born first, or Apollo. Most stories depict Artemis as born first, becoming her mother's midwife upon the birth of her brother Apollo.

At three years old, Artemis, while sitting on the knee of her father, Zeus, asked him to grant her six wishes: to remain always a virgin; to have many names to set her apart from her brother Apollo; to be the Phaesporia or Light Bringer; to have a bow and arrow and a knee-length tunic so that she could hunt; to have sixty "daughters of Okeanos," all nine years of age, to be her choir; and for twenty Nymphs as handmaidens to watch her dogs and bow while she rested. She wished to rule the mountains, and for the ability to help women in the pains of childbirth.

Artemis believed that she had been chosen by the Fates to be a midwife, particularly since she had assisted her mother in the delivery of her twin brother, Apollo. All of her companions remained virgins and Artemis guarded her own chastity closely. Her symbols included the golden bow and arrow, the hunting dog, the stag, and the moon.

In some versions of the story of Adonis, who was a late addition to Greek mythology during the Hellenistic period, Artemis sent a wild boar to kill Adonis as punishment for boasting that he was a better hunter than she. In other versions, Artemis killed Adonis for revenge. In later myths, Adonis had been related as a favorite of Aphrodite, and Aphrodite was responsible for the death of Hippolytus, who had been a favorite of Artemis. Therefore, Artemis killed Adonis to avenge Hippolytus's death. In yet another version, Adonis was not killed by Artemis, but by Ares, as punishment for being with Aphrodite.

As a young virgin, Artemis had interested many gods and men, but none of them successfully won her heart, except her hunting companion Orion, who was then accidentally killed either by the goddess herself or by Gaia.

Artemis played quite a large part in the Trojan war. Like her mother and brother, who was widely worshiped at Troy, Artemis took the side of the Trojans. At the Greek's journey to Troy, Artemis becalmed the sea and stopped the journey until an oracle came and said they could win the goddess' heart by sacrificing Iphigenia, Agamemnon's daughter. Agamemnon once promised the goddess he would sacrifice the dearest thing to him, which was Iphigenia, but broke the promise. He boasted about his hunting ability and provoked the goddess' anger. Artemis saved Iphigenia because of her bravery. In some versions of the myth, Artemis made Iphigenia her attendant or turned her into Hecate, goddess of night, witchcraft, and the underworld.

At Ephesus in Ionia (Turkey), her temple became one of the Seven Wonders of the World. Remains of the Temple of Artemis can be visited today.

Astarte

Astarte was connected with fertility, sexuality, and war. Her symbols were the lion, the horse, the sphinx, the dove, and a star within a circle representing the planet Venus. Pictorial representations often show her naked.

Astarte was accepted by the Greeks under the name of Aphrodite. The island of Cyprus, where Astarte was especially revered, supplied the name Cypris as Aphrodite's most common byname.

Astarte arrived in Ancient Egypt during the 18th dynasty, along with other deities who were worshipped by northwest Semitic people. She was especially worshipped in her aspect as a warrior goddess, often paired with the goddess Anat.

In the contest between Horus and Set, these two goddesses appear as daughters of Ra and are given in marriage to the god Set, here identified with the Semitic name Hadad. Astarte also was identified with the lioness warrior goddess Sekhmet, but seemingly more often conflated, at least in part, with Isis to judge from the many images found of Astarte suckling a small child.

In Phoenicia, Astarte appears as a daughter of Sky and Earth and sister of the God El. After El overthrows and banishes his father Sky, as a trick Sky sends to El his "virgin daughter" Astarte along with her sisters Asherah and the goddess who will later be called Ba'alat Gebal, "the Lady of Byblos." It seems that this trick does not work, as all three become wives of their brother El. Astarte bears to El children who appear under Greek names as seven daughters called the Titanides or Artemides and two sons named Pothos ("Longing") and Eros ("Desire").

Later, with El's consent, Astarte and Hadad reigned over the land together. Astarte puts the head of a bull on her own head to symbolize her sovereignty. Wandering through the world Astarte takes up a star that has fallen from the sky (a meteorite) and consecrates it at Tyre.

Athena

Athena was a parthenogenetic daughter of Metis, ("wisdom" or "knowledge"), a Titan. Other versions of her myth relate that, although Metis was of an earlier generation of the Titans, Zeus became her consort when his cult gained dominance. In order to avoid a prophecy that any offspring of his union with Metis would be greater than he, Zeus swallowed Metis to prevent her from having offspring, but she already was pregnant with Athena. Metis gave birth to Athena and nurtured her inside Zeus until Zeus complained of headaches and called for Hephaestus to split open his head with his smithing tools. Athena burst forth from his forehead fully armed with weapons given by her mother. She wields the thunderbolt and the Aegis, which she and Zeus share exclusively.

Athena never had a consort or lover and was thus known as Athena Parthenos ("Virgin Athena"). Her most famous temple, the Parthenon, on the Acropolis in Athens takes its name from this title. It was not merely an observation of her virginity, but a recognition of her role as enforcer of rules of sexual modesty and ritual mystery.

In Greek mythology, the Gorgon was a terrifying female creature. It derives from the Greek word gorgós, which means "dreadful." While descriptions of Gorgons vary across Greek literature, the term commonly refers to any of three sisters who had hair of living, venomous snakes, and a horrifying gaze that turned those who beheld it to stone. Traditionally, while two of the Gorgons, Stheno and Euryale, were immortal, their sister Medusa was not, and was slain by the mythical hero Perseus.

In a later myth, Medusa, unlike her two sister-Gorgons, came to be thought of by the Classical Greeks during the 5th century as mortal and extremely beautiful, but she lay with Poseidon in the temple of Athena and Hephaestus. Upon discovering the desecration of her temple, Athena changed Medusa's form to match that of her sister Gorgons as punishment. Medusa's hair turned into snakes, her lower body was transformed also, and meeting her gaze would turn any living man to stone. Later myths of the Classical Greeks relate that Athena guided Perseus in his quest to behead Medusa.

Bacchus

See "Dionysus" on page 140.

Ba-Kha

In Egyptian mythology, Bakha was the manifestation of the a deification of Ka ("power" or "life force") of the war god Menthu, who was worshipped in the region of Hermonthis. The name is simply Ba-Kha, which is a reference to the Ba and Akh (Akh is sometimes referred to as Khu), the components into which the Ka was split, after death (a characteristic of war). As Ka is also the Egyptian word for cattle, Bakha was said to manifest in a living bull, which, since Bakha was an aspect of a war-god, was said to be a wild bull, since these are aggressive when slightly provoked.

A wild bull was chosen and worshiped as the Bukhis incarnation of Menthu. Over time, the criteria for choosing the bull became more rigid, fixating on what had been simply the general appearance of bulls in the region, a white body and black face. When these bulls, or their mothers, died, they were mummified and placed in a special cemetery known as the Bucheum. The mothers of these bulls were considered aspects of Hathor, the mother of these deities.

Eventually, the Bakha was identified as a form of the Apis, and consequently became considered an incarnation of Osiris.

Baron Samedi

Baron Samedi is one of the Loa of Vodou. Samedi is a Loa of the dead, along with Baron's numerous other incarnations Baron Cimetiere, Baron LaCroix, and Baron Kriminel. He is the head of the Ghede family of Loa, or possibly their spiritual father. Samedi means "Saturday" in French. His wife is the Loa Maman Brigitte.

He is usually depicted with a top hat, black tuxedo, dark glasses, and cotton plugs in the nostrils, as if to resemble a corpse dressed and prepared for burial in the Haitian style. He has a white, frequently skull-like face (or actually has a skull for a face) and speaks in a nasal voice. He is a sexual Loa, frequently represented by phallic symbols and is noted for disruption, obscenity, debauchery, and having a particular fondness for tobacco and rum. Additionally, he is the Loa of sex and resurrection, and in the latter capacity he is often called upon for healing by those near or approaching death, as it is only Baron who can accept an individual into the realm of the dead.

Baron Samedi spends most of his time in the invisible realm of voodoo spirits. He is notorious for his outrageous behavior, swearing continuously and making filthy jokes to the other spirits. He is married to another powerful spirit known as Maman Brigitte, but often chases after mortal women. He is also known for his bisexuality, in chasing mortal men. He loves smoking and drinking and is rarely seen without a cigar in his mouth or a glass of rum in his bony fingers. Baron Samedi can usually be found at the crossroad between the worlds of the living and the dead. When someone dies he digs their grave and greets their soul after they have been buried, leading them to the underworld.

As well as being master of the dead, Baron Samedi is also a giver of life. He can cure a mortal of any disease or wound, if he thinks it is worthwhile. His powers are especially great when it comes to voodoo curses and black magic. Even if somebody has been afflicted by a hex which brings them to the verge of death, they will not die if the Baron refuses to dig their grave. So long as this mighty spirit keeps them out of the ground they are safe. He also ensures all corpses rot in the ground to stop any soul being brought back as a brainless zombie. What he demands in return depends on his mood. Sometimes he is content with his followers wearing black, white or purple clothes or using sacred objects; he may simply ask for a small gift of cigars, rum, black coffee, grilled peanuts or bread. But sometimes the Baron requires a voodoo ceremony to help him cross over into this world.

Bona Dea

Bona Dea ("The Good Goddess") was a divinity in ancient Roman religion. She was associated with chastity and fertility in women, healing, and the protection of the Roman state and people.

Her rites allowed women the use of strong wine and blood-sacrifice, things that were forbidden to them by Roman tradition. Men were barred from her mysteries and the possession of her true name. Given that male authors had limited knowledge of her rites and attributes, ancient speculations about her identity abound, among them that she was an aspect of Terra, Ops, the Magna Mater ("Great Mother"), or Ceres, or a Latin form of Damia. Most often, she was identified as the wife, sister or daughter of the god Faunus, thus an equivalent or aspect of the nature-goddess Fauna, who could prophesy the fates of women.

The goddess had two annual festivals. One was held at her Aventine temple; the other was hosted by the wife of Rome's senior annual magistrate, for an invited group of elite matrons and female attendants. The rites remained a subject of male religious and prurient curiosity and speculation.

Bona Dea's Roman cults were led by the Vestal Virgins, and her provincial cults by virgin or matron priestesses. She is depicted as a sedate Roman matron with a cornucopia and a snake. Approximately one third of her dedications were from men, some of whom may have been lawfully involved in her cult.

Brigid

In Irish mythology, Brigid or Brighid ("exalted one") was the daughter of the Dagda and one of the Tuatha Dé Danann. She was the wife of Bres of the Fomonians, with whom she had a son, Ruadán. She had two sisters, also named Brigid, and is considered a classic Celtic Triple Goddess.

Brigid was the powerful goddess of poetry, healing and ironsmithing. One side of her face was ugly, but the other side was beautiful. Her name represented a fiery arrow.

She is the goddess of all things perceived to be of relatively high dimensions such as high-rising flames, highlands, hill-forts and upland areas; and of activities and states conceived as psychologically lofty and elevated, such as wisdom, excellence, perfection, high intelligence, poetic eloquence, craftsmanship (especially blacksmithing), healing ability, druidic knowledge and skill in warfare. In the living traditions, whether seen as goddess or saint, she is largely associated with the home and hearth.

Ceres

In ancient Roman religion, Ceres was a goddess of agriculture, grain crops, fertility and motherly relationships. She is also linked with marriage and funeral rites. She is the patron goddess of written law.

Ceres was credited with the discovery of spelt wheat, the yoking of oxen and plowing, the sowing, protection and nourishing of the young seed, and the gift of agriculture to humankind.

She also maintained the boundaries between the realms of the living and the dead. Given the appropriate rites, she would help the deceased into afterlife as an underworld shade (Di Manes, from which the word "demons" was derived); otherwise, the spirit of the deceased might remain among the living as a wandering, vengeful ghost.

Cernunnos

Cernunnos is the horned god of Celtic polytheism. Cernunnos is often depicted as a horned or antlered figure, associated with animals and holding or wearing torcs. There is a carved wall figure in the Church of

Notre Dame in Paris that bears the name "Ernunnos," but an early drawing of the figure shows that the original sign said "Cernunnos" and that the "C" was lost, probably accidentally, during repairs to the stonework.

In Wicca and other forms of Paganism, a Horned God is revered; this divinity incorporates a number of horned or antlered gods from various cultures, including Cernunnos. The Horned God reflects the seasons of the year in an annual cycle of life, death and rebirth. In the tradition of Gardnerian Wicca, the Horned God is sometimes specifically referred to as Cernunnos, or sometimes also as Kernunnos.

Cerridwen

In medieval Welsh mythology, Cerridwen was an enchantress, mother of Morfran and a beautiful daughter, Creirwy. Her husband was Tegid Foel, and they lived in north Wales. Medieval Welsh poetry refers to her as possessing the cauldron of Poetic Inspiration (Awen) and the *Tale of Taliesin* recounts her swallowing her servant Gwion Bach, who is then reborn through her as the poet Taliesin, who, in later mythology, was a friend and confidante of King Arthur.

According to the late medieval *Tale of Taliesin* and included in some modern editions of the *Mabinogion*, Morfran was hideously ugly, so Cerridwen wanted to make him wise. She used Awen, a magical cauldron, to make a potion granting the gift of wisdom and poetic inspiration. The mixture had to be boiled for a year and a day. Morda, a blind man, tended the fire beneath the cauldron, while Gwion Bach, a young boy, stirred the concoction. The first three drops of liquid from this cauldron gave wisdom; the rest was a fatal poison. Three hot drops spilled onto Gwion's thumb as he stirred, burning him. He instinctively put his thumb in his mouth, and instantly gained great wisdom and knowledge.

Annoyed at his clumsiness, Ceridwen chased Gwion. He turned himself into a hare; she became a greyhound. He became a fish and jumped into a river; she turned into an otter. He turned into a bird; she became a hawk. Finally, he turned into a single grain of corn; she then became a hen and ate him. When Ceridwen became pregnant, she knew it was Gwion and resolved to kill the child when he was born. However, when he was born, he was so beautiful that she couldn't do it. She threw him in the ocean instead. The child did not die, but was rescued on a Welsh shore by a prince named Elffin ap Gwyddno; the reborn infant grew to became the legendary bard Taliesin.

Robert Graves adapted the myth of Cerridwen into his concept of the Threefold Goddess, in which she was interpreted as a form of the destructive side of the goddess. Graves' theory was appropriated by Wicca, in which Cerridwen plays a role as a goddess, her cauldron symbolizing feminine energy.

Cronos

See "Saturn" on page 168.

Cupid

See "Eros" on page 142.

Dagda

In Irish mythology, the Dagda ("good god") is an important father-figure and a protector of the tribe. In some texts his father is Elatha, in others his mother is Ethlinn. The Dagda was a High King of the Tuatha Dé Danann, a race of supernatural beings who conquered the Fomorians. Despite his great power and prestige, the Dagda is sometimes depicted as oafish and crude, even comical, wearing a short, rough tunic that barely covers his rump, dragging his great penis on the ground.

The Dagda had immense power, and was armed with a magic club and associated with a cauldron. The club was supposed to be able to kill nine men with one blow; but with the handle he could return the slain to life. The cauldron was known as the Undry and was said to be bottomless, from which no man left unsatisfied. Uaithne was a richly ornamented magic harp made of oak; when the Dagda played the harp, it put the seasons in their correct order. Other myths indicate it was used to command the order of battle. He possessed two pigs, one of which was always growing while the other was always roasting, and ever-laden fruit trees.

He was the father of Brigid, among several other gods and goddesses.

Damballa

In Vodou, Damballa is one of the most important of all the Loa. Damballa is the Sky God and considered the creator of all life. He is both a member of the Rada family and a root, or racine Loa. In New Orleans and Haiti he is often depicted as a serpent and is closely associated with snakes. He is considered the father of all the loa as all Spirits are aspects of Damballa. His wife and companion, the rainbow spirit Ayida Weddo, is also a Loa of creation; he is also married to Erzulie Freda. Damballa rules the mind, intellect, and cosmic equilibrium. Common altar symbols used to represent the Sky God include white cloth, owls, bones, ivory, cotton, and chameleons.

Some of his ritual songs indicate that he "carries the ancestors" on his back to Guinea (spiritual home of the Loa, and the afterlife.) As a loa of the Rada nation he is associated with the color white. His day of the week is Thursday. Damballa's offerings are very simple and he prefers an egg on a mound of flour or salt, but loves everything white, including milk, coconut and coconut milk, honey, shea butter, rice, mild cigars, bread, and cookies. Some houses also serve him with anisette and corn syrup while kola nuts are also acceptable.

Damballa is the patron protector of the handicapped, deformed, cripples, albinos, and young children. When he presents himself in possession, he does not talk, but makes hissing noises like a snake in Rada rite. But in Petro he's known as "Dumballa Nan Flambo," and you can hear him speaking through a flame, just like God spoke to Moses in the burning bush.

Demeter

In Greek mythology, Demeter is the goddess of the harvest, presiding over grains, the fertility of the earth, and the seasons. Her common surnames are Sito ("wheat") as the giver of food or corn/grain and Thesmophoros ("divine law") as a mark of the civilized existence of agricultural society. Though Demeter is often described simply as the goddess of the harvest, she presided also over the sanctity of marriage, sacred law, and the cycle of life and death. She and her daughter Persephone were the central figures of the Eleusinian Mysteries that predated the Olympian pantheon

Demeter is easily confused with Gaia or Rhea, and with Cybele, all of them embodying aspects of the pre-Hellenic Great Goddess.

The greatest gifts which Demeter gave were cereal (also known as corn in ancient Briton), the cultivation of which made man different from wild animals; and the Mysteries which give the initiate higher hopes in this life and the afterlife.

Diana

Diana ("heavenly" or "divine") was the goddess of the hunt, associated with wild animals and woodland, and also of the moon in Roman mythology. In literature she was the equal of the Greek goddess Artemis. Dianic Wicca, a largely feminist form of the practice, is named for her. Diana was known to be the virgin goddess and looked after virgins and women. She was one of the three maiden goddesses, Diana, Minerva and Vesta, who swore never to marry.

Along with her main attributes, Diana was an emblem of chastity. Oak groves were especially sacred to her.

Diana is reflected in her connection with light, inaccessibility, virginity, and her preference for dwelling on high mountains and in sacred woods. Diana therefore reflects the heavenly world in its sovereignty, supremacy, impassibility, and indifference towards such secular matters as the fates of men and states. At the same time, however, she is seen as active in ensuring the succession of kings and in the preservation of mankind through the protection of childbirth. Diana was also worshiped by women who sought pregnancy or asked for an easy delivery.

Diana was initially just the hunting goddess, associated with wild animals and woodlands. She also later became a moon goddess, supplanting the Titan goddess Luna. She was worshiped at a festival on August 13.

Today there is a branch of Wicca named for her, which is characterized by an exclusive focus on the feminine aspect of the Divine.

In Italy the old religion of Stregheria embraced goddess Diana as Queen of the Witches; witches being the wise women healers of the time. Goddess Diana created the world of her own being having in herself the seeds of all creation yet to come. It is said that out of herself she divided into the darkness and the light, keeping for herself the darkness of creation and creating her brother Apollo, the light. Diana loved and ruled with her brother Apollo, the god of the Sun.

Dionysus

Dionysus was the god of the grape harvest, winemaking and wine, of ritual madness and ecstasy in Greek mythology. He was worshiped from c. 1500—1100 BC by Mycenean Greeks: other traces of Dionysian-type cult have been found in ancient Minoan Crete. His origins are uncertain, and his cults took many forms; some are described by ancient sources as Thracian, others as Greek. He is a god of epiphany, and his "foreignness" as an arriving outsider-god may be inherent and essential to his cults. He is a major, popular figure of Greek mythology and religion, and is included in some lists of the twelve Olympians. His festivals were the driving force behind the development of Greek theater.

The earliest cult images of Dionysus show a mature male, bearded and robed. He holds a fennel staff, tipped with a pine-cone and known as a thyrsus. Later images show him as a beardless, sensuous, naked or half-naked youth: the literature describes him as womanly or "man-womanish". In its fully developed form, his central cult imagery shows his triumphant, disorderly arrival or return, as if from some place beyond the borders of the known and civilized. His procession is made up of wild female followers (maenads) and bearded satyrs. Some are armed with the thyrsus, some dance or play music. In theThracian mysteries, he wears a fox-skin, symbolizing a new life. Dionysus is represented as the protector of those who do not belong to conventional society and thus symbolizes everything which is chaotic, dangerous and unexpected, everything which escapes human reason and which can only be attributed to the unforeseeable action of the gods

He was also known as Bacchus, the name adopted by the Romans; the frenzy he induces is a bakkheia. His thyrsus is sometimes wound with ivy and dripping with honey. It is a beneficent wand but also a weapon, and can be used to destroy those who oppose his cult and the freedoms he represents. He is also the Liberator (Eleutherios), whose wine, music and ecstatic dance frees his followers from self-conscious fear and care, and subverts the oppressive restraints of the powerful. Those who partake in his mysteries are possessed and empowered by the god himself. His cult is also a "cult of the souls"; his maenads feed the dead through blood-offerings, and he acts as a divine communicant between the living and the dead.

In Greek mythology, he is presented as a son of Zeus and the mortal Semele, thus semi-divine or heroic, and as son of Zeus and Persephone or Demeter, thus both fully divine, and possibly identical with Iacchus of the Eleusinian Mysteries.

Dionysus had a strange birth that evokes the difficulty in fitting him into the Olympian pantheon. His mother was a mortal woman, Semele, the daughter of king Cadmus of Thebes, and his father was Zeus, the king of the gods. Zeus' wife, Hera, discovered the affair while Semele was pregnant. Appearing as an old crone, Hera befriended Semele, who confided in her that Zeus was the father of the baby in her womb. Hera pretended not to believe her and planted seeds of doubt in Semele's mind. Curious, Semele demanded of Zeus that he reveal himself in all his glory as proof of his godhood. Though Zeus begged her not to ask this, she persisted and he agreed. Therefore he came to her wreathed in bolts of lightning; mortals, however, could not look upon an undisguised god without dying, and she perished. It is said that Dionysus was mocked by the Titans who gave him a thyrsus (a fennel stalk) in place of his rightful sceptre. Zeus turned the Titans into dust with his thunderbolts, but only after the Titans ate everything but the heart, which was saved, according to various accounts, by Athena, Rhea, or Demeter. Zeus used the heart to recreate him in his thigh, hence he was again "the twice-born." Other versions claim that Zeus recreated him in the womb of Semele, or gave Semele the heart to eat to impregnate her.

The rebirth in both versions of the story is the primary reason why Dionysus was worshipped in mystery religions, as his death and rebirth were events of mystical reverence.

According to the myth Zeus gave the infant Dionysus into the charge of Hermes. One version of the story is that Hermes took the boy to King Athamas and his wife Ino, Dionysus' aunt. Hermes bade the couple raise the boy as a girl, to hide him from Hera's wrath.

When Dionysus grew up, he discovered the culture of the vine and the mode of extracting its juice; but Hera struck him with madness and he became a wanderer through various parts of the earth. In Phrygia the goddess Cybele, better known to the Greeks as Rhea, cured him and taught him her religious rites, and he set out on a progress through Asia teaching the people the cultivation of the vine.

Ereshkigal

In Mesopotamian mythology, Ereshkigal ("great lady under earth") was the goddess of Irkalla, the land of the dead or the underworld. Sometimes her name is given as Irkalla, similar to way the name Hades was used in Greek mythology for both the underworld and its ruler. Ereshkigal was the only one who could pass judgment and give laws in her kingdom.

The goddess Ishtar refers to Ereshkigal as her older sister in the Sumerian hymn *The Descent of Inanna* (which was also in later Babylonian myth called *The Descent of Ishtar*). Inanna or Ishtar's trip and return to the underworld is the most familiar of the myths concerning Ereshkigal.

As the sister of Ishtar and as her counterpart, she represents the symbol of nature during the non-productive season of the year. As the doctrine of two kingdoms, one of this world and one of the world of the dead, becomes crystallized, the dominions of the two sisters are sharply differentiated from one another.

In some versions of the myths, she rules the underworld by herself, sometimes with a husband subordinate to her named Gugalana. It was said that she had been stolen away by Kur and taken to the underworld, where she was made queen unwillingly.

Eros

Eros was the primordial god of sexual love and beauty. He was also worshipped as a fertility deity. His Roman counterpart was Cupid ("desire"). In some myths, he was the son of the deities Aphrodite and Ares. Eros sprang forth from the primordial Chaos together with Gaia, the Earth, and Tartarus, the underworld; according to Aristophanes' play *The Birds*, he is hatched from an egg laid by Nyx ("Night") conceived with Erebus ("Darkness").

Erzulie

There are two manifestations of the Vodoun Loa Erzulie: Erzulie Freda and Erzulie Dantor.

Erzulie Freda is the vain and flirty Goddess of love. She embodies the spirit of love, beauty, jewelry, dancing, luxury, and flowers. Gay men are considered to be under her particular patronage. She wears three wedding rings, one for each husband – Damballa, Agwe and Ogoun. Her symbol is a heart, her colors are pink, blue, white and gold, and her favorite sacrifices include jewelry, perfume, sweet cakes and liqueurs. Coquettish and very fond of beauty and finery, Erzulie Freda is femininity and compassion embodied, yet she also has a darker side; she is seen as jealous and spoiled and within some vodoun circles is considered to be lazy. She flirts with all the men, and treats all the women as rivals. She is conceived of as never able to attain her heart's most fervent desire. For this reason she always leaves a service in tears.

As Erzulie Dantor, she is often depicted as a scarred and buxom black woman, holding a child protectively in her arms. She is a particularly fierce protector of women and children. She is often identified with lesbian women. A common depiction of Erzulie Dantor is Joan of Arc, who is displayed carrying or supporting a sword. Another is as the Black Madonna of Czestochowa, as she is represented as being dark-skinned. Her colors are red, gold and navy blue; her symbols are a pierced heart and knives; and her favorite sacrifices include black pigs, griot (seasoned fried pork) and rum.

The scars on her cheek are said to be the result of a fight between her and Erzulie Freda over possession of Ti-Jean Petro (a snake loa), because the two are fierce rivals.

Faunus

In ancient Roman religion and myth, Faunus was the horned god of the forest, plains and fields; when he made cattle fertile he was called Inuus.

He came to be equated in literature with the Greek god Pan. While Pan was always depicted with horns, Faunus was not similarly endowed until the 3rd and 2nd centuries BCE.

Fauns are place-spirits (genii) of untamed woodland. Educated, Hellenizing Romans connected their fauns with the Greek satyrs, who were wild and orgiastic drunken followers of Dionysus. Festivals honoring Faunus were celebrated on February 13-15 and December 5th.

Freya

In Norse mythology, Freya (Old Norse for the "Lady") is a goddess associated with love, beauty, fertility, gold, witchcraft or sorcery, war, and death. Freya rules over her heavenly afterlife field Folkvangr and there receives half of those that die in battle, whereas the other half go to the god Odin's hall, Valhalla. Freya, who assists other deities by allowing them to use her feathered cloak, is invoked in matters of fertility and love. Scholars have theorized about whether Freya and the goddess Frigg ultimately stem from a single goddess common among the Germanic peoples; about her connection to the valkyries, female battlefield choosers of the slain; and her relation to other goddesses and figures in Germanic mythology.

Frigg

In ancient Norse mythology, Frigg was Odin's wife and a mother. She had the power of prophecy yet she never revealed what she knew. Frigg is described as the only one other than Odin who is permitted to sit on his throne and look out over the universe. Her companion is Eir, a goddess associated with medical skills.

Some scholars argue both for and against the idea that Frigg and Freya are really the same goddess, avatars of one another.

Gwydion or Gwyddien

Gwydion is a magician, hero and trickster of Welsh mythology, associated largely with his relationship with his young nephew, Lleu Llaw Gyffes. His name means "Born of Trees."

Gilfaethwy, nephew to king Math fab Mathonwy, falls in love with his uncle's virgin foot-holder, Goewin. His brother Gwydion conspires to start a war between the north and the south to give the brothers the opportunity to rape Goewin while Math is distracted. Gwydion employs his magic powers to steal a number of otherworldly pigs from the Demetian king, Pryderi, who retaliates by declaring war. Meanwhile, Gwydion and Gilfaethwy attack and rape Goewin.

Pryderi and his men march north and fight a battle between Maenor Bennardd and Maenor Coed Alun, but are forced to retreat. He is pursued to Nant Call, where more of his men are slaughtered, and then to Dol Benmaen, where he suffers a third defeat. To avoid further bloodshed, it is agreed that the outcome of the battle should be decided by single combat between Gwydion and Pryderi. The two contenders meet and "because of strength and valour and magic and enchantment," Gwydion triumphs and Pryderi is killed. Pryderi's men retreat back to their own land, lamenting over the death of their lord.

When Math hears of the assault on Goewin, he turns his nephews into a series of mated pairs of animals: Gwydion becomes a stag for a year, then a sow and finally a wolf. Gilfaethwy becomes a deer, a boar and a she-wolf. Each year they produce an offspring which is sent to Math: Hyddwn, Hychddwn and Bleiddwn. After three years, Math releases his nephews from their punishment and begins the search for a new footholder. Gwydion suggests his sister Arianrhod, who is magically tested for virginity by Math. During the test, she gives birth to a "sturdy boy with thick yellow hair" whom Math names Dylan and who takes on the nature of the seas until his death at his uncle Gofannon's hands.

Ashamed, Arianrhod runs to the door, but on her way out something small drops from her, which Gwydion wraps up and places in a chest at the foot of his bed. Some time later, he hears screams from within the chest, and opens it to discover a baby boy. Some scholars have suggested that in an earlier form of the Fourth Branch, Gwydion was the father of Arianrhod's sons.

Some years later, Gwydion accompanies the boy to Arianrhod and presents him to his mother. The furious Arianrhod, shamed by this reminder of her loss of virginity, curses the boy with a curse that only she could give him a name. Gwydion however tricks his sister by disguising himself and the boy as cobblers and luring Arianrhod into going to them in person in order to have some shoes made for her. The boy throws a stone and strikes a wren "between the tendon and the bone of its leg", causing Arianrhod to make the remark "it is with a skillful hand that the fair-haired one has hit it." At that Gwydion reveals himself, saying Lleu Llaw Gyffes, "the fair-haired one with the skillful hand,' is his name now." Furious at this trickery, Arianrhod places another curse on Lleu: he shall receive arms from no one but Arianrhod herself. Gwydion tricks his sister once again, and she unwittingly arms Lleu herself. By now Arianrhod, annoyed Gwydion's trickery, places a third curse on Lleu: that he shall never have a human wife.

Hades

Hades (meaning "the unseen") refers both to the ancient Greek underworld, the abode of Hades, and to the god of the underworld. In Homer's poems, Hades referred just to the god. Eventually, the name came to designate the abode of the dead.

In Greek mythology, Hades is the oldest male child of Cronus and Rhea. According to myth, he and his brothers Zeus and Poseidon defeated the Titans and claimed rulership over the cosmos, ruling the underworld, air, and sea, respectively; the solid earth, long the province of Gaia, was available to all three concurrently. Because of his association with the underworld, Hades is often interpreted in modern times as the personification of death, even though he was not so considered in ancient times.

In older Greek myths, the realm of Hades is the misty and gloomy abode of the dead (also called Erebus) where all mortals go. Later Greek philosophy introduced the idea that all mortals are judged after death and are either rewarded or cursed. Very few mortals could leave his realm once they entered: the exceptions, such as Heracles and Thesus, are heroic.

For Hellenes, the deceased entered the underworld by crossing the Acheron, ferried across by Charon, who charged an obolus, a small coin for passage placed in the mouth of the deceased by relatives. Paupers and the friendless gathered for a hundred years on the near shore. Greeks offered libations to prevent the deceased from returning to the upper world to haunt those who had not given them a proper burial. The far side of the river was guarded by Cerebus, the three-headed dog defeated by Heracles (the Roman Hercules). Passing beyond Cerberus, the shades of the departed entered the land of the dead to be judged.

The five rivers of the realm of Hades, and their symbolic meanings, are Acheron (the river of sorrow, or woe), Cocytus (lamentation), Phlegethon (fire), Lethe (oblivion), and Styx (hate), the river upon which even the gods swore and in which Achilles was dipped to render him invincible. The Styx forms the boundary between the upper and lower worlds.

Hades had three sisters, Demeter, Hestia and Hera, as well as two brothers, Zeus, the youngest of the three, and Poseidon, collectively comprising the original six Olympian gods. The six younger gods, along with allies they managed to gather, challenged the elder gods for power in the Titanomachy, a divine war. Zeus, Poseidon, and Hades received weapons from the three Cyclopes to help in the war: Zeus the thunderbolt, Hades the Helm of Darkness, and Poseidon the trident. The night before the first battle, Hades put on his helmet and, being invisible, slipped over to the Titans' camp and destroyed their weapons. The war lasted for ten years and ended with the victory of the younger gods. Following their victory, Hades and his two brothers, Poseidon and Zeus, drew lots for realms to rule. Zeus got the sky, Poseidon got the seas, and Hades received the underworld, the unseen realm to which the dead go upon leaving the world as well as any and all things beneath the earth. Hades obtained his eventual consort and queen, Persephone, through trickery.

Hecate

Hecate is a Greco-Roman goddess of the underworld associated with magic, witchcraft, necromancy, and crossroads, and a protector of entrances She has been associated with childbirth, nurturing the young, gates and walls, doorways, crossroads, magic, lunar lore, torches and dogs. She appears as a three-faced goddess associated with magic, witchcraft, and curses. Today she is claimed as a goddess of Wicca (particularly witches). Some Pagans refer to her as a "crone goddess," although this characterization appears to conflict with her frequent characterization as a virgin in late antiquity. She closely parallels the Roman goddess Trivia.

There was an area sacred to Hecate in the Temple of Artemis at Ephesus.

Hecate also came to be associated with ghosts, infernal spirits, the dead and sorcery. Like the totems of Hermes—herms placed at borders as a ward against danger—images of Hecate (like Artemis and Diana) were also placed at the gates of cities, and eventually domestic doorways. Over time, the association with keeping out evil spirits could have led to the belief that if offended, Hecate could also allow the evil spirits **in**. According to one view, this accounts for invocations to Hecate as the supreme governess of the borders between the normal world and the spirit world, and hence as one with mastery over spirits of the dead.

Hera

Hera was the wife and one of three sisters of Zeus in the Olympian pantheon of classical Greek mythology. Her chief function was as the goddess of women and marriage. In Roman mythology, Juno was the equivalent mythical character. The cow, and later, the peacock were sacred to her. Hera's mother was Rhea and her father was Cronus. Hera is a goddess of marriage and unions.

Portrayed as majestic and solemn, often enthroned, and crowned with the polos (a high cylindrical crown worn by several of the Great Goddesses), Hera often bears a pomegranate in her hand, emblem of fertile blood and death and a substitute for the narcotic capsule of the opium poppy.

Hera was known for her jealous and vengeful nature, most notably against Zeus's lovers and offspring, but also against mortals who crossed her, such as Pelias. Paris offended her by choosing Aphrodite as the most beautiful goddess, earning Hera's hatred.

Hephaestus

Hephaestus was a Greek god whose Roman equivalent was Vulcan. He is the son of Zeus and Hera, or according to some accounts, of Hera alone. He was the god of technology, blacksmiths, craftsmen, artisans, sculptors, metals, metallurgy, fire and volcanoes. Like other mythic smiths but unlike most other gods, Hephaestus was lame, which gave him a grotesque appearance in Greek eyes. He served as the blacksmith of the gods, and he was worshipped in the manufacturing and industrial centers of Greece, particularly in Athens. Hephaestus's symbols are a smith's hammer, an anvil and a pair of tongs, although sometimes he is portrayed holding an axe.

Hephaestus, being the most unfaltering of the gods, was given Aphrodite's hand in marriage by Zeus in order to prevent conflict over her between the other gods. Aphrodite, who disliked the idea of being married to unsightly Hephaestus, began an affair with Ares, the god of war. Eventually, Hephaestus found out about Aphrodite's promiscuity from Helios, the all-seeing Sun, and planned a trap for them during one of their trysts.

While Aphrodite and Ares lay together in bed, Hephaestus ensnared them in an unbreakable chain-link net so small as to be invisible and dragged them to Mount Olympus to shame them in front of the other gods for retribution. However, the gods laughed at the sight of these naked lovers and Poseidon persuaded Hephaestus to free them in return for a guarantee that Ares would pay the adulterer's fine. Hephaestus declared that he would return Aphrodite to her father and demand back his bride price.

Hercules

Hercules is the Roman name for the Greek god Heracles, son of Jupiter (the Roman equivalent of Zeus), and the mortal Alcmena, the wisest and most beautiful of all mortal women.

Hera was enraged at Zeus for his infidelity with Alcmena, and even more so that he placed the infant Hercules at Hera's breast as she slept and allowed Hercules to feed, which caused Hercules to be partially immortal, allowing him to surpass all mortal men in strength, size and skill. Hera held a spiteful grudge against Hercules and sent Hercules into a blind frenzy, in which he killed all of his children. When Hercules regained his sanity, he sought out the Oracle at Delphi in the hope of making atonement. The Oracle ordered Hercules to serve Eurystheus, king of Mycenae, who sent him on a series of tasks known as the Labors of Hercules. These tasks are told in this order:

1   To kill the Nemean lion.

2   To destroy the Lernaean Hydra.

3   To capture Cernean hind alive.

4   To trap the Erymanthian boar.

5   To clean the Augean stables.

6   To get rid of the Stymphalen birds.

7   To capture the Cretan bull.

8   To round up the mares of Diomeds.

9   To fetch Hippolyte's girdle, or belt.

10 To fetch the cattle of Geron.

11 To fetch the golden apples of the Hesprides.

12 To bring Cerberus from Tartarus.

While he was a champion and a great warrior, he was not above cheating and using any unfair trick to his advantage. However, he was renowned as having "made the world safe for mankind" by destroying many dangerous monsters. Hercules is noted for his great physical strength and endurance.

Hermaphrodite

Although usually not acknowledged as a deity, Hermaphrodite was said to be the child of Hermes and Aphrodite. Hermaphrodite was both male and female, having a penis and breasts. Another myth states that a nymph, Salmacis, fell in love with and pursued a mortal man who was not interested in her. She asked the gods to join them forever; the gods joined them literally together into a single person with both masculine and feminine attributes.

Along with Dionysus, Hermaphrodite is considered one of the patron saints of hermaphrodites and transgendered people.

Hermes

Hermes is the great messenger of the gods in Greek mythology and additionally a guide to the Underworld. Hermes was born on Mount Cyllene in Arcadia. An Olympian god, he is also the patron of boundaries and of the travelers who cross them, of shepherds and cowherds, of the cunning of thieves, of orators and wit, of literature and poets, of athletics and sports, of weights and measures, of invention, and of commerce in general.

He protects and takes care of all the travelers, miscreants, harlots, old crones and thieves that pray to him or cross his path. Hermes is credited as the inventor of fire. In addition to the lyre, Hermes was believed to have invented many types of racing and the sports of wrestling and boxing, and therefore was a patron of athletes. Hermes often helped travelers have a safe and easy journey. Many Greeks would sacrifice to Hermes before any trip.

In many Greek myths, Hermes was depicted as the only god besides Hades, Persephone, Hecate, and Thanatos who could enter and leave the Underworld without hindrance.

Herne

See "Cernunnos" on page 135.

Horus

Horus is one of the oldest and most significant deities in the Ancient Egyptian religion, who was worshiped from at least the late Pre-dynastic period through to Greco-Roman times. Different forms of Horus are recorded in history and these are treated as distinct gods by Egyptologists. These various forms may possibly be different perceptions of the same multi-layered deity in which certain attributes or relationships are emphasized, complementary to one another, and consistent with how the Ancient Egyptians viewed the multiple facets of reality.

The earliest recorded form is Horus the Falcon who was the patron deity of Nekhen in Upper Egypt and who is the first known national god, specifically related to the king who in time came to be regarded as a manifestation of Horus in life and Osiris in death. The most commonly encountered family relationship describes Horus as the son of Isis and Osiris but in another tradition Hathor is regarded as his mother and sometimes as his wife. Horus served many functions in the Egyptian pantheon, most notably being the god of the Sky, god of War and god of Protection.

Pyramid texts dating from the 25th century BCE describe the nature of the Pharoah in different characters as both Horus and Osiris. The Pharaoh as Horus in life became the Pharaoh as Osiris in death, where he was united with the rest of the gods. New incarnations of Horus succeeded the deceased pharaoh on earth in the form of new pharaohs.

The lineage of Horus, the eventual product of unions between the children of Atum, may have been a means to explain and justify Pharaonic power; The gods produced by Atum were all representative of cosmic and terrestrial forces in Egyptian life; by identifying Horus as the offspring of these forces identified him with Atum himself, and in identifying the Pharaoh with Horus, the Pharaoh theologically had dominion over all the world.

The notion of Horus as the Pharaoh seems to have been superseded by the concept of the Pharaoh as the son of Ra during the Fifth Dynasty of Egypt.

The Eye of Horus is an ancient Egyptian symbol of protection and royal power from deities, in this case from Horus or Ra. The symbol is seen on images of Horus' mother, Isis, and on other deities associated with her.

Horus was also said to be a god of war and hunting.

Horus was told by his mother, Isis, to protect the people of Egypt from Set, the god of the desert, who had killed his father Osiris. Horus had many battles with Set, not only to avenge his father, but to choose the rightful ruler of Egypt. In these battles, Horus came to be associated with Lower Egypt where he was worshiped, and became its patron.

One scene stated how Horus was on the verge of killing Set; but his mother (and Set's sister) Isis stopped him. Isis injured Horus, but eventually healed him.

By the 19th dynasty, the enmity between Set and Horus, in which Horus had ripped off one of Set's testicles, was represented as a separate tale. Set is depicted in an ancient papyrus as trying to prove his dominance by seducing Horus and then having intercourse with him. However, Horus places his hand between his thighs and catches Set's semen, then subsequently throws it in the river, so that he may not be said to have been inseminated by Set. Horus then deliberately spreads his own semen on some lettuce, which was Set's favorite food. After Set had eaten the lettuce, they went to the gods to try to settle the argument over the rule of Egypt. The gods first listened to Set's claim of dominance over Horus, and called his semen forth, but it answered from the river, invalidating his claim. Then, the gods listened to Horus' claim of having dominated Set, and called his semen forth, and it answered from inside Set.

But still Set refused to relent, and the other gods were getting tired from over eighty years of fighting. Horus and Set challenged each other to a boat race, where they each raced in a boat made of stone. But Horus had an edge: his boat was made of wood painted to resemble stone, rather than true stone. Set's boat, being made of heavy stone, sank, but Horus' did not. Horus then won the race, and Set stepped down and officially gave Horus the throne of Egypt. But after the New Kingdom, Set still was considered Lord of the desert and its oases.

Hyacinth

See "Apollo" on page 126.

Inanna

Inanna is the ancient Sumerian goddess of sexual love, fertility, and warfare. Her counterpart from Babylonian myth is Ishtar. Inanna can be considered the most prominent female deity in ancient Mesopotamia.

Along the Tigris and Euphrates rivers were many shrines and temples dedicated to Inanna. The temple of Eanna, meaning "house of heaven" or "house of An" was the greatest of these, where sacred prostitution was a common practice. In addition, persons with asexual or hermaphroditic bodies and feminine men were particularly involved in the worship and ritual practices of Inanna's temples. The high priestess would choose for her bed a young man who represented the shepherd Dumuzi, consort of Inanna, in a sacred marriage, celebrated during the annual ceremony of the spring Equinox.

Inanna was associated with the celestial planet of Venus. There are hymns to Inanna as her astral manifestation. It is also believed that in many myths about Inanna, including Inanna's *Decent to the Underworld* and *Inanna and Shukaletuda*, her movements correspond with the movements of Venus in the night sky. Also, because of its positioning, Venus moves irregularly across the night sky, and never travels all the way across the dome of the sky like most celestial bodies. This relates to Inanna's erratic nature.

Inanna is the goddess of love but not marriage. She is connected with extramarital sex and sensual affairs. Despite her association with mating and fertility of humans and animals, Inanna was not a mother goddess, though she is associated with childbirth in certain myths. Inanna was also associated with rain and storms and with the planet Venus, the morning and evening star, as was the Greco-Ropman goddess Aphrodite or Venus.

The story of Inanna's descent to the underworld is known from a poem on a relatively intact set of tablets.

In Sumerian religion, the Underworld was conceived of as a dreary, dark place; a home to deceased heroes and ordinary people alike. The treatment or position they achieved in the underworld was based on their behavior during their life.

Inanna's reason for visiting the underworld is unclear. The reason she gives to the gatekeeper of the underworld is that she wants to attend her brother-in-law Gugalana's funeral rites. Gugalana was the Bull of Heaven in the Epic of Gilgamesh, killed by Gilgamesh and Enkidu.

In this story, before leaving Inanna instructed her minister and servant Ninshubur to plead with the gods Enlil, Nanna, and Enki to save her if anything went wrong, because everyone that went to the Underworld never came back.

Inanna dressed elaborately for the visit, with a turban, a wig, a lapis lazuli necklace, beads upon her breast, the 'pala dress' (the ladyship garment), mascara, pectoral, a golden ring on her hand, and she held a lapis lazuli measuring rod. These garments are each representations of powerful magic she possesses. Perhaps Inanna's garments, unsuitable for a funeral, along with her haughty behaviour, make Ereshkigal suspicious.

Following Ereshkigal's instructions, the gatekeeper tells Inanna she may enter the first gate of the underworld, but she must hand over her lapis lazuli measuring rod. She asks why, and is told 'It is just the ways of the Underworld.' She obliges and passes through. Inanna passes through a total of seven gates, at each one removing a piece of clothing or jewelry she had been wearing at the start of her journey, thus stripping her of her power.

When she arrives in front of her sister, she is naked. After she had crouched down and had her clothes removed, they were carried away. Then she made her sister Ereshkigal rise from her throne, and instead she sat on her throne. The Anna, the seven judges, rendered their decision against her. They looked at her with the look of death; they spoke to her with the speech of anger; and they shouted at her with guilt. The afflicted woman was turned into a corpse, and the corpse was hung on a hook.

Ereshkigal's hate for Inanna could be referenced in a few other myths.

Ereshkigal is seen as an accidental "black sheep" of sorts. She cannot leave her kingdom of the Underworld to join the other "living" gods, and they cannot visit her in the Underworld, or else they can never return. Inanna symbolized erotic love and fertility, and contrasts with Ereshkigal.

Three days and three nights passed, and following instructions, Ninshubur went to Enlil, Nanna, and Enki's temples, and demanded they save Inanna. The first two gods refused, saying it was her own problem, but Enki was deeply troubled and agreed to help. He created two asexual figures named the gala-tura and the kur-jara from the dirt under the fingernails of the gods. He instructed them to appease Ereshkigal; and when asked what they wanted, they were to ask for Inanna's corpse and sprinkle it with the food and water of life. However, when they went to Ereshkigal, she was in agony like a woman giving birth, and she offered them what they wanted, including life-giving rivers of water and fields of grain, if they can relieve her; nonetheless they take only the corpse.

The gala-tura and the kur-jara were able to revive Inanna. Demons of Ereshkigal's followed Inanna out of the underworld and insisted that she wasn't free to go until someone took her place. They found Dimuzi, Inanna's husband. He was sitting in nice clothing underneath a tree and enjoying himself, despite his wife supposedly still being missing in the underworld. Inanna, displeased, decreed that the demons should take him and uses the same "look of death" that was previously used upon her by Ereshkigal. Dumuzi tried to escape his fate; then Dumuzi's sister, out of love for him, begged to be allowed to take his place. It was then decreed that Dumuzi would spend half the year in the underworld, and his sister would take the other half. Inanna eventually regrets sending her husband to the underworld and begins to miss him. The fertility that she controls with her godly powers begins to fade during the six months that he is in the underworld each year. This infertile time corresponds to the fall and winter months. When her husband's sister is in the underworld and Dumuzi is with Inanna, everything is filled with love and with life; this time corresponds to Spring and Summer.

The myth can be described as a union of Inanna with her own "dark side," her twin sister-self, Ereshkigal, as when she ascends it is with Ereshkigal's powers, while Inanna is in the underworld it is Ereshkigal who apparently takes on fertility powers, and the myth ends with a line in praise, not of Inanna, but of Ereshkigal. It is symbolic of an acceptance of the necessity of death to the continuance of life. It can also be interpreted as being about the psychological power of a descent into the unconscious, realizing one's own strength through an episode of seeming powerlessness, and an acceptance of one's own negative qualities.

To the ancient Mesopotamian audience, though, it is most likely that the moral of this story was that there are always consequences for one's actions. The story was about one of the gods behaving badly and other gods and mortals having to suffer for that behavior, and it would have given to an ancient listener the same basic understanding anyone today would take from an account of a tragic accident caused by someone's negligence or poor judgment: that, sometimes, life is just not fair."

Ishtar

See "Ereshkigal" on page 142 and "Inanna" on page 153.

Isis

Isis was a goddess in Ancient Egyptian religious beliefs whose worship spread throughout the Greco-Roman world. She was worshiped as the ideal mother and wife as well as the matron of nature and magic. She was the friend of slaves, sinners, artisans, and the downtrodden, and she listened to the prayers of the wealthy, maidens, aristocrats, and rulers. Isis is the goddess of motherhood, magic, and fertility.

The goddess Isis (the mother of Horus) was the first daughter of Geb, god of the Earth, and Nut, the goddess of the Overarching Sky. At some time Isis and Hathor had the same headdress. In later myths about Isis, she had a brother, Osiris, who became her husband, and she then was said to have conceived Horus. Isis was instrumental in the resurrection of Osiris when he was murdered by Set. Her magical skills restored his body to life after she gathered the body parts that had been strewn about the earth by Set.

Isis is also known as protector of the dead and goddess of children from whom all beginnings arose. In later times, the Ancient Egyptians believed that the Nile River flooded every year because of her tears of sorrow for her dead husband, Osiris. This occurrence of his death and rebirth was relived each year through rituals. The worship of Isis eventually spread throughout the Greco-Roman world, continuing until the suppression of paganism in the Christian era.

Temples to Isis were constructed in Iraq, Greece and Italy, with a well-preserved temple still standing at Pompeii.

Both priests and priestesses officiated at Isis rituals throughout its entire history. By the Greco-Roman era, many of them were healers, and were said to have many other special powers, including dream interpretation and the ability to control the weather, which they did by braiding or not combing their hair. The latter was believed because the Egyptians considered knots to have magical powers.

Isis and her sister Nephthys often were depicted on coffins, with wings outstretched, as protectors against evil. As a funerary deity, she was associated with Osiris, lord of the underworld, and was considered his wife as well as his sister.

In Osirian myth, Set held a banquet for Osiris in which he brought in a beautiful box and said that whoever could fit in the box perfectly would get to keep it. Set had measured Osiris in his sleep and made sure that he was the only one who could fit the box. Several tried to see whether they fit. Once it was Osiris's turn to see if he could fit in the box, Set closed the lid on him so that the box was now a coffin for Osiris. Set flung the box in the Nile so that it would drift far away. Isis went looking for the box so that Osiris could have a proper burial. She found the box in a tree in Byblos, a city along the Phoenician coast, and brought it back to Egypt, hiding it in a swamp. But Set went hunting that night and found the box. Enraged, Set chopped Osiris's body into fourteen pieces and scattered them all over Egypt to ensure that Isis could never find Osiris again for a proper burial. Isis and her sister Nephthys went looking for these pieces, but could only find thirteen of the fourteen. Fish had swallowed the last piece, his phallus, so Isis made him a new one with magic, putting his body back together after which they conceived Horus.

In order to resurrect Osiris for the purpose of having the child Horus, it was necessary for Isis to "learn" magic (which long had been her domain before the cult of Ra arose), and so it was said that Isis tricked Ra into telling her his "secret name" by causing a snake to bite him, for which only Isis had the cure. The names of deities were secret and not divulged to any but the religious leaders. Knowing the secret name of a deity enabled one to have power of the deity. That he would use his "secret name" to "survive" implies that the serpent had to be a more powerful deity than Ra. The oldest deity known in Egypt was Wadjet, the Egyptian cobra, whose cult never was eclipsed in Ancient Egyptian religion. As a deity from the same region, she would have been a benevolent resource for Isis. The use of secret names became central in late Egyptian magic spells, and Isis often is implored to "use the true name of Ra" in the performance of rituals. By the late Egyptian historical period, after the occupations by the Greeks and the Romans, Isis became the most important and most powerful deity of the Egyptian pantheon because of her magical skills.

Janus

In Roman religion and mythology, Janus is the god of beginnings and transitions; also of gates, doors, doorways, roads, city gates, or boundaries, endings and time. Most often he is depicted as having two heads, facing opposite directions: one head looks eastward and the other westward. Symbolically they look simultaneously into the future and the past, back at the last year and forward at the new.

Because of his initial nature he was frequently used to symbolize change and transitions such as the progression of past to future, of one condition to another, of one vision to another, the growing up of young people, and of one universe to another. He was also known as the figure representing time because he could see into the past with one face and into the future with the other.

According to a legend, he had received the gift to see both future and past from the god Saturn.

The Winter solstice was thought to happen on December 25. Shortly afterward, on January 9, a sacrifice of a sheep was offered to Janus. Cakes made of spelt and salt were offered to the god and consumed. Ovid states that in most ancient times there were no animal sacrifices and gods were propitiated with offerings of spelt and pure salt.

Juno

Juno was an ancient Roman goddess, the protector and special counselor of the state. She is a daughter of Saturn and the sister and wife of the chief god Jupiter and the mother of Mars and Vulcan. Her Greek equivalent is Hera. She often appeared armed and wearing a goatskin cloak. The traditional depiction of this warlike aspect was assimilated from the Greek goddess Athena.

Her central role as a goddess of marriage. She is also connected with the idea of vital energy, and eternal youthfulness. Two additional qualities associated with the interrelated aspects of the function of Juno include cyclical renewal of time in the waning and waxing of the moon and protection of delivery and birth. Through her association with the moon, she governed the feminine physiological functions, menstrual cycle and pregnancy.

Jupiter

In ancient Roman religion and myth, Jupiter (or Jove) was the king of the gods, and the god of sky and thunder. He is the equivalent of Zeus in the Greek pantheon.

The largest temple in Rome was that of Jupiter Optimus Maximus on the Capitoline Hill. Here, Romans worshipped him alongside Juno and Minerva, forming the Capitoline Triad. When Hadrian built Aelia Capitolina on the site of Jerusalem, a temple to Jupiter Capitolinus was erected in the place of the destroyed Temple in Jerusalem.

The Loa

The Loa are the spirits of the Vodoun religion practiced in Louisiana, Haiti, Benin, and other parts of the world. They are also referred to as Mystères and the Invisibles. They are considered to be intermediaries between Bondye (Bon Dieu, or "good god") – the Creator, who is not part of the physical world – and humanity. Unlike saints or angels however, they are not simply prayed to, they are served. They are each distinct beings with their own personal likes and dislikes, distinct sacred rhythms, songs, dances, ritual symbols, and special modes of service. Contrary to popular belief, the loa are not deities in and of themselves; they are intermediaries for a distant Bondye.

The *Rada Loa* are generally the older, more beneficent spirits, and are associated with the gods of Africa. They include Legba, Loko, Ayizan, Anaisa Pye, Dhamballa Wedo, and Ayida Weddo, Erzulie Freda, LaSirene, and Agwe. Their traditional color is white (as opposed to the specific colors of individual Loa).

The *Petro Loa* are generally the more fiery, occasionally aggressive and warlike Loa, and are associated with Haiti and the New World. They include Erzulie Dantor, Marinette, Ogoun, and Met Kalfu (Maitre Carrefour, "Master Crossroads"). Their traditional color is red.

Originating from the Congo region of Africa, the *Kongo Loa* include the many Simbi loa, and also includes the much dreaded Marinette, a fierce and much feared female loa.

Originating from Nigeria (specifically the Yoruba speaking tribes) the *Nago Loa* includes many of the Ogoun spirits.

The *Ghede Loa* are the spirits of the dead. They are traditionally led by the Barons (LaCroix, Samedi, Cimitiere, Kriminel) and Maman Brigitte. The Ghede as a family are loud, rude (although rarely to the point of real insult), sexual, and usually a lot of fun. As those who have lived already, they have nothing to fear, and frequently will display how far past consequence and feeling they are when they come through in a service - eating glass, raw chili peppers, and anointing their sensitive areas with chili rum for example. Their traditional colors are black and purple.

Lugh

In Irish mythology, Lugh ("skilled in many arts") was a sun god associated with war and skillfulness, much like Mercury.

As a young man Lugh travels to Tara to join the court of Nuada, the king of the Tuatha Dé Danann. The doorkeeper will not let him in unless he has a skill with which to serve the king. He offers his services as a wright, a smith, a champion, a swordsman, a harpist, a hero, a poet and historian, a sorcerer, and a craftsman, but each time is rejected as the Tuatha Dé Danann already have someone with that skill. But when Lugh asks if they have anyone with all those skills simultaneously, the doorkeeper has to admit defeat, and Lugh joins the court and is appointed Chief Ollam of Ireland. He wins a flagstone-throwing contest against Ogma, the champion, and entertains the court with his harp. The Tuatha Dé Danann are at

THE MALE PAGAN | 161

that time oppressed by the Fomorians, and Lugh is amazed how meekly they accept this. Nuada wonders if this young man could lead them to freedom. Lugh is given command over the Tuatha Dé Danann, and he begins making preparations for war.

When the sons of Tuireann, Brian, Iuchar and Iucharba kill his father, Cian (who was in the form of a pig at the time), Lugh sets them a series of seemingly impossible quests. They achieve them all, but are fatally wounded in completing the last one. Despite Tuireann's pleas, Lugh denies them the use of one of the items they have retrieved, a magic pigskin which heals all wounds. They die of their wounds, and Tuireann dies of grief over their bodies.

Using the magic artifacts the sons of Tuireann have gathered, Lugh leads the Tuatha Dé Danann in the second battle against the Fomorians. Nuada is killed in the battle by Balor. Lugh faces Balor, who opens his terrible, poisonous eye that kills all it looks upon, but Lugh shoots a sling-stone that drives his eye out the back of his head, wreaking havoc on the Fomorian army behind. After the victory Lugh finds Bres, the half-Fomorian former king of the Tuatha Dé Danann, alone and unprotected on the battlefield, and Bres begs for his life. If he is spared, he promises, he will ensure that the cows of Ireland always give milk. The Tuatha Dé Danann refuse the offer. He then promises four harvests a year, but the Tuatha Dé Danann say one harvest a year suits them. But Lugh spares his life on the condition that he teach the Tuatha Dé Danann how and when to plow, sow and reap.

Lugh's sling rod was the rainbow and the Milky Way which was called "Lugh's Chain." He also had a magic spear (named Areadbhar), which, unlike the sling-rod, he had no need to wield since it was alive and thirsted so for blood that only by steeping its head in a potion of pounded fresh poppy seeds could it be kept at rest. When battle was near, it was drawn out; then it roared and struggled against its thongs, fire flashed from it, and it tore through the ranks of the enemy once slipped from the leash, never tired of slaying

Mars

Mars was the Roman god of war and also an agricultural guardian. Under the influence of Greek culture, Mars was identified with the

Greek god Ares, whose myths were reinterpreted in Roman literature and art under the name of Mars. But the character and dignity of Mars differed in fundamental ways from that of his Greek counterpart, who is often treated with contempt and revulsion in Greek literature. While Ares was viewed primarily as a destructive and destabilizing force, Mars represented military power as a way to secure peace, and was a father of the Roman people.

Although Ares was the son of Zeus and Hera, Mars was the son of Juno alone. Jupiter had usurped the mother's function when he gave birth to Minerva directly from his forehead (or mind); to restore the balance, Juno sought the advice of the goddess Flora on how to do the same. Flora obtained a magic flower and tested it on a heifer who became fecund at once. She then touched Juno's belly, and impregnated her. Juno withdrew to Thrace and the shore of Marmara for the birth.

As an agricultural god, Mars directs his energies toward creating conditions that allow crops to grow, which may include warding off hostile forces of nature. As an embodiment of masculine aggression, he is the force that drives wars — but ideally, war that delivers a secure peace.

Mercury

Mercury was a messenger and a god of trade. Mercury had essentially the same aspects as Hermes, wearing winged shoes and a winged cap, and carrying the caduceus, a herald's staff with two entwined snakes that was Apollo's gift to Hermes. He was often accompanied by a cockerel, herald of the new day, a ram or goat, symbolizing fertility, and a tortoise, referring to Mercury's legendary invention of the lyre from a tortoise shell.

Like Hermes, he was also a messenger of the gods and a god of trade, particularly of the grain trade. Mercury was also considered a god of abundance and commercial success. He also led newly-deceased souls to the afterlife. Additionally, Ovid wrote that Mercury carried Morpheus' dreams from the valley of Somnus to sleeping humans.

Mercury's festival was celebrated on May 15th.

Minerva

Minerva was the Roman goddess whom Romans from the 2nd century BC onwards equated with the Greek goddess Athena. She was the virgin goddess of poetry, medicine, wisdom, commerce, weaving, crafts, art, schools, war, magic, and the inventor of music. She is often depicted with her sacred creature, an owl, which symbolizes her ties to wisdom.

While Minerva was worshiped throughout Italy, she was equated with a warlike character, like Athena, only in Rome. The Romans celebrated her holiday from March 19-23.

Neptune

Neptune was the god of water and the sea in Roman mythology. He is similar but not identical to the Greek god Poseidon. In the Greek-influenced tradition, Neptune was the brother of Jupiter and Pluto, each of them presiding over one of the three realms of the universe, Heaven, Earth and the Underworld.

Unlike the Greek Oceanus, titan of the world-ocean, Neptune was associated as well with fresh water. For Latins, who were not a seafaring people, the primary identification of Neptune was with freshwater springs, lakes and rivers.

The festival of Neptunalia was celebrated on July 23rd, at the height of summer. This festival was a time of general free and urestrained merrymaking during which men and women mixed without the usual traditional Roman social constraints. This character of the festival as well as the fact that Neptune was offered the sacrifice of a bull points to an agricultural fertility context.

Odin

In ancient Norse mythology, Odin was an ambivalent deity, associated with poetry and inspiration as fury, madness and the wanderer. Odin sacrificed his eye at Mimir's spring in order to gain the Wisdom of Ages. Odin gives to worthy poets the mead of inspiration, made by the dwarfs. He is associated with the concept of the Wild Hunt, a noisy, belligerent movement across the sky, leading a host of slain warriors. Odin is also associated with trickery, cunning, and deception.

Odin was the father of Thor and Frigg.

Osiris

Osiris was an Egyptian god, usually identified as the god of the Afterlife, the underworld and the dead. He is classically depicted as a green-skinned man with a pharoah's beard, partially mummy-wrapped at the legs, wearing a distinctive crown with two large ostrich feathers at either side, and holding a symbolic crook and flail.

Osiris was the oldest son of the Earth god Geb, and the sky goddess Nut, as well as being brother and husband of Isis, with Horus being his posthumously begotten son. He was also associated with the epithet "Khenti-Amentiu," which means "Foremost of the Westerners" – a reference to his kingship in the land of the dead. As ruler of the dead, Osiris was also sometimes called "king of the living," since the Ancient Egyptians considered the dead "the living ones."

Osiris was not only a merciful judge of the dead in the afterlife, but also the underworld agency that granted all life, including sprouting vegetation and the fertile flooding of the Nile River. He is described as the "Lord of love," "He Who is Permanently Benign and Youthful," and the "Lord of Silence."

Osiris, who died only to be resurrected, represented continuity and therefore stability. He represents regeneration and rebirth, and immortality.

Pan

In Greek religion and mythology, Pan is the god of shepherds and flocks, of mountain wilderness, hunting and rustic music, as well as the companion of the nymphs. His name originates within the Greek language from the word meaning "to pasture." He has the hindquarters, legs, and horns of a goat, in the same manner as a faun or satyr. He is recognized as the god of fields, groves, and wooded glens; because of this, Pan is connected to fertility and the season of spring. The ancient Greeks also considered Pan to be the god of theatrical criticism.

In Roman religion and mythology, Pan's counterpart was Faunus, a nature god who was the father of Bona Dea, who was sometimes identified as Fauna.

Pan is famous for his sexual powers, and is often depicted with a phallus.

One of the famous myths of Pan involves the origin of his pan flute, fashioned from lengths of hollow reed. Syrinx was a lovely water-nymph. As she was returning from the hunt one day, Pan met her. To escape from his attentions, she ran away; he pursued her until she came to her sisters who immediately changed her into a reed. When the air blew through the reeds, it produced a plaintive melody. The god, still infatuated, took some of the reeds, because he could not identify which reed she became, and cut seven pieces (or according to some versions, nine), joined them side by side in gradually decreasing lengths, and formed the musical instrument bearing the name of his beloved Syrinx. Pan was seldom seen afterward without it.

Echo was a nymph who was a great singer and dancer and scorned the love of any man. This angered Pan, a lecherous god, and he instructed his followers to kill her. Echo was torn to pieces and spread all over earth. The goddess of the earth, Gaia, received the pieces of Echo, whose voice remains repeating the last words of others. In some versions, Echo and Pan first had one child: Iambe. Pan also loved a nymph named Pitys, who was turned into a pine tree to escape his relentless pursuit.

Pan's greatest conquest was that of the moon goddess Selene. He accomplished this by wrapping himself in a sheepskin to hide his hairy black goat form, and drew her down from the sky into the forest where he seduced her.

Persephone

See also "Proserpina" on page 166.

Poseidon

Poseidon, in ancient Greek mythology, was the god of the sea, and, as "Earth-Shaker," of earthquakes. He was integrated into the Olympian gods as the brother of Zeus and Hades. Poseidon has many children.

In his benign aspect, Poseidon was seen as creating new islands and offering calm seas. When offended or ignored, he supposedly struck the ground with his trident and caused chaotic springs, earthquakes, drownings and shipwrecks. Like Dionysus, who inflamed the maenads (the female followers of Dionysus), Poseidon also caused certain forms of mental disturbance. He was blamed for certain types of epilepsy.

Priapus

In Greek mythology, Priapos (Latinized as Priapus), was a minor rustic fertility god, protector of livestock, fruit plants, gardens and male genitalia. Priapus was best noted for his large, permanent erection, which gave rise to the medical term priapism.

Priapus was the son of Aphrodite by Dionysus, or son of Dioysus and Chione, perhaps as father or son of Hermes, son of Zeus or Pan, depending on the source.

According to legend, in revenge for the hero Paris having the temerity to judge Aphrodite more beautiful than her, Hera cursed him with impotence, ugliness and foul-mindedness while he was still in Aphrodite's womb. The other gods refused to allow him to live on Mount Olympus and threw him down to Earth, leaving him on a hillside. He was eventually found by shepherds and was brought up by them.

Priapus joined Pan and the satyrs as a spirit of fertility and growth, though he was perennially frustrated by his impotence. In a ribald anecdote told by Ovid, he attempted to rape the nymph Lotis but was thwarted by an ass, whose braying caused him to lose his erection at the critical moment and woke Lotis. He pursued the nymph until the gods took pity on her and turned her into a lotus plant. The episode gave him a lasting hatred of asses and a willingness to see them destroyed in his honor. The emblem of his lustful nature was his permanent erection and his giant penis.

Priapus continues to be invoked as a symbol of health and fertility. Some scholars believe that the common garden gnome is a descendent of Priapus.

Priapus' role as a patron god for merchant sailors in ancient Greece and Rome is that of a protector and navigational aide.

Proserpina

Proserpina was the daughter of Ceres, the goddess of agriculture and crops, and Jupiter, the god of sky and thunder. She is the goddess of springtime, a Roman equivalent of Persephone.

In order to bring love to Pluto, Venus sent her son Cupid to strike Pluto with one of his arrows. Proserpina was in Sicily, where she was playing with some nymphs and collecting flowers, when Pluto came out from the volcano Etna. He abducted her in order to marry her and live with her in the underworld of which he was the ruler. Pluto was also her uncle, being Jupiter's (and Ceres's) brother. She is therefore Queen of the Underworld.

Her mother Ceres, the goddess of agriculture or of the Earth, went looking for her in vain in every corner of the earth, but wasn't able to find anything but a small belt that was floating upon a little lake made with the tears of the nymphs. In her desperation Ceres angrily stopped the growth of fruits and vegetables, bestowing a curse on Sicily. Ceres refused to go back to Mount Olympus and started walking on the Earth, creating a desert at every step.

Worried, Jupiter sent Mercury to order Pluto (Jupiter's brother) to free Proserpina. Pluto obeyed, but before letting her go he made her eat six pomegranate seeds, because those who have eaten the food of the dead could not return to the world of the living. This meant that she would have to live six months of each year with him, and stay the rest with her mother. This story was undoubtedly meant to illustrate the changing of the seasons: when Ceres welcomes her daughter back in the spring the earth blossoms, and when Proserpina must be returned to her husband it withers.

Ptah

In Egyptian mythology, Ptah called the world into being after dreaming about creation and speaking it. His name means "opener," in the sense of opener of the mouth. The ceremony of opening the mouth, performed by priests at funerals to release souls from their corpses, was said to have been created by Ptah. Atum was created by Ptah to rule over creation.

Ptah is portrayed as a bearded mummified man, often wearing a skull cap, with his hands holding an *ankh*, *was*, and *djed*, the symbols of life, power and stability, respectively. It was believed that Ptah manifested himself in the Apis bull. He might have originally been a fertility god because of this.

He was considered the god of craftsmen, and in particular stone-based crafts. Eventually, due to the connection of these things to tombs, the craftsmen at Thebes regarded him so highly as to say that he controlled their destiny. Consequently, Ptah also became a god of regeneration, first among the craftsmen, then the population as a whole.

Rhiannon

In Welsh mythology, Rhiannon ("great queen") is best known from *The Mabinogion,* a collection of medieval Welsh tales, in which she makes her first appearance on a pale, mysterious steed and meets King Pwyll, whom she later marries. She was accused of killing and devouring her infant son, and in punishment she was forced to assume the guise of a horse and to carry visitors to the royal court. According to another myth, she was made to wear the collars of asses about her neck in the manner of a beast.

Saturn

Saturn was a major Roman god of agriculture and harvest, whose reign was depicted as a Golden Age of abundance and peace. He was known as the Roman god of justice and strength. He held a sickle in his left hand and a bundle of wheat in his right. His mother was Terra and his father was Caelus. He was identified in classical antiquity with the Greek deity Cronus, and the mythologies of the two gods are commonly mixed.

To honor Saturn, a great feast called the Saturnalia was held during the winter months around the time of the winter solstice. It was originally only one day long, taking place on December 17, but later lasted one week. During Saturnalia, roles of master and slave were reversed, moral restrictions loosened, and the rules of etiquette ignored.

The first inhabitants of the world were the children of Terra (Mother Earth) and Caelus (Father Sky). These creatures were very large and man-like, but without human qualities. They were the qualities of Earthquake, Hurricane and Volcano living in a world where there was yet no life. There were only the irresistible forces of nature creating mountains and seas. They were unlike any life form known to man.

Three creatures born of Terra were monstrously huge with one hundred hands and fifty heads. Three others were individually called Cyclopes, because each had only one enormous eye in the middle of their foreheads. Then there were the seven Titans, formidably large and none of whom were a purely destructive force. One was actually credited with saving man after creation.

Caelus hated the children with the fifty heads. As each was born, he imprisoned it under the earth. Terra was enraged by the treatment of her children by their father and begged the Cyclopes and the Titans to help her put an end to the cruel treatment. Only one Titan, Saturn, responded. Saturn lay in wait for his father and, depending on the source, either castrated him or sliced him into a thousand pieces with his sickle. From Caelus' blood sprang the Giants, a fourth race of monsters, and the Erinyes (the Furies), whose purpose was to punish wrongdoing. They were referred to as "those who walk in darkness" and were believed to have writhing snakes for hair and eyes that cried blood. Though eventually all the monsters were driven from Earth, the Erinyes were to remain until the world is free of sin.

It was prophesied that one day Saturn would lose power when one of his children would depose him. To prevent this from happening, each time his wife Ops delivered a child, Saturn would immediately devour it. When her sixth child, Jupiter, was born, Ops had him spirited away to the island of Crete. She then wrapped a stone in his swaddling clothes. Saturn devoured it, thinking it was the child. When Jupiter was grown, he secured the job of cup-bearer to his father. With the help of Terra, his grandmother, Jupiter fed his father a potion that caused him to vomit up Jupiter's five immortal siblings, Vesta (Hestia), Ceres (Demeter), Juno (Hera), Pluto (Hades), and Neptune (Poseidon), who were still alive in their father's stomach.

The god Saturn was believed to rule the planet Saturn. One aspect of Saturn and its ruling sign, Capricorn is the settling of accounts. The time of the winter solstice is when the Sun enters the sign Capricorn. Astrologically, Saturn's function is contraction, which gives Saturn (called since ancient times "The Greater Malefic") a somewhat polarized role against Jupiter (called "The Greater Benefic") in astrology. Saturn and Jupiter are considered natural neutrals, but under closer relations become enemies. Saturn is considered cold (slow) and dry (separate) whereas Jupiter is considered warm (speedy) and moist (inclusive). Where there is light Saturn brings darkness, where there is heat Saturn brings cold, where there is joy Saturn brings sadness, where there is life Saturn brings death, where there is luck Saturn brings misfortune (and sometimes heavy consequences for bad judgment or mistakes), where there is unity Saturn brings isolation, where there is knowledge Saturn brings fear, where there is hope Saturn brings skepticism and stalling. However these effects are not always negative. Saturn's properties of contraction and "crystallization" are said to create solidness in the world and give lasting form to everything physical and principle. Saturn is considered the only planet that doesn't cause over-expansion when negatively aspected with Jupiter, but rather causes Jupiter's expansion to abate.

Tammuz

See "Adonis" on page 125.

Thor

In ancient Norse mythology, Thor is a hammer-wielding god associated with thunder, lightning, storms, oak trees, strength, destruction, fertility, healing, and the protection of mankind.

Scandinavian folk belief that lightning frightens away trolls and ettins (supernatural giants) appears in numerous Scandinavian folktales, and reflects Thor's role in fighting such beings.

Thor is associated with a hammer (or axe) that was able to strike as firmly as he wanted, whatever his aim, and the hammer would never fail, and if he threw it at something, it would never miss and never fly so far from his hand that it would not find its way back, and when he wanted, it would be so small that it could be carried inside his tunic.

Pendants with a distinctive shape that represents Thor's hammer have been found frequently in ancient Norse burial grounds. It is believed that Norse pagans wore these pendants or amulets in much the same way a Christian would wear a cross pendant.

Thor is associated with men's habitation and possessions, and with well-being of the family and community. This included the fruitfulness of the fields, and Thor, although pictured primarily as a storm god in the myths, was also concerned with the fertility and preservation of the seasons. In our own times, little stone axes from the distance past have been used as fertility symbols and placed by the farmer in the holes made by the drill to receive the first seed of spring.

Venus

See "Aphrodite" on page 127.

Vesta

Vesta was the virgin goddess of the hearth, home and family in Roman religion. Vesta's presence was symbolized by the sacred fire that burned at her hearth and temples. Her closest Greek equivalent is Hestia.

Vesta's fire was guarded at her Temples by her priestesses, the Vestales (we know them today as the Vestal Virgins). Every March 1 the fire was renewed. It burned until 391, when the Emperor Theodosius I forbade public pagan worship. One of the Vestales mentioned in mythology was Rhea Silvia, who with the god Mars conceived Romulus and Remus, who founded the city of Rome.

The Vestales were one of the few full-time clergy positions in Roman religion. They were drawn from the patrician class and had to observe absolute chastity for 30 years. It was from this that the Vestales were named the Vestal Virgins. They could not show excessive care of their person, and they were not allowed to let the sacred fire go out. The Vestal Virgins lived together in a house near the Forum. On becoming a priestess, a Vestal Virgin was legally emancipated from her father's authority and swore a vow of chastity for 30 years. This vow was so sacred that if it were broken, the Vestal was buried alive in the Campus Sceleris ("Field of Wickedness"). It is likely that this is what happened to Rhea Silvia. They were also very independent and had many privileges that normal women did not have. They could move around the city but had to be in a carriage.

The festival of Vestalia was held from June 7-15.

It was in the house and home that Vesta was most important because she was the goddess of the hearth and of fire. Vesta was particularly important to women of the household as the hearth was the place where food was prepared and next to it the meal was eaten with an offering being thrown into the fire to divine the future from the way it burned.

Vulcan

Vulcan is the god of beneficial and hindering fire, including the fire of volcanoes in ancient Roman religion. He is known as Sethlans in Etruscan mythology. He was worshipped at an annual festival on August 23 known as the Volcanalia. Vulcan was identified with the Greek god of fire and smithery, Hephaestus.

It is recorded that during the Vulcanalia people used to hang their cloths and fabrics under the sun. This habit might reflect a theologic connection between Vulcan and the divinized sun. Another custom observed on this day required that one should start working at the light of a candle, probably to propitiate a beneficial use of fire by the god.

The Roman concept of the god is connected to the destructive and fertilizing powers of fire. Another meaning of Vulcan is related to male fertilizing power.

Vulcan was considered as the manufacturer of art, arms, iron, jewelry and armor for various gods and heroes, including the thunderbolts of Jupiter. He was the son of Jupiter and Juno, and husband of Maia and Venus.

As the son of Jupiter and Juno, the king and queen of the gods, Vulcan should have been quite handsome, but baby Vulcan was small and ugly with a red, bawling face. Juno was so horrified that she hurled the tiny baby off the top of Mount Olympus.

Vulcan fell down for a day and a night, landing in the sea. Unfortunately, one of his legs broke as he hit the water, and never developed properly. From the surface, Vulcan sunk like a pebble to the depths where the sea-nymph, Thetis, found him and took him to her underwater grotto, and raised him as her own son.

Vulcan had a happy childhood with dolphins as his playmates and pearls as his toys. Late in his childhood, he found the remains of a fisherman's fire on the beach and became fascinated with an unextinguished coal, still red-hot and glowing.

Vulcan carefully shut this precious coal in a clamshell and took it back to his underwater grotto and made a fire with it. On the first day, Vulcan stared at this fire for hours on end. On the second day, he discovered that when he made the fire hotter with bellows, certain stones sweated iron, silver or gold. On the third day he beat the cooled metal into shapes: bracelets, chains, swords and shields. Vulcan made pearl-handled knives and spoons for his foster mother, he made a silver chariot for himself, and bridles so that seahorses could transport him quickly. He even made slave-girls of gold to wait on him and do his bidding.

Later, Thetis left her underwater grotto to attend a dinner party on Mount Olympus wearing a beautiful necklace of silver and sapphires, which Vulcan had made for her. Juno admired the necklace and asked as to where she could get one. Thetis became flustered causing Juno to become suspicious and, at last, Juno discovered the truth: the baby she had once rejected had grown into a talented blacksmith.

Juno was furious and demanded that Vulcan return home, a demand that he refused. However, he sent Juno a beautifully constructed chair made of silver and gold, inlaid with mother-of-pearl. Juno was delighted with this gift but, as soon as she sat in it her weight triggered hidden springs and metal bands sprung forth to hold her fast. The more she shrieked and struggled the more firmly the mechanical throne gripped her; the chair was a cleverly designed trap.

For three days Juno sat fuming, trapped in Vulcan's chair; she couldn't sleep, stretch, or eat. Jupiter finally saved the day by promising that if Vulcan released Juno he would give him a wife, Venus, the goddess of love and beauty. Vulcan agreed and married Venus. He later built a smithy under Mount Etna on the island of Sicily. It was said that whenever Venus is unfaithful, Vulcan grows angry and beats the red-hot metal with such a force that sparks and smoke rise up from the top of the mountain to create a volcanic eruption.

Zeus

In Greek mythology, Zeus is the "Father of Gods and men" who ruled the Olympians of Mount Olympus as a father rules a family. He was the god of sky and thunder in Greek mythology. His Roman counterpart was Jupiter and his Etruscan counterpart was Tinia. His symbols are the thunderbolt, eagle, bull, and oak.

Cronus sired several children by Rhea: Hestia, Demeter, Hera, Hades, and Poseidon, but swallowed them all as soon as they were born, since he had learned from Gaia and Uranus that he was destined to be overcome by his own son as he had overthrown his own father— an oracle that Zeus was to hear and avert. But when Zeus was about to be born, Rhea sought Gaia to devise a plan to save him, so that Cronus would be punished for his acts against Uranus and his own children. Rhea gave birth to Zeus in Crete, handing Cronus a rock wrapped in swaddling clothes, which he promptly swallowed.

After reaching manhood, Zeus forced Cronus to disgorge first the stone (which was set down at Pytho under the glens of Parnassus to be a sign to mortal men, the Omphalos) then his siblings in reverse order of swallowing. In some versions, Metis gave Cronus bitter herbs to force him to disgorge the babies, or Zeus cut Cronus' stomach open. Then Zeus released the brothers of Cronus, the Gigantes, the Hecatonchires and the Cyclopes, from their dungeon in Tartarus, after killing their guard, Campe.

As a token of their appreciation, the Cyclopes gave him thunder and the thunderbolt, or lightning, which had previously been hidden by Gaia. Together, Zeus and his brothers and sisters, along with the Gigantes, Hecatonchires and Cyclopes overthrew Cronus and the other Titans, in the combat called the Titanomachy. The defeated Titans were then cast into a shadowy underworld region known as Tartarus. Atlas, one of the Titans that fought against Zeus, was punished by having to hold up the sky.

After the battle with the Titans, Zeus shared the world with his elder brothers, Poseidon and Hades, by drawing lots: Zeus got the sky and air, Poseidon the waters, and Hades the world of the dead (the underworld). The ancient Earth, Gaia, could not be claimed; she was left to all three, each according to their capabilities, which explains why Poseidon was the "earth-shaker" (the god of earthquakes) and Hades claimed the humans that died.

Gaia resented the way Zeus had treated the Titans, because they were her children. Soon after taking the throne as king of the gods, Zeus had to fight some of Gaia's other children, the monsters Typhon and Echidna. He vanquished Typhon and trapped him under Mount Etna, but left Echidna and her children alive.

Zeus was brother and consort of Hera. By Hera, Zeus sired Ares, Hebe and Hephaestus, though some accounts say that Hera produced these offspring alone. Some also include Eileithyia and Eris as their daughters. The conquests of Zeus among nymphs and the mythic mortal progenitors of Hellenic dynasties are famous. Olympian mythography even credits him with unions with Leto, Demeter, Diana and Maia. Among mortals were Semele, Io, Europa and Leda.

Many myths render Hera as jealous of his amorous conquests and a consistent enemy of Zeus' mistresses and their children by him. For a time, a nymph named Echo had the job of distracting Hera from his affairs by incessantly talking; when Hera discovered the deception, she cursed Echo to forever repeat the words of others.

List of the Gods/Goddesses in the Ancient Egyptian Pantheon

This list contains the currently known gods and goddesses in the ancient Egyptian pantheon, and how they were worshiped.

Each region of ancient Egypt had its own pantheon of gods and goddesses:

- ✓ The Ennead of *Heliopolis*, meaning the nine – consisted of Atum, Geb, Isis, Nut, Osiris, Nephthys, Set, Shu, and Tefnut.

- ✓ The Ogdoad of *Hermopolis*, eight deities who were worshiped in four female-male pairs; the females were associated with snakes and the males with frogs: Naunet and Nu, Amaunet and Amun, Kauket and Kuk, Hahtet and Huh.

- ✓ The Ptah-Sekhmet-Nefertem triad of *Memphis*.

A number of major deities were considered as the creator of the cosmos. These include Atum, Ra, Amun (Amen) and Ptah among others, as well as some composite forms of these Gods, such as Amun-Ra. Each deity was responsible for an aspect of creation. The combination of aspects defined human existence.

Aken – ferryman to the underworld

Aker - deification of the horizon

Am-heh - minor underworld god

Ammit – crocodile-headed devourer in Duta, not a true deity

Amun or **Amen** – "the hidden one," a local creator deity later married to Mut after rising in importance

Amunet – female aspect of the primordial concept of air in the Ogdoad cosmogony; depicted as a cobra snake or a snake-headed woman

Andjety - god thought to be a precursor to Osiris

Anhur - god of war

Ankt - a minor war goddess

Anput - female aspect of Anubis

Anti - god of ferrymen

Anubis or **Yinepu** – dog or jackal God of embalming and tombs; the caretaker who watches over the dead

Anuket - gazelle-headed goddess of the Nile River, the child of Satis and among the Elephantine triad of deities

Apep or **Apophis** – evil serpent of the Underworld and enemy of Ra; formed from a length of Neith's spit during her creation of the world

Apis – bull deity worshiped in the Memphis region

Ash - god of oases and the vineyards of the western Nile Delta

The **Aten** – sun god worshiped primarily during the period of Atenism in the eighteenth dynasty when Pharoah Amenhotep IV (Akhenaten) introduced monotheistic worship

Atum – a creator deity, and the setting sun

Babi - baboon god associated with death and virility

Banebdjedet - ram god of fertility

Ba-Pef - minor underworld god

Bastet – protector of the pharaoh and solar goddess, depicted as a lioness, house cat, cat-bodied or cat-headed woman

Bat – cow goddess who gave authority to the king; her cult originated in Hu and persisted widely until absorbed as an aspect of Hathor after the eleventh dynasty

Bata - bull god

Bes – dwarfed demigod associated with protection of the household, particularly childbirth, and entertainment

Chenti-cheti - crocodile god

Geb –god of the Earth, first ruler of Egypt and husband of Nut

Ha - god of the western deserts

Hapi or **Hapy** – deification of the annual flooding of the Nile, associated with fertility

Hathor or **Hethert** – cow or cow-goddess of the sky, fertility, love, beauty and music

Hatmehit - fish goddess, originally a deification of the Nile River

Hedetet - scorpion goddess, later incorporated into Isis

Heka - deification of magic

Hemen - falcon god

Heqet – frog or a frog-headed goddess of childbirth and fertility

Hemsut - goddess of fate and protection

Heryshaf - ram god

Horus or **Heru** – falcon-headed god of the sky, pharaohs, war and protection

The four sons of Horus - personifications of the four canopic jars used to hold the internal organs after mummification

Hu - deification of the first word

Huh - deification of eternity

Iabet - goddess of the east, consort of Min and cleanser of Ra

Iah - god of the moon

Iat - minor goddess of milk and, by association, of nurturing and childbirth

Imenet - goddess of the necropolis west of the Nile

Isis or **Aset** – goddess of magic, motherhood and fertility and consort of Osiris; represented as the throne

Iusaaset – a primal goddess described as "the grandmother of all of the deities"

Kebechet - deification of embalming liquid

Kephri – the scarab beetle or scarab-headed god of rebirth and the sunrise

Kneph - a creator deity

Khnum – ram-headed creator god of the flooding of the Nile River

Khonsu – god of youth and the moon

Kuk –frog-headed personification of darkness, whose consort or female form was the snake-headed Kauket

Maahes – lion-headed god of war and weather.

Ma'at – goddess who personified concept of truth, balance, justice and order

Mafdet – goddess who protected against snakes and scorpions

Mehen - protective snake god which coils around the sun god Ra during his journey through the night

Menhit – goddess of war, associated with Sekhmet

Meret - goddess associated with rejoicing, singing and dancing

Meretseger – cobra-goddess of tomb builders and protector of royal tombs

Meskhenet – goddess of childbirth and the creator of each person's Ka, a part of their soul, which she breathed into them at the moment of birth

Min – god of fertility and lettuce, often represented as a man with an erect penis

Mnevis – the sacred bull of Heliopolis

Monthu - falcon god of war

Mut – mother goddess, associated with the waters from which everything was born

Nefertem - god of healing and beauty

Nehebkau - guardian of the entrance to the underworld

Neith – goddess of creation, weaving, war and the dead

Nekhbet – vulture goddess; patron of pharaohs and Upper Egypt

Neper - androgynous deification of grain

Nephthys or **Nebthet** – goddess of death, night and lamentation; the nursing mother of Horus and the pharaohs

Nu – deification of the primordial watery abyss

Nut – goddess of the sky and heavens

Osiris or **Wesir** – merciful judge of the dead in the afterlife and consort of Isis

Pakhet – a synthesis of Sekhmet and Bast

Petbe - god of revenge

Ptah – creator deity, also a god of craft

Qebui – god of the north wind

Ra – the sun, also a creator deity, whose chief cult center was based in Heliopolis

Rem - fish god who fertilizes the land with his tears

Renenutet - deification of the act of giving a true name during birth

Saa or **Sia** - deification of perception

Satet – goddess of war, hunting, fertility and the flooding of the Nile River

Sekmet – lioness goddess of destruction, pestilence and war; fierce protector of the pharaoh, and later as an aspect of Hathor

Seker or **Sokar** - falcon god of the necropolis at Memphis

Serket – scorpion goddess of healing stings and bites

Seshat – goddess of writing, astronomy, astrology, architecture, and mathematics; depicted as a scribe

Set or **Seth** – god of the desert, storms and foreigners; later god of chaos

Shai - deification of the concept of fate

Shed - savior deity

Shezmu - god of execution, slaughter, blood, oil and wine

Shu - personification of air

Sobek – crocodile God of the Nile; patron of the military

Sobkou - messenger god

Sopdet - deification of the star Sothuis (Sirius)

Sopdu - personification of the scorching heat of the sun

Ta-Bitjet - scorpion goddess identified as the consort of Horus

Tatenen - god of the primordial mound

Taweret – hippopotamus goddess of pregnant women and protector during childbirth

Tefnut – goddess of moisture, moist air, dew and rain.

Tenenet - goddess of beer

Thoth or **Djehuty** – ibis-headed god of the moon, drawing, writing, geometry, wisdom, medicine, music, astronomy and magic

Unut - snake goddess

Wadjet – snake goddess and protector of Lower Egypt

Wadj-wer – fertility God and personification of the Mediterranean Sea and the lakes of the Nile Delta

Weneg - plant god supporting the heavens

Werethekau - personification of supernatural powers

Wepwawet – jackal god of warfare and hunting

Wosret – a localized guardian Goddess, protector of the young God Horus; an early consort of Amun, later superseded by Mut

12

Conclusions

We Pagan men have it pretty good!

My survey indicated that after making a considered and thoughtful choice about how they wanted to express both their masculinity and their humanity, Pagan men felt that they consciously manifested exactly what was appropriate into their lives.

I have definitely felt for many years that Pagan men are content with the path they chose. I have known only a few men who, for various reasons, were Pagan for a time and then found another path to be more satisfying to them. Many of the men who responded to my survey indicated that they knew they were Pagans when they were very young children. There was always a sense that this path was the only one that made sense to them.

Here are some of the conclusions that I have drawn from the responses to the survey and from discussions with Pagan men over the years:

Overall, Pagan men are more satisfied with their lives than men in Abrahamic religions.

Pagan men are generally stable, loving partners, regardless of whether their relationship is heterosexual, gay or bisexual.

In general, Pagan men do not suffer from a sense of guilt or shame. They accept themselves, as they are, without wishing to be someone else. They accept others in the same way.

Gay and bisexual men feel a sense of welcome and acceptance in

Pagan traditions that does not exist in Abrahamic religions. This sentiment was expressed so often that it should have just been a checkbox at the top of the survey to make it easier for the men who responded to more easily articulate the thought.

Pagan men are more willing to accept so-called "feminine" energies, to do chores or jobs that are often considered "women's work," and they do it without drama or hidden agenda.

In relationships, Pagan men are more likely to participate in a more equal partnership. Most of them do not feel that "men should go out to work and women should stay home, barefoot and pregnant."

Pagan men realize that their partner is a full human being, on equal footing, with the same joy and sorrow that they experience. They do not consider men to be superior to women in any way that is important or meaningful.

Pagan men overwhelmingly believe in reincarnation. Life is a temporary situation. Those issues that cannot be resolved in this life will be resolved in another lifetime. Nothing is important enough to make them forget their spiritual connection to universal energy, regardless of how negative it looks while they are experiencing it.

Pagan men will attempt anything. Nothing in the physical world is permanent. To move on, one simply has to start. Pagan men are not afraid of starting something new.

Pagan men are loving, gentle men who encourage their male children to express their softer emotions. In my experience, this is not a group of football-loving, beer-guzzling he-man woman-haters who express all of the negative qualities of their masculinity and few (if any) of the positive ones.

Over the years, I have had deep and genuine friendships with many Pagan men. They value these relationships and work hard at them.

Pagan men understand that they can work practical magick to change aspects of their lives that they want to change. They rarely feel powerless; often the only time this happens is when a loved one becomes seriously ill and their normal response is fear and a sense of ineffectiveness. However, when they finally snap out of that state, they get down to business with the tools of their tradition to attempt to make a change. Many times their work is successful. And when it is not, they understand that other people have master plans for their lives that might not include being on the planet for eighty years.

On the same note, most Pagan men are not fearful of death. They realize that anything that is born will also someday die. It's part of the natural cycle of life, death and rebirth. Therefore, death is not a sad occasion, but instead a time to honor the person who has passed over and celebrate a life well lived, and then to move on to new adventures that will include new people.

Only a handful of the hundreds of men that I surveyed and with whom I have spoken over the years said that they felt their lives were chaotic or out of control. Even for these few men, there was little sense that the loss of control was a negative. In fact, several men said that they realized that the chaos they experienced (or continue to experience) is part of a life-long learning process. They are manifesting those issues in their lives that their spirit wanted to manifest. They felt protected, either by guardian spirits, their higher self, or the God and Goddess. The state of not being in complete control was something they welcomed, even though it often made their lives more difficult.

In general, Pagan men are happier with the quality of their lives and with the choices that they have made. Unlike those who feel like victims or who whine about anything that does not go as they would prefer, Pagan men accept the responsibility for everything they experience.

One man said, "As a living, breathing Pagan, there is no concept that I can identify with whatsoever that 'shit happens.' What we get in life, we need to get. Maybe we don't understand why. That's because we are living in the physical world where not everything is immediately apparent. But after death, it all becomes clear. Those things that you would prefer happening to someone else are most likely the experiences from which you can best grow and evolve as a human. There's nothing negative about that."

Thank You!

I want to offer thanks to all of those men who took time from their busy lives to answer the questions on the survey, and to add so much valuable insight through their additional comments. I also want to thank the hundreds of Pagan men I have personally met and talked with throughout the 42 years that I have experienced as a Pagan man. Every comment was a valuable signpost along the way. Life is easier when someone who has experienced the same issue or resolved the same problem can tell you how he did it. While those who offer advice are often ignored, those who simply state what they experienced and allow others to draw their own conclusions and use that experience as they see fit are a valuable resource.

Without all of this valuable input, this book could not have been written. Research on the internet and in books is possible, but not always accurate. The men who took the survey, and those with whom I've spoken over time, were brutally honest about their experience as Pagan men. It was genuinely satisfying to see that the Pagan lifestyle is viewed so positively by the men who live it. There was little sense of men questioning their life choices, or second-guessing. Looking back is always far easier than looking forward, but Pagan men overwhelmingly live in the present, with an eye on the future. They consider the past to be valuable material for learning, but their past does not dictate their future. They welcome change. They seek it every day. Where there is chaos, they make a hearty attempt to find meaning. It doesn't work every time, but it's far better than sitting around bemoaning a life that looks dismal from the vantage point of the moment.

Pagan men learn early in life to listen to other Pagan men. Life is easier when the journey is shared. At times, life can be overwhelming; it is exactly at those times when your friendship and camaraderie with other Pagans, both male and female, becomes vitally important.

I sincerely hope that this book provides some insight along your path. Blessings to you!

13

Appendix —
Magickal Correspondences

The Appendix contains lists of magickal correspondences that you can use as an aid in your rituals or practical magick. Remember, these are aids — not requirements. For example, you can use a candle of any color and as long as you focus your will and intention properly, any color will work. If you feel your results might be enhanced by using some of these magickal correspondences, feel free to adapt them.

Obviously, none of this is chiseled in stone. Always use what works for you!

Wood

Here is a list of various tree species and their suggested correlations. As with any tool, how you feel about it personally is of the utmost importance. This table is intended to be a guide for those Pagans who need some background information, not a list of absolutes. Everything is relative!

If a substitute is included, you can use that species of wood instead.

Species of Trees and Their Energetic Quality

Tree Species	Masculine Energy	Feminine Energy	Deity Associations	Used for:
Alder	X		Bran	Astral protection, journeys, spiritual growth, self-confidence, bravery, teaching
Apple		X	Venus, Rhiannon, Elves and Fairies	Fertility, peace, joy, abundance, love, working with fairy realm, psychic vision, peace, harmony
Ash		X	Neptune, Mercury, Odin, Gwydion, Yggdrasil	Communication, intelligence, wisdom, curiosity, prevent unwanted change, protection, prosperity, healing Substitute: Cedar, Rowan
Basswood		X	Aphrodite, Arianrhod	Creativity, love and attraction, healing, enchantment
Beech		X	Apollo, Oberaash	Divination (runes are often beechwood), mental balance, connection to ancestors and ancient wisdom Substitute: Spruce
Birch		X	Druids, Thor, Diana, Cerridwen	New beginnings, birth or rebirth, renewal, heal wounds, calm emotions, protection, working with the moon
Cedar		X	Persephone	Cleanse negativity, create sacred spaces, longevity, protection, preservation Substitute: Ash
Cherry	X	X	Artemis, Morrigan, Tyr, Mars, Aries, Herne, Ambash	Centering and grounding, divination, healing, love, hunting, working with animals and familiars, detection and amplification

Tree Species	Masculine Energy	Feminine Energy	Deity Associations	Used for:
Elder	X		Cailleach Beara	Banishment, magick, cause change, healing, prosperity, protection from evil, and work with fairies Substitute: Elderberry
Elm		X	Crone (Great Goddess)	Fertility, passage through death and rebirth, invoke the Goddess, stability, grounding, spellwork
Fir	X	X	Dagda, Druids	Aid and improve divination Substitute: Oak
Hawthorn	X		Olwen, Aquarius, Vashaan	Protection of homes, psychic protection, creativity, self-confidence, patience, conceal magick, male potency, fairy magick
Hazel		X	Aphrodite, Danus, Arianrhod	Magickal knowledge, love, creativity, cause change, art, wisdom, intelligence, navigation, wrath, optimism, manifestation
Hemlock	X	X	Mars, Lugh, Tammuz, Thor	Transfer power, protection against lightning and poisons, aid sleep, ease losses related to death, calm emotions, revenge, beauty, unconditional love, sacrifice, reincarnation, sex magick Substitute: Holly
Hickory	X		Lugh, Apollo	Abundance, acquisition, leadership
Honey Locust	X	X	Inanna, Ishtar, Cernunnos	Protection, binding, beauty and physical appearance, work with fairies
Holly	X	X	Mars, Lugh, Tammuz, Thor	Transfer power, protect against lightning and poisons, aid sleep, ease losses related to death, calm emotions, revenge, beauty, unconditional love, sacrifice, reincarnation, sex magick Substitute: Hemlock

Tree Species	Masculine Energy	Feminine Energy	Deity Associations	Used for:
Ivy	X		Herne, Pan, Cernunnos, the Green Man	Strength, optimism, spiritual growth, protection, guard against spirits and elementals, business, healing, cooperation, promote success in new endeavors
Lilac	X	X	Pan	Love, romance, passion, communication, concentration, sexuality, protection during travel
Maple	X	X	Apollo, Pan, Isis, Diana, Venus	Spiritual healing, intellect, travel, communication, beauty, binding, abundance, attract gold and love
Oak	X		Dagda, Druids	Truth, knowledge, protection, vitality and long life, mental focus, improve intuition and observation, bravery, leadership, prosperity, strength, fidelity Substitute: Fir
Osage Orange	X		Diana, Isis, Ishtar, Inanna, Osiris	Repel pests, prevent rot, astral healing, work with spirit and animal guides, pursuit of goals and pleasure
Poplar	X		Venus	Diverse energy that can be used for any task, evocation, redirection, banishing, hope, rebirth, divination
Pine	X		Artemis, Ariadne, Rhea, Cybele, Druantia, Erigone, Dionysus, Bacchus, Merlin, Pan, Attis	Birth, abundance, health, fortune, fertility, love, prosperity, protect the home, purification, divination, eliminate negativity, ease guilt

Tree Species	Masculine Energy	Feminine Energy	Deity Associations	Used for:
Redwood	X	X	Thor, Orion	Access universal energy, permanence, connect with nature/wild animals/hunting, eternal life (redwood roots never die and continue to sprout)
Rowan	X	X	Brigid, Thor	Meditation, open and clear the mind, power, protection from harm, attraction, spiritual enlightenment, life force, divination and prophecy, flirtation and romance Substitute: Ash
Sassafras	X	X	Hygieia	Cure physical ailments, increase hunger, provide restful sleep, digestion, prosperity
Spruce	X		Apollo, Oberaash	Divination (runes are often beechwood), mental balance, connection to ancestors and ancient wisdom Substitute: Beech
Vine	X	X	Herne, Pan, Cernunnos, Diana, Inanna	Spiritual initiation, work with fairies, joy, excitement, rebirth, authority, sacred knowledge
Walnut (Black)	X	X	Vashaan, Zeus, Jupiter, Thor, Vishnu	Astral travel, weather working, avert lightning strikes, wind, breath, motivation, transitions
Willow		X	Diana, Hecate, Astarte, Ceriddwen, Arianrhod, Rhiannon, Omulan	Cycles of death and rebirth, develop or strengthen will, change, vitality, ensure success with magick, love, emotion, increase psychic ability, divination, aid souls of recently deceased

Tree Species	Masculine Energy	Feminine Energy	Deity Associations	Used for:
Yew		X	Artemis, Persephone, Hecate, Astarte, Odin, Crone Goddess	Immortality, rebirth, protection, longevity, change, divinity, strength, guard souls of the deceased, rules the underworld, perseverence

How a tree grows indicates its possible uses for ritual and magick. Trees that reach high into the sky can be used for spirituality, growth, and improvement of any type. Trees that have weeping branches can be used to alleviate sadness or elevate mood. Trees that are spiky or thorny can be used projectively to combat problems or sooth disruptive energy. Trees that have a strong odor, like cedar, pine or spruce, are associated with projective energy, healing and comfort. If the odor is strong, the energy of the tree is more projective than if it were a weaker odor. Trees bearing fruit promote love, joy and abundance.

Because plants are living, sentient beings, each individual plant has qualities that are its own, just like humans. This is why it is often advisable to go out into the woods and find a tree of the type with which you want to work. Cutting your own branch from a living tree (after asking the tree for its help and its gift of the branch) increases the amount of energy contained in that piece of wood. Although some Pagans advocate using dead wood that has dropped from the tree naturally, I feel that once the life force has left the wood, it limits its usefulness for magick and ritual.

Trees and plants are unlike humans in one important way. If you cut an arm off a human, it won't grow back. But if you cut a branch from a tree, the tree simply creates a new branch, either in the same spot on the trunk or somewhere else.

Metals

Here is a list of various metals and their suggested correlations. As with any tool, how you feel about it personally is of the utmost importance.

This table is intended to be a guide for those Pagans who need some background information, not a list of absolutes. Everything is relative!

Metals can be associated with all forms of deity. Consider the results you seek from the ritual or spell and choose a metal that contains that vibration.

Metals and Their Energetic Quality

Metal	Masculine Energy	Feminine Energy	Associations
Gold	X		Sun, daylight, strong projective energy, vitality, success, happiness
Silver		X	Night, moonlight, strong receptive energy, sensitivity, family, children
Copper	X	X	Unconditional love, art
Brass	X		A combination of copper and zinc. Unconditional love, art, resolution, determination
Iron and Steel	X		Determination, solidity, union
Bronze	X		A combination of copper and tin. Unconditional love, art, communication, understanding, action
Tin	X	X	Communication, understanding, action
Lead	X	X	Containment, reduction, suppression, self-fulfillment, divine awareness, spirituality

Color

The human eye can discern an incredibly vast range of color. For example, consider the differences between baby blue, sky blue, florescent blue and midnight blue. If you look at a color sample that contains blues, you can easily recognize whether the blue is sky blue or midnight blue. If you're painting a room, the hue you pick can have significant impact.

The same is true for how you use color for rituals or spellcasting. While the use of one color over another does not guarantee the results you would like to occur, you can use color as a tool to help your subconscious link to universal energy.

Color correspondences are variable in different parts of the world. For example, in the USA, we link money and wealth with the color green, because the reverse side of our paper money is printed with green ink. In another country that does not use green ink, that same correspondence would be much less effective. Australian certificates are printed using a reddish-brown ink. A Pagan in Australia would probably have better results using that color instead of green.

As with any issue in the Pagan realm, you are the ultimate source. If you believe that a rosy pink will attract wealth, then use that color. The influences that you hold as truth within yourself are always the correct ones, for you, in that particular time and space. Those influences change over time and perhaps as you move about in the world. Always use what feels right.

Another sticky point is in attempting to clearly define a color. If you gave three people an unlimited palette of colors and asked them to paint an area of blue, pink and green, it is very likely that the three samples would differ significantly. For example, there could be light blue, dark blue, and indigo blue, each of which is a good descriptive of the color blue for the person who chose them. There is no absolute list for color. The list of color correspondences outlined here can provide a jumping off point to help you determine what might work in your specific case. In working different rituals, you might choose several different shades or hues of a color because one seems to fit the ritual more appropriately. Allow your intuition to influence your choices.

Note: The list of color correspondences below is based on one that I printed a while back from a website, but did not note the website URL. I have updated this list over time. If you are the owner of the website, please contact the publisher.

Color Correspondences

Color	Used for:
Black	Completion; endings; closing of doors; psychic work; death; repel negativity; protection; spirit contact; truth; remove discord or confusion; reversing; releasing; repel negative thoughtforms.
Brown	Earth elemental; animal health; endurance; steadiness; houses and homes; physical objects; overcoming uncertainty and hesitancy; attract money and financial success; concentration; ESP; intuition; study.
Blue (dark)	West; the goddess; water elemental; inspiration; truth; dreams; protection; change; impulse; fidelity; deep emotion; peace; meditation; changeability; psychic ability.
Blue (light)	Healing; patience; happiness; psychic awareness; quests; intuition; opportunity; tranquility; understanding; eliminate depression; safe journey; harmony in the home; peace.
Gold	The god; solar energy; physical strength; power; success; mental growth; improve skills; healing energy; fortune; divination; creative work; intuition; money; fast luck; attract higher influences.
Gray	Faerie magic; travel to other realms; vision quests; veiling and concealing; cancellation; hesitation; competition.
Green	North; money; fertility; growth; employment; earth elemental; herb magick; luck; healing; balance; prosperity; courage; nature type faerie-magick; garden blessing; abundance; generosity; renewal; marriage.
Greenish-yellow	To negate; discord, sickness, jealousy, cowardice, anger, animosity.
Indigo	Meditation; spirit communication; working with karma; balance; learn ancient wisdom; neutralize magick created by others; eliminate slander, lies or undesirable competition.
Lavender	Spiritual development; psychic growth; divination; sensitivity to other realms; blessings.
Magenta	Sudden change; spiritual healing, exorcism. Has a very high spiritual vibration that tends to work quickly, so usually used with other colors.
Orange	The god; attraction; stimulation; energy; healing; vitality; encouragement; adaptability; luck; clearing the mind; dominance, sudden change; change of luck.

Color	Used for:
Pink	Love; peace; femininity; friendship; honor; morality; emotional love; affection; romance; spiritual awakening; healing of the spirit; togetherness.
Purple	Power; dignity; spiritual development; meditation, spirituality; intuition; ambition; spirit communication; tension; business progress; healing severe diseases; occult wisdom; success; idealism; improve psychic ability; eliminate bad luck; drive away evil; honors.
Red	South; protection; strength; issues with the blood; passion; courage; health; power; fire elemental; sexuality; vigor; energy; enthusiasm; willpower; to conquer fear or laziness.
Silver	The goddess; lunar magick; remove negative forces; open astral gates; conduct energy; meditation; creative work; protection; money; psychic development; success; balance; eliminate negative energy; stability; victory.
Violet	Self-improvement; intuition; success in searches; creativity.
White	Represents the self; protection; purification; full moon magick; purity; innocence; centering; truth; sincerity; meditation; peace; power of a higher nature; greater attainments in life; spirituality.
Yellow	East; air elemental; intellect; creativity; learning; change; confidence; attraction; harmony; clairvoyance; charm; imagination; power of the mind; gentle persuasion; action.

The qualities of color are often associated with candles, among other tools. Many Pagans believe that using a candle of a color that corresponds to the intention behind its employment increases the chances for effectiveness. However, remember that candles, like any other tools, are useful for focusing and directing energy. They have no extra or special quality; they are simply an adjunct to your will and intention.

Animals

Certain animals are associated with either a god or goddess archetype. Here are some of the more common interpretations. The list is arranged alphabetically.

Masculine (God)	Feminine (Goddess)
Boar	Bear
Bull	Cat
Eagle	Dog
Fish	Horse
Snake	Owl
Stag	Rabbit
Wolf	Spider

Astrology

In astrology, various cosmic bodies are associated with either God or Goddess energy. Here are some of the more common interpretations.

Masculine (God)	Feminine (Goddess)
Sun	Moon
Mercury	Venus
Earth	Mars
Neptune	Jupiter
Uranus	Saturn
The Milky Way Galaxy	Pluto

Index

A

Abderus 54
Abrahamic religions 3, 37, 59, 63
  definition 4, 50
absolute belief 83
abundance 162, 168, 186, 187, 188,
  190, 193
abyss 179
acceptance 181
accessing energy
  feminine 98
  masculine 98
  universal 189
Acheron 146
Achilles 54, 146
acquisition 187
action 191, 194
act of giving a true name during birth
  179
adaptability 193
adapting Goddess rituals for men 96
additional tools 106
Adonis 122, 125, 128, 130
Aegis 131
affection 194
afterlife 139, 144, 162, 164, 179
Agamemnon 130
aggression 129, 132
agnostics 3
agriculture 135, 168
Agwe 143, 160
aid souls of recently deceased 189

air 104, 106, 110, 176, 179, 194
air (Gardnerian Wicca) 104
Aken 175
Aker 175
Akh 132
Alaha 129
albinos 138
Alcmena 149
alder 186
alive and abundant 41
alleviate sadness 190
altar 117
  placement 118
  Wiccan 118
Ambash 186
ambition 194
Ameinias 54
Amen 175, 176
Am-heh 175
Ammit 176
Ampelus 54
amplification 186
amulets 115
Amun 175, 176, 180, 126
Amunet 176
Amun-Ra 126, 175
Anaisa Pye 160
Anat 131
ancestors 186, 189
Anchises 127
ancient wisdom 186, 189, 193
Andjety 176

androgynous 178
anger 193
Anhur 176
animals 41, 135, 186
  correspondences 194
  guides 188
  health 193
animism 4
animosity 193
Ankt 176
Anna 154
annual regeneration 42
Anput 176
antlered 135
Anubis 176
Anuket 176
anvil 148
Apep 176
Aphrodite 54, 122, 125, 127, 128, 130,
    142, 148, 150, 153, 166, 186,
    187
Aphroditus 54
Apis 128, 133, 167, 176
Apollo 54, 55, 57, 122, 125, 126, 129,
    140, 162, 186, 187, 188, 189
Apophis 176
Appendix 185
apple 186
Aquarius 187
Aradia 122
archetypes 7, 9, 39, 42, 55, 57, 121,
    125, 194
  definition 46
architecture 179
Ares 126, 127, 128, 130, 142, 148,
    162, 174
Ariadne 188
Arianrhod 122, 145, 186, 187, 189
Aries 186
aristocrats 156
armor 172
arms 172
arrow 135

art 163, 172, 191
Artemides 131
Artemis 55, 122, 125, 126, 127, 129,
    139, 147, 186, 188, 190
artisans 148, 156
artistic aspect 47
Asatru 3, 47, 49, 105
Asclepius 125, 127
Aset 177
asexual priests 153
ash 186, 189
Ash 176
Asherah 131
aspects of the divine 122
Astarte 122, 127, 130, 189, 190
astral
  body 75
  healing 188
  protection 186
  travel 189
  world 75
astrology 179
astronomy 179, 180
Aten 176
athame 103, 104
  and blood 105
  length 104
  uses 104
atheists 3
Athena 122, 125, 131, 132, 141, 159,
    163
athletes 150
athletics 150
Atlas 174
Attis 188
attract
  higher influences 193
  money 193
attraction 186, 189, 193, 194
Atum 151, 167, 175, 176
authority 59, 189
Avalon 58
Awen 136

axe 148
Ayida Weddo 138, 160
Ayizan 160

B

Ba 132
Ba'alat Gebal 131
Babi 176
Babylonian 153
  deities 125
Bacchus 132, 140, 188
bad 85
Bakha 132
balance 48, 178, 193, 194
  in Wicca 10
Banebdjedet 176
banishing 188
  and sulfur 107
  stress 107
Ba-Pef 176
Barbara Straub 42
Baron Cimetiere 133
Baron Kriminel 133
Baron LaCroix 133
Barons 160
Baron Samedi 133
basswood 186
Bast 179
Bastet 176
Bat 176
Bata 176
battle 129, 137, 144
bear 195
beauty 51, 54, 135, 142, 143, 144, 146,
      147, 177, 178, 187, 188
beech 186, 189
beer 180
beeswax 110
beginnings 41, 158, 186
belief and reality 34
bell 109
berdache 58
berries 119

Bes 176
besom 108
between the worlds 58
binding 113, 187, 188
birch 186
birth 41, 159, 178, 186, 188
birth, death and rebirth 4, 109
bisexuality 133
bisexual men 13, 40, 53, 56
black 68, 193
Black Madonna of Czestochowa 143
black magic 134
blacksmith 148
black walnut 189
Bleiddwn 145
blessings 109, 193
blockages in magick 96
blood 78, 106, 148, 179, 194
  and athames 105
bloodshed 128
blue (dark) 193
blue (light) 193
boar 195
Bohr's Theory of Energy 32
boldness 129
boline 104, 106
  and blood 106
  uses 106
Bona Dea 134, 164
Bon Dieu 159
Bondye 159
bones 138
Book of Mirrors 112
Book of Shadows 111
  uses for 111
borders 140, 147, 148
Born of Trees 144
boundaries 135, 150, 158
bounty 109
boxing 150
Bran 186
Branchus 54
brass 114, 191

bravery 46, 130, 186, 188
bread 134
breasts 150
breath 189
Bres 135
brews 109
Brighid 135
Brigid 135, 137, 189
bring rain to crops 42
bronze 114, 191
broom 108
broom (plant) 108
brown 193
Buddhists 2
bull 131, 132, 173, 176, 178, 195
business 188, 194

C

Cadmus of Thebes 141
caduceus 162
Caelus 168
Cailleach Beara 187
cakes 143
Calliope 125
Callisto 55
calm emotions 186, 187
calm seas 165
Campe 174
cancellation 193
candles 110
Capitoline Triad 159
care 140
caretaker 176
cat 195
cattle 132, 143
cauldron 109, 136, 137
cedar 186, 190
Celtic 49, 105
censer 106
centering 186, 194
ceramic 106
cereal 139
Cerebus 146

Ceres 134, 135, 166, 167, 169
Ceriddwen 189
Cernunnos 41, 122, 135, 187, 188, 189
Cerridwen 110, 122, 136, 186
chalice 102, 104, 105
chameleons 138
champion 150
change 39, 158, 189, 190, 193, 194
changeability 193
change of luck 193
changing reality 8
chaos 179, 183
chaotic 140
charms 115, 194
Charon 125, 146
chastity 134, 139
cheating 150
Chenti-cheti 177
cherry 186
childbirth 126, 129, 139, 147, 153, 177, 178, 180
children 191
Chione 166
choosing an ethical path 70
Christianity 37
chromosomes
  and sexuality 45
  and spirituality 40
Chrysippus 54
cigars 134
Cimitiere 160
cingulum 113
circle 59
city gates 158
clairvoyance 194
clay 115
cleanse negativity 186
clearing the mind 193
clockwise 108
closing of doors 193
cobra 178
cockerel 162
Cocytus 146

codes of behavior 84
coffee 134
coffins 157
cold and desolate 41
color
  and magick 68
  correspondences 191
  for candles 110
  of cingulum 113
  using in magick and ritual 192
combat problems 190
comfort 190
comical 137
commerce 150, 163
  success in 162
common sense 11
communication 186, 188, 191
  with spirits 194
communion 74
community 170
companion of the nymphs 164
compassion 45, 143
competition 193
completion 193
concealing 193
concentration 188, 193
conduct energy 194
confidence 194
confusion 193
conquer
  fear 194
  laziness 194
conscious 86
consecration of tools 102
containment 191
continuity 164
control
  spirits 104
  weather 157
cooperation 188
Copenhagen Interpretation 32
copper 191
cornucopia 134

corpse 133
correspondences
  animals 194
  astrological 195
  colors 191
  metals 190
  woods 185
cosmic equilibrium 138
cotton 138
courage 45, 128, 129, 193, 194
cow 148, 176, 177
cowardice 193
cowherds 150
crafts 163, 169
craftsmanship 135
craftsmen 148, 168
create
  new islands 165
  sacred spaces 186
creation 77, 140, 167, 178
creative
  aspect 47
  visualization 75
  work 193
creativity 186, 194
creator 138, 176, 178, 179, 125
Creirwy 136
crescent moon 106
cripples 138
crocodile 177, 179
crone 122, 147, 187, 190
Cronus 127, 137, 140, 146, 148, 168,
    173, 174
crops 41, 162
crossroads 133, 147
crude 137
crystal 114
  and wands 104
  balls 119
  points 114
cunning 163
cup 105
Cupid 125, 137, 142, 167

cures physical ailments 189
curiosity 186
curses 134
cutting 106
Cybele 139, 142, 188
cycle
  of life and death 138
  renewal of time 159
Cyclopes 127, 147, 169, 174
Cyparissus 55, 127
Cypris 128, 130
Cytherea 128

D

Dagda 135, 137, 187, 188
Damballa 138, 143
Damballa Wedo 160
Damia 134
dancing 140, 143, 178
danger 140, 147
Danus 187
Danuzi 41
Daphnis 54
darkness 140, 178
daylight 191
dead 133, 141, 142, 146, 147, 164,
  176, 178
death 41, 133, 136, 138, 144, 146, 148,
  176, 178, 183, 187, 193
  and rebirth 189
debauchery 133
deception 163
deep emotion 193
defining magick 77
deformed 138
deities
  and sexuality 123
  unnamed or unknown 125
deity-centered 3
delivery 139, 159
Demeter 138, 141, 142, 144, 147, 169,
  173, 175
depression 193

descent
  of Inanna 142
  of Ishtar 142
  to the underworld 154
desert 152, 157, 179
desire 131, 142
destruction 137, 170, 179
detection 186
determination 191
develop will 189
dew 180
Diana 57, 139, 142, 147, 175, 186,
  188, 189
difficulty in accessing masculine traits
  for women 49
digestion 189
dignity 194
Di Manes 135
Dimuzi 155
Dionysus 41, 54, 122, 125, 140, 144,
  150, 166, 188
directing 101
  energy 114
disapproval 56
discord 6, 128, 193
disease 133
disruption 133
disruptive energy 190
diversity of paths 59
divination 109, 119, 186, 188, 189,
  193
divine
  awareness 191
  feminine 3
  law 129, 138
  manifestation of male energy 41
  masculine 3
divinity 190
Djehuty 180
doctrine 63
dogma 63
dogs 129, 147, 195
dominance 193

doorways 109, 147, 158
doubt 79
doves 128, 130
downtrodden 156
drawing 180
dreadful 132
dream
  interpretation 119, 157
  world 78
dreams 193
drinking 133
drive away evil 194
drownings 165
Druantia 188
Druidism 49
Druids 3, 186, 187, 188
Dumballah Nan Flambo 138
Dumuzi 153
Dustin Hoffman 81
Dylan 145

E

eagle 173, 195
Eanna 153
Earth 104, 111, 114, 131, 163, 177,
  193, 195
earth-centered 3
earthquakes 165, 168
ease guilt 188
East 177, 194
Echidna 174
Echo 165, 175
ecstasy 140
egg 138, 142
Egyptian deities 125
Eileithyia 175
Einstein's Theory of Relativity 31
Eir 144
El 131
Elatha 137
Elder 124
elder (wood) 187
electrical energy. 52

elementals 78, 104, 188
Elephantine triad 176
Eleusinian Mysteries 138, 142
elevate mood 190
Elffin ap Gwyddno 137
eliminate
  bad luck 194
  depression 193
  negativity 188, 194
  slander 193
eliminate negativity 107, 109
elm 187
eloquence 54, 135
Elves 186
embalming 176, 177
E=mc2 31
emotional love 194
emotions 186, 187, 189
empathy 51
employment 193
enchantment 186
enchantress 136
encouragement 193
endings 41, 158, 193
endurance 150, 193
energetic realms 77
energy 31, 193, 194
  definition 31
  that can be used for any task 188
England 113
Enki 154
Enkidu 154
Enlil 154
Ennead of Heliopolis 175
entertainment 177
enthusiasm 194
entrance 147
  to the underworld 178
Enyalius 128
Enyo 128
Eos 125
Ephesus 130, 147
epilepsy 166

epiphany 140
equal partners 182
Erebus 142, 146
erection 166, 178
Ereshkigal 122, 142, 154
Erigone 188
Erinyes 169
Eris 128, 175
Eros 54, 125, 128, 131, 142
Erotes 54
Erymanthus 126
Erzulie 143
  Dantor 143, 160
  Freda 138, 143, 160
Esbats 10
ESP (extra-sensory perception) 193
eternal
  life 177
  youthfulness 159
eternal life 189
eternity 177
ethics 84
  for Pagans 63
  in magick 68
Ethlinn 137
ettins 170
Europa 175
Euryale 54, 132
Eurystheus 149
evil 9
evocation 188
evoke good energy 109
exalted one 135
excellence 135
excitement 189
execution 179
exorcism 193
extramarital sex 153
extrasensory perception 33
eye of Horus 152

F

faerie magick 193

faggots 55
fair 10
fairies 42, 186, 187, 189
faith 29, 30
falcon 177, 178, 179
familiars 186
family 171, 191
fate 177, 179
  of women 134
Fates 129
father 137, 138
Fauna 134, 164
fauns 144, 164
Faunus 134, 143, 164
fear 128, 140, 194
feminine
  animal associations 195
  energy 9, 57, 60, 137
  men 153
  physiological functions 159
femininity 194
feminists 10
fertility 41, 42, 128, 130, 134, 135,
       142, 143, 144, 153, 156, 162,
       164, 166, 167, 170, 176, 177,
       178, 179, 180, 122, 186, 188,
       193
  of the earth 138
  of the land 179
fidelity 188, 193
fields 143, 164
financial success 193
fir 187, 188
fire 104, 106, 110, 146, 148, 150, 171,
       172, 194
  in Gardnerian Wicca 104
fish 177, 179, 195
flagellate 114
flames 135, 138
flaming faggot 55
flirtation 189
flocks 164
flooding 177, 178, 179

Flora 162
flowers 143
focus 101
foliage 42
folk magick 73, 80
Folkvangr 144
food of the dead 167
force 78
foreigners 179
forest 143
fortune 188, 193
foul-mindedness 166
four sons of Horus 177
freedom 129
free will 81
fresh water 163
Freya 144
friendship 194
Frigg 144, 163
frog 177, 178
fruit 166
fruitfulness 170
fruit trees 137
full moon magick 194
funeral rites 135
funerary 128
Furies 169
fury 163

G

Gaia 130, 139, 142, 146, 151, 165, 174
galaxy 195
Ganymede 55, 144
garden gnome 166
gardens 166, 193
Gardnerian Wicca 114
gates 147, 158
gay men 13, 40, 53, 56, 58, 143
Geb 156, 164, 177
gender 45
generosity 193
genii 144
gentle 182

geometry 180
Gerald Gardner 46
ghosts 135, 147
Gigantes 174
Gilfaethwy 144
Gilgamesh 154
giver of life 133
Glastonbury 113
Glaucus 55
goat 162
goblet 105
god 193
    animal associations 195
god and goddess resource list 123
goddess 109, 193, 194
    animal associations 195
    of children 156
Goddess Above 122
goddess-based rituals
    adapting for Pagan men 96
Goddess Below 122
Goddess of the Future 122
Goddess of the Past 122
Goddess of the Present 122
Goddess Within 122
God of Light 122
God of Shadow 122
gods and goddesses 121
Goewin 144
Gofannon 145
gold (color) 193
gold (metal) 114, 144, 188, 191
good 85
Good God 137
Good Goddess 134
Gorgon 132
grain 105, 128, 135, 138, 178
grandmother 177
grapes 140
gray 193
Great Goddess 187
Great Horned God 40, 116
Great Lady Under Earth 142

Great Mother 134
green 193
greenery 41
Green Man 3, 41, 42, 122, 188
green-yellow 193
grimoire 112
grounding 186
groves 164
growth 39, 42, 166, 190, 193
guardian 180
guardian angel 81
guard souls of the deceased 190
Gugalana 142, 154
guidelines for a Pagan life 64
guilt 56, 181
Gwion 136
Gwyddien 144
Gwydion 144, 186

H

Ha 177
habitation 170
Hadad 131
Hades 127, 146, 151, 156, 165, 169, 173, 174
Hadrian 159
halt storms 109
handfasting 108
handicapped 138
Hapi 177
happiness 191, 193
Hapy 177
harlots 150
harmony 186, 194
  in the home 193
harp 137
harvest 106, 138, 140, 161, 168
  grasses 105
hate 146
Hathor 128, 133, 151, 156, 176, 177, 179
Hatmehit 177
hawthorn 187

hazel 187
healers 139
healing 134, 135, 170, 178, 186, 188, 190, 193, 194
  of the spirit 194
  severe diseases 194
  stings and bites 179
  wounds 186
health 166, 188, 194
heart 143
hearth 135, 171
Heaven 7, 163
heavens 179, 180
Hebe 174,
Hecate 125, 130, 147, 151, 189, 190
Hecatonchires 174
Hedetet 177
hedonists 3
Heka 177
Helios 125, 148
Hell 7
Hemen 177
hemlock 187
Hemsut 177
Hephaestus 127, 128, 131, 132, 148, 172, 174
Heqet 177
Hera 126, 127, 128, 141, 147, 148, 149, 152, 159, 162, 166, 169, 173, 174, 175
Heracles 54, 146, 149
herb magick 193
herbs 111, 116
Hercules 149
herds 128
Hermaphrodite 150
hermaphrodites 54, 150
hermaphroditic priests 153
Hermaphroditus 54
Hermes 54, 125, 141, 147, 150, 162, 166
Herne 41, 42, 151, 186, 188, 189
hero 144

Heru 177
Heryshaf 177
hesitation , 193
Hestia 147, 152, 169, 171, 173
heterosexual men 13, 40, 56
Hethert 177
hex 134
hickory 187
hidden one 176
high dimensions 135
higher self 81, 82, 84
highlands 135
high priest 59
high priestess 59
hill-forts 135
Himeros 54
Hindus 2
Hippolytus 127, 130
hippopotamus 180
holly 187
home 135, 171, 193
honey 140
honey locust 187
honors , 194
hope 188
horizon 175
horned 135
horns 143
horse 128, 130, 195
Horus 131, 151, 156, 162, 164, 177,
     179, 180
Horus and Set 152
hostile forces of nature 162
house cat 176
household 176
houses 193
how magick works 33
how ritual works 33
Hu 177
Huh 177
human babies 41
humanity 181
humility 45

hunger 189
hunt 41, 139
hunting 130, 152, 164, 179, 180, 186,
     189
hurricane 168
Hyacinth 54, 127, 153
Hychddwn 145
Hyddwn 145
Hygieia 189
Hylas 54
Hymenaios 54

I

Iabet 177
Iacchus 141
Iah 177
Iambe 165
Ianthe 55
Iapis 54
Iat 177
ibis 180
idealism 194
ignorant savage 3
Ilithyia 126
imagination 194
Imenet 177
immortality 149, 164, 190
  of the spirit 4
impassibility 139
impotence 166
improvement 190
improve skills 193
impulse 193
inaccessibility 139
Inanna 41, 122, 142, 153, 187, 188,
     189
incarnation 57
incense 106, 111
increase hunger 189
indifference 139
indignation 129
indigo 193
industry 148

infernal spirits 147
initiation 114
innocence 194
Ino 141
inscribing candles 106
inspiration 136, 163, 193
instant magick 124
intellect 138, 188, 194
intelligence 135, 186
intention 79, 185
  in magick 72
intuition 11, 188, 193, 194
Inuus 143
invention 150
invisibility 147
Invisibles 159
invoking the Great Horned God 42
Io 175
Iolaus 54
Iphigenia 130
Iphis 55
Irkalla 142
iron 172, 191
ironsmithing 135
Isaac Bonewits 3
Isaac Newton 31
Ishtar 41, 142, 153, 156, 187, 188
Isis 42, 58, 131, 152, 156, 164, 171,
      177, 179, 188
Iusaaset 177
ivory 138
ivy 140, 188

J

jackal 180
Janus 41, 158
jealousy 56, 143, 148, 193
jewelry 114, 143, 172
Joan of Arc 143
journal 111
  uses for 111
journeys , 186
Jove 159

joy 186, 189, 190
  in rituals 95
judge of the dead 42, 146, 164, 179
judgment 9, 142
Juno 148, 158, 159, 162, 169, 172
Juno's chair 173
Jupiter 149, 159, 162, 163, 166, 167,
      169, 172, 173, 189
Jupiter (planet) 195
justice 168, 178

K

Ka 132
Kabbalah 115
Kalais 55
Kali 122
karma 80, 193
  and magick 65
Kauket 178
Kebechet 177
Kephri 178
Kernunnos 136
Khnum 178
Khonsu 178
Khu 132
King Athamas 141
kingship 128
Kneph 178
knives 143
knowledge 131, 135, 188
Kore 122
Kriminel 160
Kuk 178
Kydoimos 129

L

Labors of Hercules 149
LaCroix 160
Lady 144
Laius 54
lakes 163
  and Mediterranean Sea 180
lame 148

lamentation 146, 178
LaSirene 160
lavender
  color 193
  herb 107
laws 135, 142
laziness 194
lazy 143
lead
  crystal 106
  metal 105, 191
leadership 187, 188
learning 194
Leda 175
Legba 160
lesbianism 53
lesbians 54, 58, 143
Lethe 146
Leto 126, 127, 129, 175,
lettuce 178
liberator 140
lies 193
life 41, 136, 138, 164, 167
  death and rebirth 136, 183
  force 8, 132, 189
  path 79, 80
light 139, 140
lightning 170, 174, 187, 189
lilac 188
lion 130, 178
lioness 131, 176, 179
liqueurs 143
literature 150
Little Big Man 81
livestock 41, 42, 166
Lleu Llaw Gyffes 144
Loa 159
  Kongo 160
  Nago 160
  Petro 160
  Rada 159
logic 11
Loko 160

longevity 186, 190
longing 131
long life 188
loss
  of control 183
  of the Goddess 50
Lotis 166
love 10, 48, 51, 143, 144, 147, 153,
        177, 181, 182, 186, 187, 188,
        189, 190, 191, 194
Lower Egypt 152
loyalty 54
luck 193
Lugh 122, 160, 187
Luna 122, 139
lunar
  lore 147
  magick 194
luxury 143
lyre 150, 162

M

Maahes 178
Ma'at 178
Mabinogion 136, 168
Mabon 122
madness 163
maenads 140, 165
Mafdet 178
magenta 193
magic 30, 144, 147, 156, 163, 177, 180
magician 144
magick
  correspondences 185
  definition 75, 77
  failure 80
  folk 73
  instant 124
  manipulative 80
  negative 80
  practical 73
  spiritual 73
Magna Mater 134

Maia 172, 175
Maiden 122
maiden goddesses 139
maidens 156
Maitre Carrefour 160
majestic 148
making magick more effective 79
male
  genitalia 166
  lovers 54
  role in Paganism 37
Maman Brigitte 133, 160
manifesting 33, 35, 57, 77, 181
manipulation 68, 78, 84
manslaughters 129
manufacturing 148
maple 103, 188
Margot Adler 58
Marinette 160
marriage 108, 135, 138, 148, 159, 193
Mars 159, 161, 171, 186, 187
  planet 195
Martha Stewart 61
masculine
  aggression 162
  animal associations 195
  archetypes 46
  energy 9, 39, 45
masculinity 129, 181
master 168
Master Crossroads 160
mastery over spirits 148
mathematics 179
Math fab Mathonwy, 144
mating 153
mature men 47
Max Planck 33
mead of inspiration 163
meadowlands 42
medical skills 144
medicine 163, 180
meditation 119, 189, 193, 194
Medusa 132

meeting the Green Man 42
Mehen 178
men and spirituality 37
Menhit 178
menstrual cycle 159
mental
  balance 186, 189
  disturbance 166
  focus 188
  growth 193
  power 194
Menthu 132
merchant sailors 166
Mercury 160, 162, 167, 186
Mercury (planet) 195
Meret 178
Meretseger 178
Merlin 188
Meskhenet 178
Mesopotamia 153
messages 179
messenger of the gods 162
metallurgy 148
metals 104, 148
  corresondences 190
meteorite 131
Metis 131, 174
Met Kalfu 160
midwife 129
military 179
milk 177
Milky Way 195
Min 177, 178
mind 138
Minerva 139, 159, 162
mirrors 119
miscreants 150
Mnevis 178
moisture 180
money 35, 193, 194
monotheism 2, 4
Monthu 178
moon 41, 82, 129, 139, 177, 178, 180,

186
moonlight 191
morality 84, 194
Morda 136
Morfran 136
Morgan 122
Morpheus 162
Morrigan 186
mortar and pestle 116
mother 122, 133, 144, 156
  goddess 178
motherhood 156, 177
Mother Theresa 87
motivation 189
mountains 129
  wilds 164
Mount Cyllene 150
Mount Olympus 149
mummification 177
music 140, 163, 177, 180
Mut 176, 178, 180
myrtles 128
Mystères 159
mystery 132

N

naked 130
name (Pagan) 116
Nanna 154
Narcissus 54
narcotics 148
nature 48, 156, 189
  sprites 42
nature-based 3
Nebthet 178
necromancy 147
necropolis 177, 179
Nefertem 178
negation 193
negative vibrations
  clearing with smudging 107
negativity 193
Nehebkau 178

Neils Bohr 32
Neith 176, 178
Nekhbet 178
Neper 178
Nephthys 157, 178
Neptune 163, 169, 186
  planet 195
Nerites 55
neutralize magick 193
new life 140
Newtonian Physics 31, 33
night 130, 178, 191
Nike 128
Nile River 176
Ninshubur 154
Nisus 54
Nordic 114
Norse 49, 105
North 118, 193
nourishing 135
Nu 179
Nuada 160
nursing mother 178
nurturing 10, 45, 147, 177
Nut 156, 164, 177, 179
nymphs 167, 175
Nyx 142

O

oafish 137
oak 137, 173, 188
  groves 139
  trees 170
oases 176
Oberaash 186, 189
oblivion 146
obolus 146
obscenity 133
observation 188
occult wisdom 194
Oceanus 163
Odin 144, 163, 186, 190
Ogdoad of Hermopolis 175

Ogoun 143, 160
oils 111, 179
old crones 150
Olwen 187
Omphalos 174
Omulan 189
open astral gates 194
opener 167
open or clear the mind 189
opportunity 193
oppression in Abrahamic religions 46
Ops 134, 169
optimism 188
oracle 130
  at Delphi 127, 149
orange 188
  color 193
orators 150
order 178
Orion 130, 189
Orpheus 55
osage orange 188
Osiris 41, 42, 126, 133, 151, 156, 162,
      164, 176, 177, 179, 188
other realms 193
Ouija 119
Ouranos 125
overcoming uncertainty 193
owls 138, 163, 195

P

Pagan
  definition 1
  name 116
  principles vs practice 48
  tools 101
Paganism 1
  definition 7
  today 9
PaganSpace 13
pain 114
Pakhet 179
Pan 41, 54, 122, 125, 143, 164, 166,

        188, 189
pan flute 165
pantheistic 3
pantheon 4, 7, 125
paraffin candles 110
Paris 148, 166
parthenogenetic 131
Parthenon 131
particle energy 32
passion 56, 188, 194
patience 193
Patroclus 54
patrons of homosexual love 54
peace 162, 168, 186, 193, 194
peacock 148
peanuts 134
Pelias 148
Pelops 55
penis 137, 150, 166, 178
pentacle 102, 103, 104
  ritual purpose 104
pentagram 104
percentage of male pagans in groups
      27
perception 179
  of reality 34
perfection 135
perfume 143
permanence 189
Persephone 122, 125, 138, 141, 147,
      151, 165, 167, 186, 190
Perseus 132
perseverence 190
personal spiritual development 8
persuasion 194
pervert 3
pestilence 179
Petbe 179
pewter 105, 106, 114
phallus 165
pharoahs 151, 177
Phlegethon 146
Phoenician deities 125

Phrygia 142
physical
  ailments 189
  appearance 187
  objects 193
  strength 150, 193
  world 75
piety 126
pine 188, 190
pink 194
Pitys 165
plains 143
plants 42, 166, 180
pleasure 188
plowing 135, 161
Pluto 163, 167, 169
  planet 195
poetry 135, 163
poets 150
poisons 187
polarity 52, 58, 59
  definition 52
Polemos 129
polos 148
Polyeidos 55
polytheism 3
pomegranate 148, 167
Pompeii 157
poor 126
poplar 188
portal 41
Poseidon 55, 132, 146, 147, 149, 152,
    163, 165, 169, 174
possessions 170
Pothos 54, 131
power 45, 51, 60, 132, 137, 167, 187,
    189, 193, 194
  in Paganism 38
powerful 10
practical magick 8, 57, 73, 182, 185
  cleaning up afterward 91
  for others 90
pregnancy 139, 159, 180

preservation 186
  of mankind 139
  of the seasons 170
prevent
  rot 188
  unwanted change 186
priapism 166
Priapos 166
Priapus 166
primary tools 103
primordial mound 180
primordial watery abyss 179
progress in business 194
projective energy 9, 190, 191
promote
  flow of positive energy 107
  good energy 109
prophecy 144, 189
Proserpina 166
prosperity 186, 188, 189, 193
Prosymnus 54
protection 109, 134, 135, 151, 170,
    177, 186, 187, 188, 190, 193,
    194
  during travel 188
  from harm 189
  of the home 188
  of the household 176
protector 42, 137, 140, 158, 176, 179,
    180
  of the dead 156
  of the underworld 42
  of tombs 178
  of women and children 143
provider 42
provide restful sleep 189
Pryderi 145
Psyche 128
psychic
  ability 189, 193, 194
  awareness 193
  development 194
  growth 193

vision 186
work 193
Ptah 167, 175, 179
Ptah-Sekhmet-Nefertem triad of
    Memphis 175
purification 188, 194
purify ritual space 109
purity 194
purple 194
pursuit of goals 188
Python 127

Q

Qebui 179
Quantum Entanglement 33
quantum physics 8, 31, 75, 83, 89
quartz 114
Queen of the Underworld 167
quests 193

R

Ra 131, 152, 157, 175, 176, 177, 178,
    179, 122, 123
rabbit 195
racing 150
rain 153, 180
ram 162, 177
randomness 32
reality and belief 34
reap 161
reater attainments in life 194
rebirth 41, 136, 141, 164, 178, 186,
    188, 189, 190
receptive energy 9, 191
Reconstructionist traditions 49
red 194
redemption 7
redirection 188
reduction 191
  of goddess energy 38
redwood 189
refine 101
regeneration 164, 168

reincarnation 4, 109, 182, 187
rejoicing 178
relationships 135
releasing 193
religion
  definition 5
Rem 179
remove
  confusion 193
  discord 193
  negative forces 194
Remus 171
Renenutet 179
renewal 186, 193
repel
  negative thoughtforms 193
  negativity 193
  pests 188
resins 106, 116
resolution 191
resource list
  gods and goddesses 123
restrictions in magick 67
resurrection 133
revenge 130, 179, 187
reversing 193
Rhea 139, 141, 142, 146, 148, 173,
    174, 188
Rhea Silvia 171
Rhiannon 168, 186, 189
Rhonda Byrne 83
rhyme
  in ritual and magick 97
rhythm
  in ritual and magick 97
ritual 8, 30, 59, 93, 111
  cleansing 108
  definition 93
  madness 140
  magick 185
  space 117
  vs practical magick 94
rivals 143

rivers 163
roads 158
robes 115
Robin Hood 42
romance 188, 189, 194
Romulus 171
rosemary 107
rowan 186, 189
Ruadán 135
rulers 156
rules 63
rum 133, 134
runes 119, 186
rustic music 164

S

Saa 179
sacred
  knowledge 189
  law 138
sacrifice 187
safe journey 193
sage 107
Salmacis 150
salt 107
Samedi 160
same-sex pairings 54
sand 107
sassafras 189
Satet 179
Satis 176
Saturn 158, 159, 168
Saturn (planet) 106, 169, 195
satyrs 140, 144, 164, 166
savior 179
scarab beetle 178
scarred 143
schools 163
science 29
scorching heat of the sun 179
scorpion 177, 178, 179
scourge 114
scribe 179

scrying 109, 119
sculptors 148
sea 165
sea-nymph 172
searching 194
seas 145
seashells 119
seasons 137, 138
  of the year 136
Seax Wicca 114
secrecy 144
secret of the universe 29
Seker 179
Sekhmet 131, 178, 179
Sekmet 179
Selene 122, 125, 165
self 194
self-confidence 186
self-fulfillment 191
self improvement 194
self-limitation in magick 70
Semele 141, 175
semen 152
sensitivity 191
sensual affairs 153
Serket 179
serpent 138, 176
Seshat 179
Set 131, 152, 156, 179
  and Horus 152
Seth 179
Sethlans 172
setting sun 176
severe disease 194
sex 133
sex magick 187
sexual 133
  energy 58
  love 142
  modesty 132
  orientation and energy 40
  powers 164
  preferences 45

sexuality 45, 55, 130, 131, 188, 194
  and deity 123
  and Paganism 13
  definition 45
  vs gender 45
Shai 179
shame 181
Shed 179
shepherds 150, 164
Shezmu 179
shipwrecks 165
Shu 179
Shukaletuda 153
Sia 179
sickle 105
sickness 193
Silvanus 55
silver (color) 194
silver (metal) 106, 114, 191
Silver Ravenwolf 49
Simbi 160
sincerity 194
singing 178
singulum 113
sinners 156
Sirius 179
Sito 138
sixth sense 33
size 149
skill 149, 160
sky 131, 151, 159, 177, 179
slander 193
slaughter 179
slave 156, 168
sleep 187, 189
smithery 172
smithing tools 131
smith's hammer 148
smoking 133
smudge sticks 107
smudging 107
  cautions for using 107
snake 134, 178, 180, 195

snakes 132, 138, 178
Sobek 179
Sobkou 179
Sokar 179
solar energy 193
solemn 148
solidity 191
solitary Pagans 71
sooth disruptive energy 190
Sopdet 179
Sopdu 179
sorcery 78, 144, 147
sorrow 146
soul 178
South 194
sovereignty 139
sow 161
sowing 135
soy candles 110
space 33, 75, 77, 80
  and ritual 118
sparrows 128
Spear 114
special counselor of the state 158
spellcasting 73, 111
spellcraft 80
sphinx 130
spider 195
spirit 48, 188
  communication 193, 194
  contact 193
  guide 81
spiritual
  awakening 194
  body 75
  development 193, 194
  enlightenment 189
  growth 186, 188
  healing 188, 193
  initiation 189
  magick 57, 73
  path
    definition 6

spirituality 190, 191, 194
  definition 5
spoiled 143
sports 150
Spring 164
springs 165
springtime 166
spruce 186, 189, 190
stability 164, 167, 194
stable 181
staff 104, 114
stag 129, 195
stang 104, 114
star 130, 131
Starhawk 49
statues 116
steadiness 193
steel 191
Stheno 132
stimulation 193
stone 104, 114, 116, 168
storms 153, 170, 179
Stregheria 139
strength 45, 54, 128, 149, 168, 170,
      188, 190, 193, 194
strengthen will 189
Stuart Farrar 49
study 193
Styx 146
subconscious 86, 89
  how to access 87
success 191, 193, 194
  in new endeavors 188
  in searches 194
  with magick 189
succession of kings 139
suckling 131
sudden change 193
sulfur
  in rituals or magick 106
Sumerian 153
  deities 125
summon spirits 114

sun 41, 140, 176, 179, 191, 195
sunrise 178
superficiality
  in Pagans and Wiccans 47
supernatural powers 180
suppression 191
supremacy 139
survey 13, 101, 181
swans 128
sword 105
  uses 105
Syrinx 165

T

Ta-Bitjet 179
Taliesin 136
tallow 110
Tammuz 41, 122, 170, 187
Tarot 119
Tartarus 142, 174,
Tatenen 180
Taweret 180
teaching 186
technology, 148
Tefnut 180
Tegid Foel 136
Temple of Artemis 147
Tenenet 180
tension 194
Terra 134, 168
terror 128
Thanatos 151
theater 140
theatrical criticism 164
Themis 127
Theory of Relativity 31
The Secret 83
Thesmophoros 138
Thesus 146
the Thracians 55
Thetis 172
thieves 150
Thor 163, 170, 186, 187, 189

Thoth 180
Thracian mysteries 140
Threefold Goddess 137
throne 177
thunder 159, 170
thunderbolt 131, 173, 174
thuribles 106
thyrsus 140, 141
Ti-Jean Petro 143
time 33, 41, 75, 77, 80, 158
  and ritual 118
  cyclical renewal 159
timing 82
tin 191
Tinia 173
Titan 131
Titanides 131
Titans 141, 146, 169, 174
Tityos 127
tobacco 133
togetherness 194
tomb 168, 176
  builders 178
tongs 148
tools 101
  additional or secondary 106
  consecrating 102
  how to use 103
  primary 103
  working with god 118
  working with goddess 119
torches 147
torcs 135
tortoise 162
total faith 83
trade 162
tranquility 193
transfer power 187
transformation 77
transgendered 150
transitions 41, 158, 189
transvestites 54
travel 188

travelers 150
travel to other realms 193
trees 42
  fruit-bearing 190
  spiky 190
  strong odor 190
  tall 190
  thorny 190
  weeping 190
trickery 144, 147, 150, 163
triple goddess 122, 135
Trivia 147
Troilus 54
trolls 170
truth 178, 188, 193, 194
Tuatha Dé Danann 135, 137, 160
twice-born 141
twigs 119
two spirits 58
Typhon 174
Tyr 186

U

ugliness 51, 135, 136, 166
uncertainty 193
unconditional love 187, 191
understanding 191, 193
underworld 41, 130, 133, 135, 142,
    146, 150, 151, 154, 163, 164,
    175, 176, 178, 190
undesirable competition 193
unexpected 140
unfaltering 148
unforeseeable action 140
Unicorn Books 42
union 148, 191
universal energy 57, 182
unseen 146
Unut 180
unwanted guests 109
upland areas 135
Uranus 127, 174
Uranus (planet) 195

using
  dead wood 190
  tools 103

V

Valhalla 144
valkyries 144
value judgments 85
vanity 143
Vashaan 187, 189
vegetation 41, 42
veiling 193
vengeful 10, 148
Venus 127, 130, 153, 167, 171, 172,
    173, 186, 188
Venus (planet) 153, 195
Vesta 139, 169, 171
Vestales 171
Vestal Virgins 134, 171
vibration 109
vibrational rates 75
victory 128, 194
vigor 194
vine 41, 189
vineyards 176
violence 128
violet 194
virgin 129, 131, 139, 147, 171
  goddess 163
virginity 139
virility 128, 176
Vishnu 189
vision quests 193
visualization
  creative 75
vitality 159, 188, 189, 191, 193
volcanoes 148, 168, 172
Vulcan 148, 159, 172
vulture 178

W

Wadjet 158, 180
Wadj-wer 180

walls 147
walnut 189
wand 102, 103, 104, 114
wanderer 142, 163
war 6, 128, 130, 132, 144, 151, 152,
    162, 163, 176, 177, 178, 179,
    125
war-cry 129
warfare 135, 180
warlike 159
warrior 49, 105, 131, 150
  spirit 47
water 105, 109, 178, 193
water-nymph 165
watery abyss 179
wave energy 32
wealth 87, 156
weapons 131, 140
weather 178, 189
weaving 163, 178
weights and measures 150
welcome 181
well-being of the family 170
Weneg 180
Wepwawet 180
Werethekau 180
Wesir 179
West 193
wheat 138
Wheel of the Year 10, 39
white 68, 194
white sage 107
why is magick spelled with a K? 78
Wicca 1, 37, 49
  Dianic 139
Wiccan Rede 64
wife 156
wild animals 139, 189
Wild Hunt 41, 163
wild places 41
will 185
willow 103, 189
willpower 194

wind 179, 189
Windsor Great Park 42
wine 140, 179
winemaking 140
wisdom 131, 135, 136, 163, 180, 186
wise 136
wit 150
witchcraft 55, 130, 144, 147
Witches Voice 13
woe 146
wolf 195
womb 46, 105, 109
women 56, 139, 148, 171
  and fundamentalist Christianity 51
  and Islam 51
  and orthodox Judaism 51
wood 104, 115, 116, 185
wooded glens 164
wooden tools 102
woodlands 41, 42, 139
Wookey Hole 113
word as bond 103, 104
working
  with fairy realm 186
  with Goddess archetypes 40
  with masculine energy 51
Wosret 180
wound 133
wrestling 150
writing 179, 180

Y

year and a day 108
yellow 194
yew 190
Yggdrasil 186
Yinepu 176
young children 138
youth 178

Z

Zeus 55, 125, 126, 127, 128, 129, 131,
  141, 146, 147, 148, 159, 162,
  165, 166, 173, 189
zombie 134
Zsusana Budapest 49

www.ingramcontent.com/pod-product-compliance
Lightning Source LLC
Chambersburg PA
CBHW070347090426
42733CB00009B/1321